Entrepreneur® **MENTOR** SERIES

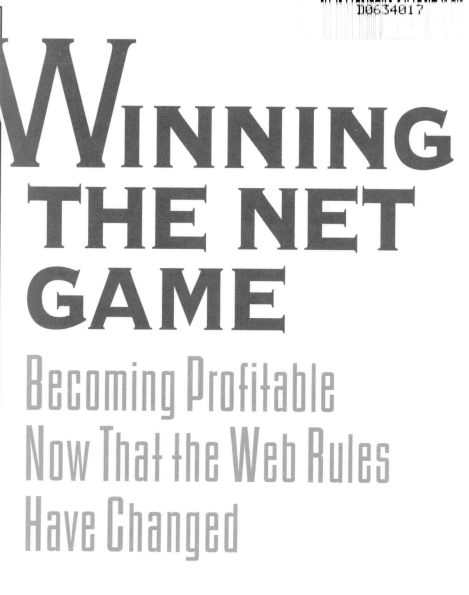

# WINNING THE NET GAME

## Becoming Profitable Now That the Web Rules Have Changed

# CAROLINE HOWARD

**EP**
Entrepreneur®
Press

Editorial Director: Jere L. Calmes
Cover Design: Beth Hanson-Winter
Composition and Production: Eliot House Productions

**Library of Congress Cataloging-in-Publication**
Howard, Caroline.
    Winning the net game: becoming profitable now that the web
rules have changed/Caroline Howard.
        p.  cm.        (Entrepreneur mentor series)
    Includes bibliographical references and index.
    ISBN 1-891984-48-9
        1. Electronic commerce. 2. Internet industry. 3. World Wide Web.
    I. Title. II. Series.
        HF5548.32 H69 2002
        658.8'4—dc21                                           2002019167

Printed in Canada

10 09 08 07 06 05 04 03 02                    10 9 8 7 6 5 4 3 2 1

# Table of Contents

# *Acknowledgments*

I have had the great fortune to work with several wonderful people during the process of writing this book. First, I want to thank Jayne Spence for guiding me through the initial steps of the project. I am especially grateful to Jayne for leading me to my superb agent, Michael Snell. His knowledge and experience were critical to the development of the project and to finding a publisher. I want to thank Les Ottolenghi and his brother, Hugo, for their help in developing the initial concept and proposal. Jere Calmes and Karen Billipp have been invaluable to the project. Their ideas and insights improved the project immensely. In advance I want to thank those who have agreed to read this book and provide a testimonial.

On a personal note, I want to thank my husband, Peter, and children, Anne and Tommy. Your generosity and patience enabled me to get where I am. You are the joys of my life, and I love you. I also want to thank my mother for her never-ending support. I could not have surmounted the difficulties along the path to this book without the fellowship of my wonderful friends and family. Their love and energy have been the source of my growth. I want to especially acknowledge the incredible warmth and kindness I have received from my cousins on both coasts. You have meant so much to my life. To my father and others sadly departed: your spirit is a part of me and who I am. Thank you for being part of my life.

# *Preface*

I was having lunch with a friend the other day. We were discussing the new and exciting paths our careers were taking. She is opening a new business, and I told her about this book. Upon hearing that I wrote a book about Web-based business, she exclaimed, "How did you learn about such a complex topic? I thought about using the Internet in my business but decided it would be too expensive and complicated."

Hearing similar comments from very intelligent and knowledgeable business people gave rise to the idea for this book. Every day I see small businesses senselessly waste money and time when simple and inexpensive Web solutions would enable them to reduce costs, increase profits, and better serve their customers. The owners and managers of these businesses are either unaware of the Web's potential or, like my friend, think it would be too difficult and costly to use in their business.

These small business people do not understand that Web-based commerce is just technically-enhanced business. It is based on the same fundamental business principles that have governed business for thousands of years. The Web is a powerful business tool that can provide a competitive advantage to those businesses that embrace it.

Unfortunately, many small business people act as if Web-based commerce is something foreign. They seem to think that their businesses can thrive without using the Web. For some this may be true, but a number are failing to see the marketplace reality, that using the Internet is critical to the survival of many businesses.

This book will show you how you can use the Web to improve the profitability and effectiveness of your small business. There are "how to" directions on ways to achieve enormous benefits quickly and easily without incurring great expense. There are also suggestions for implementing more expensive and complex Web applications.

The Web has immense potential for small business, and now you can tap into this potential to empower your business.

# E-COMMERCE OR DIE
## *Surviving in the Global Village*

WINNING IN OUR CHANGING AND CHALLENGING
21ST CENTURY MARKETPLACE.

*For many years, a widow and her four children worked on their farm and sold produce in their profitable farm stand. Their property was located on a popular route that led from the city to the seashore. Each summer the farm stand made more than enough money for the family to live on. During the off-season, they ran a profitable flower business. As the only florists for miles, they could depend on selling local residents flower arrangements for holidays, weddings, and other special occasions. The children had grown up, married, and had families of their own. Each had built a house on a portion of the property. They were very comfortable and assumed that the farm stand would support their families for generations.*

*Unfortunately, times were changing. Recently, a highway provided a faster, more direct route from the city to the shore, resulting in less passing traffic. As beach communities developed into business centers, previous summer communities were becoming year-round residences.*

*Development further decreased summer traffic and brought competition from small grocers, supermarkets, and superstores. At first the family did not worry as their flower business was expanding to cover the reduction in farm stand sales. Recently, however, fewer people were buying flowers from the farm stand and were instead purchasing their arrangements over the Internet.*

*The widow was worried that the farm stand would not support their expanding family. She wondered how long they could continue to prosper or if she should*

*Hype abounds, certainly. But at the same time, something startling is taking place. In stage one of the information age, computers proliferated and made us more productive. We're now in stage two: Computers and the world's telecommunications networks have converged on the Internet to collapse distance and time more than anything that has gone before. This new connectivity broadens and deepens the ability of people to interact—a profound transformation that goes to the heart of society, culture, and humanity. It's a disruptive, revolutionary change. We are wiring the planet and creating a single digital marketplace in which everyone can connect and do business in ways never before dreamed possible.*

—TREVER R. STEWART, "A CAUSE FOR
RATIONAL EXUBERANCE"

*sell her farm to the real estate conglomerate that expressed interest.*

▲　▲　▲

## Challenges of the 21st Century

The challenges faced by the widow and her family are similar to those facing many companies as we enter the 21st century. While business fundamentals remain the same, the competitive landscape is changing. The Internet and electronic commerce (e-commerce) are radically changing the ways we conduct business, and many organizations will not survive these changes. To thrive and win in this electronic marketplace will require learning these new ways of business while not forgetting basic business principles.

As more commerce is conducted on the Internet, many businesses will be forced to participate or risk their demise. Harvard Business School's David Yoffie predicts that "We won't be talking about Internet companies five years from now as everyone will either be on the Internet or out of business." In order to survive in business "companies that do not want to participate in Internet commerce may be forced to do so," says Shikhar Ghosh in "Making Business Sense of the Internet." Engaging in Internet commerce will be critical to the survival of many businesses.

Unfortunately, just participating in Internet commerce is not enough. You not only need to do it; you need to do it well. To do it well requires understanding the endless opportunities available on the Web. You need to understand how to make money. Succeeding on the Web means bringing in more money than you spend.

You may be skeptical about Internet commerce. There has been so much hype about e-commerce, and the reality is that many high profile Internet businesses have failed. Much can be learned from their mistakes. Many of the Internet pioneers forgot that business success means making more than you spend. They failed to adhere to basic business principles. They generated Web traffic and investor financing rather than revenue. They did not take advantage of the potential cost savings on the Web, and instead incurred exorbitant expenses without the revenue or solid projections to justify their spending. They seemed to forget that being in business means making a profit.

This book is about how you can use the Web for making money and reducing costs. Not only does the Internet open up channels for increasing profits, it provides ways to decrease costs. As competition becomes more and more cutthroat, using the power of the Internet for both becomes increasingly critical to the future success of your business.

Small businesses reap huge benefits from the Web according to the Small Business Administration. Small businesses that utilized the Web had average revenues of $3.79 million compared with $2.72 million for all small businesses. Similarly, *American City Business Journals* reports that small businesses that use the Internet have grown 46 percent faster than those that do not. Arlene Weintraub of *BusinessWeek e.biz* predicts that much of the growth in e-commerce will come from small business.

The purpose of this book is to show you how to develop a successful e-business. You will see what others are doing on the Internet and receive step-by-step guidance on how you can take advantage of the endless opportunities to make money and reduce costs on the Web.

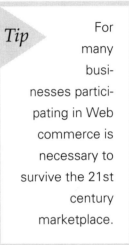

*Tip* For many businesses participating in Web commerce is necessary to survive the 21st century marketplace.

*If yesterday's game was about revenue generation at all costs, then today's is about being as aggressive as you can with cost-saving strategies. Let's face it. Every company is learning to do more with less.*

*—PHILIP SAY, "SEVEN GREAT B2B MARKETING INITIATIVES"*

> *While the newspapers and news sites fill their space with dotcom layoffs and closures, the Web audience continues to quietly grow.*
>
> —DAVID WALKER,
> *"BEHIND THE GLOOM"*

## What Are the Most Important Changes?

The World Wide Web and other communication technologies are changing the way we purchase goods, obtain information, and conduct commerce. While local businesses have traditionally competed with each other to sell their goods and services, they must now compete in the global electronic marketplace. Both business buyers and consumers can now go on the Web and quickly determine where to get the lowest prices for a particular good or service. Small businesses are therefore facing a much more powerful consumer. In the words of Jeff Bezos, founder of Amazon.com, "The balance of power is shifting away from business and to the consumer." Using the Internet, customers can obtain price information and advice from a wide variety of vendors, customers, and independent sources. They can purchase goods and services, check product availability, examine prototype products, or send and receive customer feedback comments on a large variety of products. This means businesses will have to develop strategies to address the needs of these more powerful customers.

When purchases are made using the Web, it no longer matters whether the businesses or customers are located near or far from each other. Customers can choose to purchase from a local merchant or supplier or they can order goods or services from anywhere in the world. On the Web, the context of the customer relationship changes from one based on face-to-face interactions to one based on electronic exchanges of information. Merchants and their customers can no longer depend on the demeanor and other physical cues that provide us with information about each other. With electronic exchanges, we no longer develop business relationships based on personal contact.

On the Web, price often becomes the primary, and sometimes only, criteria for selecting where to purchase goods and services. Unfortunately, small businesses are unable to benefit from the volume discounts, economies of scale, and power of larger companies. They may be unable to compete effectively on price alone and must find new bases on which to compete in this new electronic business world. They need to find ways to add value to their goods and services as well as find new ways to develop trusting and loyal customer relationships using electronic rather than face-to-face interactions. Arthur B. Sculley and W. William A. Woods, authors of "B2B Exchanges," predict that the rise of electronic commerce will force most businesses to reinvent themselves.

*Y*ou should recognize the fact that you are global, in the sense that you very likely have global competitors, so you are in a competitive global marketplace whether you've addressed those issues or not.

—*ADVANCINGWOMEN.COM, "GOING GLOBAL...STUDY YOUR MARKETS, DEVELOP A STRATEGIC PLAN"*

## What Is the Solution?

For many, small business survival in the new environment will require participation in e-commerce and using the Internet to reduce costs and add value to their goods and services so they can meet the needs of both business and individual retail customers. Both large and small businesses can use the Internet to gather the necessary customer information to effectively compete in a marketplace of empowered consumers. The Internet enables all companies to sell products and services locally, nationally, or globally. They can gather the data needed to better anticipate and meet consumer demands through increasing levels of personalization and customization. The Internet has also allowed businesses to lower costs through increased efficiency and productivity. Businesses can use the Web to develop mutually beneficial relationships with those in their value chain including suppliers, consumers, business customers, competitors,

*Tip*

The Small Business Administration defines a small business as one with fewer than 500 employees.

> *We believe that, just as early tremors warn of an impending earthquake, the upheaval in securities markets that Internet-based, electronic trading systems are causing is a signal of the huge changes that are to come in every major industry. The fact that electronic systems are shaking the very foundations of centuries-old stock exchange institutions should be a warning to us that no industry or company, however established it may be, will be spared. Every business will be shaken by this Internet quake.*
>
> —ARTHUR B. SCULLEY AND W. WILLIAM A WOODS, "B2B EXCHANGES"

**Tip** Small businesses with a Web site have higher revenues than those that do not.

and regulators. Through these links, organizations are able to fill and deliver customer orders more quickly, improve customer service, better forecast customer demands, develop faster cycle times, and lower order-processing costs. Small businesses can use these links to gain power and compete with larger organizations.

## How Can this Book Help?

This book shows you how you can successfully compete in this new business climate by discussing how to succeed in the e-commerce world while not exceeding your budget. *Winning the Net Game* presents an easy to follow, step-by-step approach for small businesses to implement inexpensive and immediately profitable Web strategies. You will learn how you can use the Web to lower your costs, improve your internal business processes, add value to your products and services, develop loyal customer relationships, and profitably form partnerships with other businesses. Simple instructions are provided on how small businesses can use a number of affordable, innovative, and profitable strategies for selling goods and services to individual customers or businesses. Different Web venues are described including:

- *Business to Customer (B2C) Commerce.* Transactions between businesses and individual customers. Businesses selling to other nonbusiness consumers.
- *Business to Business (B2B) Commerce.* Transactions between businesses. Businesses selling to other business customers.
- *Business to Government (B2G) Commerce.* Transactions between businesses and government entities— businesses selling to the government.

- *Government-to-Business (G2B), Government-to-Consumer (G2C) Commerce.* Government using the Web to provide services and sell to businesses and consumers

- *Government-to-Government (G2G) Commerce.* Government organizations using the Web for transactions with each other.

- *Business-to-Employee (B2E) Commerce.* Businesses using the Web for transactions with employees.

- *Peer-to-Peer (P2P) Commerce.* Consumers interacting directly with each other on the Web.

The book begins by giving you basic information to help you get going on the Web as quickly, inexpensively, and profitably as possible. Chapter 1 shows you how you can quickly and inexpensively create a profitable Web presence and expand if you want to. Chapter 2 talks about deciding where you want to go on the Web and how to get there. In Chapter 3 you learn how you can pay for it. Chapter 4 presents basic concepts in Web design along with advice on how to develop a successful Web site. Chapter 5 presents some lessons from the past and talks about how you use them to improve your chances of success.

Next, the book describes the different ways business is performed on the Web. Chapter 6 presents an overview of the business marketplaces and models for doing business. Chapters 7 and 8 show how business models are implemented in the retail sphere and business sphere, respectively. Chapters 9 and 10 present new implementations in the government and peer-to-peer worlds.

The following chapters discuss some ways you can use the Web to save money. You can use the money to automate your supply chains, and interact internally and with your customers to improve the efficiency and

> *E-valuations Research surveyed 500 small businesses and found that the majority indicated a strong likelihood to build commerce-enabled Web sites. Of those already running transaction Web sites, 92 percent said they believed the Internet gave them a competitive edge.*

> *Tip* Customers are empowered on the Web. They can purchase goods/services and compare prices globally.

*U*.S. tax authorities expect 35 million U.S. tax forms to be logged online this year, up 20 percent from last year. Jupiter Research's latest online consumer survey suggests the proportion of U.S. households online will grow by four to six percent a year up to 2005, when fully 74 percent of households will have Internet access.

—DAVID WALKER, "BEHIND THE GLOOM"

*Tip* There are new, innovative models for doing business on the Web.

effectiveness of your processes. Chapter 11 and Chapter 12 show how you can use the Web to manage your value chain and save money on purchasing both as a consumer and business buyer. Chapter 13 discusses automating accounting, one of the most obvious applications of computers. Unfortunately, compatibility issues are still prevalent. Chapter 14 discusses how you can save a lot of money, improve employee morale, and improve relationships with customers, suppliers, employees, and other business partners by posting information on Intranets, Extranets, and the Internet.

Customer relationships are important to Web success. The book discusses critical customer relationship concepts, how to know your customer better, and how to market to both business and consumer customers. You will learn how to market to customers, develop trust, and gain loyal customers in the absence of face-to-face interactions.

The final section prepares you to succeed today and remain successful into the future. Business alliances are becoming more necessary on the Web. Global and mobile commerce are here and getting stronger. And success today and tomorrow means being adaptable and willing to change with the altered business landscape. The chapters are followed by an appendix and glossary that describe the basic technologies that you need to know to understand this new world and the language of the Internet.

## Summary

For many businesses, e-commerce is becoming necessary for survival. They need to learn new ways of doing business and replace those based on face-to-face interactions and local competition. Businesses need to learn how to add value to their goods and services, meet customer needs through customization and personalization, and use electronic means to develop relationships. They need to learn to use the Web to make money, increase their revenues, and decrease their costs.

This book shows you how you can compete in this new environment. New ways of doing business and how they impact you are discussed. You'll find specific instructions for taking advantage of the many opportunities available in the electronic marketplace so that you can succeed in e-commerce.

> *N*ow's the time to build an Internet presence. Most of the competition is in retreat, services cost less, the formulas for success are clearer—and the audience just keeps growing.
>
> —*DAVID WALKER,* *"BEHIND THE GLOOM"*

## Web Sources for More Information

▶ **About.com** (www.about.com) provides articles, links, advice, and other information on B2B marketing and a host of other business topics.

▶ **Brint.com** (www.brint.com) is a free membership organization that provides links to articles, information, and vendors. White pages describing aspects of B2B commerce are posted on the site.

▶ **B2BmarketingBiz** (www.b2bmarketingbiz.com) includes articles, information, and numerous links to B2B marketing sites.

▶ **Clickz.com** (www.clickz.com) provides articles, links, advice, and other information on B2B marketing and many other e-commerce areas.

▶ **Digitrends** (www.digitrends.net) offers articles and other information on the Internet and digital commerce.

▶ **Entrepreneur.com** (www.entrepreneur.com) provides a wide array of resources and information for entrepreneurs and small businesses.

▶ **ZDNet.com** (www.zdnet.com) provides articles, links, advice, and other information on a number of e-commerce and business topics.

# JUMPSTARTING YOUR FUTURE
## *Simple Steps for Getting Started*

HOW TO ESTABLISH A WEB PRESENCE. ◄

*he opening of the highway resulted in an immediate reduction in farm stand sales. While local customers continued to buy their produce from the farm stand, the new highway reduced passing traffic and thus, the number of potential customers. As long as the farm stand was located on the main route to the shore, the family had been able to maintain a high sales volume by selling to travelers. Since shore traffic had been rerouted to the new highway, the family lost a lot of their customers. The family worried that they would not be able to reach their dream of supporting future generations with the farm stand.*

*To make matters worse, their flower business was no longer profitable. Overall flower sales were down, and they were donating an increasing volume of unsold flowers to neighboring hospitals and assisted living facilities. The bulk of recent flower sales came from the beautiful floral arrangements the daughter had designed for several weddings. She grew orchids and loved putting together the flowers for friends' weddings. She had given wedding arrangements as gifts to a few friends and was getting orders for more from guests at those weddings. Unfortunately, the small number of orders was not nearly enough to make up for the lost flower and farm stand sales.*

*The family was desperate to find new ways to expand their market and replace the lost sales. They seemed to be hearing and reading about e-commerce everywhere and decided to look into the alternatives.*

*Tip* By being smart about how you spend, you can establish a profitable business for minimal upfront costs.

> *Dotcoms may be going down in flames every day, but a surprising group of Web survivors is emerging unscathed: small businesses, the mighty mini-dots. With just a handful of employees and annual sales of $5 million or less, these intrepid independents are doing what almost none of their venture-capital-funded brethren could: make money online.*
>
> —ARLENE WEINTRAUB,
> "THE MIGHTY MINI-DOTS"

By now it is clear that it is absolutely necessary to develop a presence on the World Wide Web. This chapter and subsequent chapters describe the choices and steps needed to turn your ideas into profits by quickly and cheaply building your Web presence. You can build a profitable Web site for a very small investment and then develop your Internet strategy further. Or you can immediately build a powerful Web site that will enhance every aspect of your small business. This chapter will take you through the steps necessary to choose a Web host (location).

## Where Do You Start?

Getting on the Web does not necessarily mean high upfront costs. You can get on the Web for $100 or less. By starting small you can test the water without committing to a large budget for Web site development or hosting fees. You can also choose to not have your own site but just sell your products on the sites of others.

Minimal investment does not necessarily mean minimal return. A simple Web page can be very profitable. For example, you can decrease your customer service costs by directing customers to your Web site for answers to frequently asked questions and solutions to common problems. You can use your Web site as "brochureware," an online version of your brochure and business card, and as a press vehicle for describing your business, promoting your products and services, and persuading potential customers to choose your products. According to ami-Partners, most small businesses with Web sites have online brochure type sites. Of the 22 percent of small businesses with Web sites in the year 2000, only 8 percent were engaging in e-commerce transactions.

You can reduce your cost of doing business by developing a more complex site without incurring major costs. Some hosting companies, charging about $25 per month, will provide software for setting up a retail site (shopping cart software) at no extra charge. Printing a product or service catalog on the Web can be much cheaper than printing and mailing your catalog to thousands of customers. You can also save on developing your Web site by using the free or low cost options available through many Web hosts. If you are inclined to do it yourself, you can build the site with an easy-to-learn software package.

## The Right Address in the Right Neighborhood

If you decide that having a Web site is for you, one of the most important questions you need to ask is "Where do I want my Web site to appear?" Your first job is to select your Web host.

Selecting a Web host depends on the answers to the following questions:

- What would you like in a domain name?
- What features and functions do you want?
- How will you develop the site?
- How much traffic do you expect to get?
- How much technical support do you need?
- How much do you want to spend on your Web site?

## Choosing Your Domain Name

It is important to choose your domain name before you choose a Web site host for your online business. Some services, especially free or inexpensive ones, may give you a long, difficult to remember, and hard to spell name.

*M*ini-dots are proving that profits can be made without much investment. 'Because we didn't get venture capital, we didn't get the opportunity to waste a ton of money,' says Jeffrey Johnson, owner of Underneath.com, an undergarment company. His business earned $30,000 last year on sales of more than $620,000 for the first profitable year in three years in business.

—ARLENE WEINTRAUB, "THE MIGHTY MINI-DOTS"

*Tip* In the case of dot-coms, smaller may be better. "Mini-dots" have been surprise money makers.

Before selecting a service, you will want to know your assigned name if that is an important factor in your ability to do business or attract customers.

You can select your own Internet name or Uniform Resource Locator (URL). You must then check to see if your selected name is available or being used by someone else. If it is available, reserve it through Internic. By going on their Web site, www.internic.com, you can check for availability and pay a small annual fee of $35 to register your selected name.

## Features and Functions

To select the right host for your Web site you need to first decide what you want to do with the site, then match the features and functions offered by different hosts with those you want. Some questions to ask include:

- Does their site support File Transfer Protocol (FTP)?
- Can an online store be set up? Does it support shopping carts?
- What e-mail services does it support? Can your e-mail address be your domain name? Can your e-mail address be set to automatically reply with a preset message (autoresponder)? Are multiple POP e-mail addresses offered? Can e-mail be forwarded?
- What types of credit card processing does the host support?
- What are the limitations on disk space?
- What are the limitations on use (advertising, etc.)?
- What is the availability of technical support?
- Is the support 24 hours a day, 7 days a week, or something less? What type of support is available? If you are doing business on the site having ample support is critical.

*Tip* A great way to avoid repeating the mistakes of others is to consult user reviews on a site like hostreview.com, thesitewizard. com, and webhostlist.com.

- What are the technical capabilities of the network? What type of hardware, software, and connections do they support?

- What do they support in terms of Web page development? Do they provide help with Web page development? Does the site support Microsoft FrontPage in its entirety, Dreamweaver, and other Web development packages?

- Does their site support Common Gateway Interface (CGI)?

- Is it a secure site? Does it have Secure Sockets Layer (SSL) for credit card security?

- How reliable is the network? If you do business on your site it is critical that the network not be out of service.

## Location, Location, Location

Options for Web hosts include:

- Trade association or network of associations
- Free or inexpensive Web hosts
- Internet Service Providers (ISPs)
- Portals and Virtual Communities
- Application Service Providers (ASPs)

### Trade Associations and Business Communities

For businesses that belong or would consider belonging to a trade association, these associations are an excellent way to gain a presence on the Web. Trade associations offer very cheap Web page development and Web hosting fees. These sites allow you to keep your Web page on their site for a nominal fee, often between $50 and $100 per year. For example, ISCT, a trade association of

> *T*rust for Historic Preservation, which tracks business in city downtown districts, reports that Main Street merchants have logged an average 12.8 percent increase in sales since launching their Web sites.
>
> —ARLENE WEINTRAUB, "THE MIGHTY MINI-DOTS"

> **Tip** To get a URL listing—"www.your name.com"—requires that you pay a monthly hosting fee. You must also register and reserve your domain name with Interdic ($35 per year).

*ISCT, an association of chemical cleaners, will develop a Web page for members for $75 and host the page for an annual fee of $50. They offer members a choice of three different styles for the $75 charge. If members want to develop a custom page the fee is $35 per hour. ISCT provides members with reasonably priced consulting services. Their Web site also features a stain removal guide to attract and retain visitors.*

chemical cleaners, allows its members to set up a Web page for a $75 one-time fee and $50 annually.

Other nonprofit associations (i.e., chamber of commerce) and commercial sites (i.e., 1 Hour Hosting) offer similar services. In addition to Web site hosting, these business communities often offer help with site development. On many sites, a simple Web page is included with the membership fee. Others charge small fees for Web pages or offer consulting on Web site development for low hourly rates. For example, ISCT offers additional Web development consulting for $35 an hour, far below the normal marketplace consulting rate. A listing of trade associations can be found on American Society of Association Executives (ASAE) Directory of Trade Associations info.asaenet.org/gateway/OnlineAssocSlist.html.

In addition to their reasonable rates, trade associations and business communities tend to have a lot of traffic and many links to other sites. With such a low fees and good visibility, many businesses find it riskier not to do anything. Even a business without an advertising budget can see how easily the site could quickly pay for itself by generating a few leads or projecting a positive corporate image.

### Free or Inexpensive Web Hosts

There are a number of communities that allow free or inexpensive Web hosting. Free sites (i.e., www.tcfb.com) offer free hosting and are supported by selling banner advertising. Free or inexpensive sites (see www.all-free-isp.com) are not usually as good at providing the Web site and application development more likely to be available through trade associations, business communities, and e-commerce sites. A directory of Web hosts and prices can be found on ClickhereFree.com (www.clickherefree.com), BudgetWeb.com (www.budgetweb.com),

ISP-for-free (www.isp-for-free.com), and Free ISP (www.all-free-isp.com). Ratings of these services can be found at www.all-free-isp.com/ratings.php.

### Internet Service Providers (ISPs)

Most ISPs (AOL, Mindspring, Earthlink, etc.) will allow members to have a simple Web page. There is usually no additional charge to the member's monthly fee. Like free or inexpensive sites, ISPs usually do not offer much in the way of application support.

### Portals and Virtual Communities

A number of portals are beginning to provide services specifically designed for small business. These sites focus on providing merchants with a place to sell their products and services. For example, virtual shopping communities allow B2C through a free virtual shopping mall such as hugeclick.com. Some companies, like Bigstep.com and eCongo.com, offer free basic e-commerce, and sell supplementary services such as advertising assistance, business services, and customer analysis. Other companies, Yahoo! and Excite@Home, have virtual superstores that offer reasonably priced e-commerce. Shopping malls charge inexpensive Web fees and may even offer assistance in developing the page. Setting up an online catalog can be costly, but many sites offer free shopping cart software in their monthly charge. Unfortunately, these stores may provide cataloging capabilities but not many other individualized services. A specialized type of portal or vortal can be a way to attract customers from that industry.

### Application Service Providers (ASP)

ASPs allow small businesses to enter the Internet marketplace with limited investment. These companies set

*Tip* Free sites can be great but for many they are not really free due to hidden costs and irritations.

*Tip* Being a part of the right community, such as a portal or trade association, may increase your traffic.

up, host, and manage applications and data on the Internet. Companies can pay subscriptions for expensive applications software rather than having to purchase it for themselves. ASPs range from large Enterprise Resource Programs (ERP) to smaller niche companies.

## Doing Business without a Web Site

If after reading this chapter you are still not convinced that you need a Web site you can do business on the Internet without one. People who have never run a business are making money by selling a large variety of things using auction sites. Without the Web, it would not be feasible for as many people to profit from selling odds and ends, collectibles, antique toys, and specialty items. Using e-mail is also a popular Internet marketing tool that does not require a Web site. Again, most businesses using e-mail probably do have a Web site and refer to their URL in the e-mail message. E-mail messages containing information describing offerings and special offers are a very inexpensive way for businesses to market products. Once an e-mail address is added to a mailing list, there is no extra cost for e-mailing that individual.

## Summary

This chapter has shown how you can develop a Web presence without spending a lot of money. Now that you have established your initial Web presence, or at least gotten a better idea of the alternatives, you are ready to develop your business. The next chapter will help you make your business successful and avoid mistakes.

> *B*y 2004, the tiniest businesses (those with fewer than 10 employees and less than $3 million in annual sales) will constitute 10 percent of United States Gross Domestic Product (GDP).
>
> —ARLENE WEINTRAUB, "THE MIGHTY MINI-DOTS"

*Tip* You can participate in e-commerce even if you don't have a Web site.

---

### *Chapter Key Points*

🔑 You can develop a profitable Web site for minimal investment.

🔑 Location is very important in determining what you can do and what traffic you will get.

🔑 You need to decide what features you want to have.

🔑 Your Web site name can also be an important component.

🔑 There are many options for developing your Web site.

🔑 You can do business on the Web without having your own Web site.

## Web Sources for More Information

▶ **BudgetWeb.com** (www.budgetweb.com) offers information on low cost ISPs.

▶ **Clickherefree.com** (www.clickherefree.com) provides information and listings of free ISPs.

▶ **Ebiz.com** (www.ebiz.com) provides information and links to help you get started in e-commerce.

▶ **Host review.com** (www.hostreview.com) offers reviews of hosts and user comments.

▶ **ISP-for-free.com** (www.isp-for-free.com) lists information ratings for ISPs.

▶ **Lyco's Web Monkey** (www.webmonkey.com) has a tutorial and other helpful information to get you started in e-commerce. It lists free ISPs in local areas and nationally.

▶ **The Web Wizard.com** (www.thewebwizard.com) provides tips and advice on building a Web site and how to maximize effectiveness on the Web. User ratings and reviews are also provided.

# E-COMMERCE 201
## *Defining Your Destiny*

TO GET WHERE YOU WANT TO GO, YOU NEED TO KNOW WHERE IT IS. ◀

*The widow worried that the farm stand would not continue to support the family now that the highway had been built. She wondered how her children, now adults, would survive financially. She asked the children to think about the future of the business and scheduled a meeting to discuss their ideas.*

*At the meeting each child talked about their image of the family's business in the future. The oldest son believed they should continue the farm stand business as they had in the past. The daughter suggested developing and selling new products at the farm stand including some baked goods from a local bakery, handmade crafts, and garden decorations.*

*The second son suggested they consider closing the farm stand and concentrate their efforts on supplying produce and flowers to area businesses. He suggested they find ways to take their products to the customer by selling through local grocery and convenience stores. The younger daughter suggested that they expand the flower business by selling through a Web site.*

*While the widow found value in each of the ideas presented, she was concerned that each child expressed a different idea for the future. The ideas of the older two would preserve the farm stand. The younger two saw the business expanding by selling products elsewhere. The widow wondered how they could build a successful business with such different images of the future business. How could they begin the journey into the future with such different destinations in mind?*

▲   ▲   ▲

## Knowing Where You Want to Go...

Before developing a Web presence or undertaking any new business, you need to decide what you want to do and how you want to do it. Stephen Covey said it best in his book, *The 7 Habits of Highly Effective People* (Simon and Schuster), "Begin with the end in mind." To get somewhere you need to first decide where you want to go and then develop a plan to get there.

To better understand business strategy, let's compare it to how you would plan a family vacation. What are the steps you need to take to make the vacation a success? First, you need to agree on what type of vacation the family wants. Even if some in the family decide to travel separately, everyone needs to agree on the final destination. While the adults in the family actually choose the vacation destination, having a happy vacation may depend on the adults' ability to persuade the children that the vacation will be great. The odds of having a good vacation will be improved if the adults can communicate and sell the vacation plans to the children.

In business, the top executive (or executives) formulate a *vision* or image of what they want the business to be. If everyone supports and works toward the vision it increases the probability of success in reaching that destination. Since many of you already have an image of your ideal business, your task may be to clearly articulate it and motivate others to attain the vision.

What are some of the characteristics of a good vision? First, a good vision should answer the following questions:

> *V*ision without action is merely a dream. Action without vision just passes the time. Vision with action can change the world.
>
> —JOEL ARTHUR BARKER,
> "THE POWER OF VISION" VIDEO

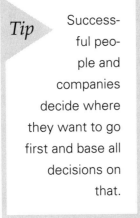

*Tip*  Successful people and companies decide where they want to go first and base all decisions on that.

## Communicating Strategic Visions
## Oxford Health Plans

Oxford Health Plans Inc. of Trumbull, Connecticut knows the power of communicating strategic visions. They have a peer-review process to make sure all information technology (IT) staffers and senior business executives share a common view and focus of strategic company initiatives. According to CIO and senior Vice President Art Gonzales,

"When all the business stars are aligned, heavenly things start to happen...in the past, Oxford had IT resources dedicated to specific business units. Now, we deliver across the entire organization. The corporate initiative allows both sides to focus on projects."

—*George V. Hulme, "Sharing Lunch: Key to Keeping Business and IT Goals in Sync," InfoWeek*

- What do we want to accomplish?
- What are our aspirations for the business?
- What do we want our business to become in the future?
- What is our ideal business?

According to Mason, Rowe, and Dickel in their text, *Strategic Management: A Methodological Approach* (Addison-Wesley):

"Vision needs to be:

- Simple, clear, and easily understood by most of the people.
- Distant enough in time to allow for dramatic changes but close enough to gain commitment from the organization. The vision must convey a sense of urgency.
- Able to focus the organization with respect to scope and time. The vision should focus the

organization on the right things, particularly the things it does best.

- Frequently articulated by top management to gain a solid consensus that the vision is desirable and achievable. The CEO must personify the vision and live by it. The vision must challenge the entire organization. Presentation of the vision is very important."

The process of vision formulation can be accomplished quickly. In his video, *The Power of Vision* (Chart House International), Joel Barker describes how a large corporation can complete the vision process in two sessions of three hours each. A small business should be able to complete the vision process in even a shorter amount of time.

## What Will You Do to Get There?

After formulating and agreeing on a vision of the final family vacation destination, you need to decide how everyone is going to get to the vacation destination. You need to discuss what everyone is willing to do to get there. How much are you willing to spend? How much time do you want to spend traveling? What types of transportation will you take? Is someone unwilling to fly or travel by boat? In business, this is called the mission.

Your mission should answer the following questions:

- What are the company's essential values?
- How is the company going to achieve the vision?
- What are we willing to do to get there?

### Where Are You Now?

Once you decide where you want to go and what you will do to get there, you need to look at where you are.

> *There is no more powerful engine driving an organization toward excellence and long-range success than an attractive, worthwhile, and achievable vision of the future, widely shared.*
>
> —BURT NANUS, AUTHOR, VISIONARY

*Tip* To have your vision be effective you must clearly communicate it to others.

Without knowing your current location you can't plan the route to get to where you are going. In business, knowing where you are means understanding the current internal and external environment. You need to understand your strengths and weaknesses both internally and externally. You need to identify opportunities and vulnerabilities. A clear understanding of strengths and weaknesses will help you to maximize benefits while minimizing risks. You may be able to identify potential failures before you begin.

Questions you should ask include:

- What are the resources (financial, technical, skill, people, expertise, equipment, etc.) the company can commit to the project?

- What is the nature of your competitive and regulatory environment?

- What opportunities and threats are present in your current environment?

- Does your vision make sense in light of the company's current situation? Does the company have the resources needed to proceed?

- Is your organization ready for e-commerce? Is top management behind the project?

## Don't Skip the Competitive and Market Analysis

Don't forget to look at your competition. Do you have much competition? Can you expect it in the future? What is the basis on which you will beat your competition? Is your product or service better, cheaper, or higher quality?

As recommended by Michael Porter in his well-known Five Forces Model, look at your power relative to

*A good mission statement is a critical element in defining your business and communicating its true goals to its customers, vendors, employees, and owners. For example, if you believe customer satisfaction and customer service are important to you, then say so in the mission statement. If growth and profits are important, say so. If you want employees treated fairly and creativity rewarded, then say that too.*

—SEAN CARLTON, "BUILDING A SUCCESSFUL BUSINESS IN 2001"

*Tip* Decide what is important. First the vision, then what you will do to get there.

> *D*ecisions on strategies to pursue should be anchored by the mission.... A banking firm is a financial institution in its mission statement, a food and cigarette manufacturing conglomerate is a multinational consumer goods provider, a Save the Bay group is an environmental watchdog. The mission defines the unique purpose that makes the company different from others of its type.
>
> —MICHAEL W. PITTS,
> "BIZStrat Strategic Management"

your competitors, customers, suppliers, and buyers of your products and services. Do you have resources and advantages not shared by your competitors? Do they have advantages that you do not have? Are your suppliers anxious to meet your needs? Are they dependent on your business or do they have numerous other companies' to which they can sell their supplies? Do your customers need your particular product or do other companies products meet their needs? Can other companies persuade your customers to switch to them? Can other products or services be easily substituted for yours?

If you have a novel idea, can other companies enter this market easily? If so, you will want to take steps to prevent this or reconsider your ideas.

Finally, make sure that the market exists for your company and that you have a good chance of survival before entering or expanding your business. By looking at the competition and market you will increase your likelihood of succeeding in your industry.

## Getting There

On a trip, the next step is to look at how to get there. You can use either a map or your knowledge of the area to develop that plan or you can get directions on getting there. In business, you develop strategies, goals, and objectives. The strategies describe the overall course of action an organization will be taking to achieve the organization's vision. Like the route traveled to a vacation destination, the route taken may change in response to the environment. For instance, goals and objectives are similar to the landmarks you pass while traveling to your vacation destination. When you reach a landmark you know that you are going the right way. If you fail to

*Tip*    Getting there means knowing where you are now.

encounter the landmarks as expected, check to make sure you are going in the right direction to eventually reach your destination. In business, goals and objectives take the place of landmarks. They are targets or results that you set as indications your company is proceeding towards its vision. Goals are long-term, usually one year or more. Objectives are short-term, measurable results. It is important that the objectives are measurable (i.e., profits of a specific dollar amount, percent market share increase) so you can determine in the short term whether you are taking the correct actions to attain your goals and eventually, your vision. Without each of these steps there is little chance that you will reach your final destination.

## Developing a Plan for Your E-Commerce Business

In business, you develop a business plan. This is not to suggest that you always need a full-scale business plan but it can be invaluable to develop at least a mini business plan. A plan will help you focus your business, and you will need it to apply for most financing. It is therefore important to go through the mechanics of doing a plan.

Business plans serve several purposes. Entrepreneurs and CEOs may use proposals to convince venture capitalists and other potential investors to put money into the business. Alternatively, employees may use a proposal to convince management to undertake a new project. No matter what your intent, forming a business plan forces you to thoroughly analyze the feasibility of your visions so that you can achieve success. Taking a few hours to put your ideas on paper and look at what will work and won't work will pay dividends in the end. If you need

> *If you don't know where your business is going, you sure won't get there. So before you invest your time, money, and sanity in a business that goes nowhere, think through in detail what your business will do, what strengths you'll use, what obstacles you'll face, how much money it will take, and how much money you'll make.*
>
> *—KEN YOUNG, "MANAGERS FAIL DOTCOM FIRMS"*

*At the very core of starting a new—or guiding an existing—small business should be a well prepared business plan. Even if it is never used externally, the process of developing a good business plan forces the entrepreneur to ask questions and evaluate key aspects that might otherwise later blindside the company. Of course, when/if the firm opts to seek loans or other capital investment, the business plan will play a significant role.*

—BIZPLANS.COM, "BUSINESS PLANS"

*Tip* ▷ Using a business plan software program makes developing a plan both easier and cheaper than other alternatives.

financing you are likely to need a business plan to complete the financial application process.

You have several alternatives for developing your plan. First, you can hire someone else to write it for as little as $500 or as much as $10,000. Not only does this make it easier for you, but it helps ensure that your plan looks professional. You can find referrals to business plan writers at www.BizBuyer.com and other Web sites.

You can also use software to develop the plan yourself. This is an easy alternative and is likely to result in a professional looking plan. The cost should be from $50 to $100. Business Plan Pro® is a popular package. If you do not need a full business plan Bplan.com's miniplan is an excellent choice, and it is free. The components of the miniplan are sufficient for many uses. Using software is much easier than writing the plan from scratch as it serves as a guide and offers prompts and suggestions for your particular type of business.

Business plan programs are an excellent way to develop a business plan. The cost is minimal for many plans, and they provide a time saving, organized format. Bplans.com, BizBuyer.com, and many other Web sites provide information on e-commerce business plans.

### Differences between the E-Commerce Plan and a Traditional Business Plan

An obvious difference between an e-commerce business plan and a traditional one is the length. E-business plans should be much shorter than a traditional plan. While a traditional plan can be 100 pages, a plan for an e-business should be no more than 30.

Also, e-commerce is new and you may be the first to open your type of business on the Web. There is little or no historical data available and your financial section and market analysis may be less extensive than in a plan for a brick and mortar business. However, you must adequately explain the business concept and how it will be profitable.

There are many formats for a business plan. The most important elements include:

- *Executive summary.* Assume the people reading your plan will be too busy to read the entire plan. Provide a summary that describes the basics of your plan.

- *Business description.* This section should describe your products and/or services. Make sure that you include a description outlining how you plan to make money (your business model) and why it will be profitable.

- *Competitive analysis.* You should include a description of the present competition and anticipated future competition. How will you differentiate your products/services in the marketplace?

- *Market plan.* What is your target market? What is your competition? Do you have any ideas for entering the market?

- *Financial information.* What are your projections for expected costs, expected revenues, break-even analysis, and other financial factors?

- *Conclusions.* A short paragraph in the plan that summarizes and reinforces important points.

## Summary

Getting where you want to go requires a vision of your destination, decisions about how you want to get there,

> *Tip* When writing your business plan consider your audience. If they are not technical and/or Internet experts make sure you explain all technical terms so they can understand your business.

> *M*apping out your biz plan on paper will help you see the real picture (like will this bring home the bacon?). And a business plan is a "must have" if you'll be courting investors or lenders. It may seem like a chore, but consider that if you aren't willing to see that your business works on paper, what are your chances in the real world?
>
> —*Dwain Thomas in Ken Young's "Managers Fail Dotcom Firms"*

> *An e-strategy covers three dimensions. The first is to develop the business model, or define how you will make money. The second is to determine the "customer experience" because you have to learn how to interact with your customers online—which is a new concept because the things traditional retailers know about their customers are based on the traditional "in person" model. And the third is assessing your technology options, because you must know which technologies will best bring your internet strategy to life.*
>
> —*JOE GAGNON IN EMELIE RUTHERFORD'S "TO E OR NOT TO E"*

*Tip* Use your plan to make sure your idea is profitable, not just clever.

and a plan for doing it. This chapter has explained how you can take these essential steps in an easy, effective manner.

You take these steps as your first on the path to making your dreams and ideas a reality. The next chapter provides tips on financing your business.

## Chapter Key Points

- The first step in reaching your desired destination is to articulate your vision. Where do you want to go?

- Next comes your mission. How do you want to get there?

- Before you can decide what you need to do to get to your destination you need to know where you are. Analyzing your current environment, especially the competition, is essential.

- Specific strategies, goals, and objectives come next.

- Develop a plan—a business plan—showing how you will get there.

- A business plan is necessary for many financing applications.

## Web Sources for More Information

▶ **BizBuyer.com** (www.bizbuyer.com) has referrals and links to business products and information.

▶ **Bizplus.com** (www.bizplus.com) provides links and information on business planning and strategy.

▶ **Bplans.com** (www.bplans.com) offers free and for-fee business planning software. Its free mini-plan package is excellent.

▶ **Ebiz101.com** (www.ebiz101.com) provides information and links on business planning and strategy.

▶ **Enow.com** (www.enow.com) offers articles, links, and information about e-commerce.

▶ **ZDNet.com** (www.zdnet.com) contains articles, links, and information on a range of business topics.

*Online retailers are still just retailers. Sure it's a little different, but they have to follow the same business and economic rules as their brick and mortar peers. You still have to research, plan, manage, and finance carefully no matter if you are online or on Main Street. Kind of reassuring, isn't it?*

*—ABOUT.COM, "LEARN FROM DOTCOM FAILURES"*

# SHOW ME THE MONEY
## *How to Finance Your E-Business*

YOU HAVE AN IDEA. NOW YOU NEED TO GET THE MONEY TO DO IT. ◀

*T*he oldest daughter was very excited. She had just described her ideas for a Web business to her uncle who had offered to lend her $25,000 to get started. The daughter and her older brother had been trying to get financing from local banks. Even though they knew many of the bankers well, they had not been able to convince the bankers to loan the money. The bankers were concerned due to the siblings' lack of experience with e-commerce and had been further frightened by the numerous farm failures in the headlines. After such discouraging experiences with institutional sources, the uncle's offer seemed like the perfect answer.

The mother was not so sure. She recalled her father getting a loan from his brother to purchase the farm. She remembered the arguments, her mother's tears, and not seeing her cousins for several years. Her father and his brother had different ideas about the implications of the loan. Her father thought he would simply pay the brother each month like he would have paid a bank. Her uncle felt the loan gave him the right to express his opinions on how to run the farm. He would visit daily to check on how things were being done. He gave her father's employees instructions, often in contradiction to her father's orders. The brothers argued continuously. Finally, her father made enough money to pay back her uncle's loan and told him to leave the farm. They did not speak again for years.

*The widow had concerns that her children's arrangement with their uncle could end similarly. She advised them to carefully consider the personal risks before taking the loan. She insisted that they each get attorneys to draw up legal documents describing the loan terms in great detail.*

▲  ▲  ▲

Once you have decided what you want to do, how will you afford it? This chapter presents a variety of ways to finance your Web strategy and discusses the advantages and disadvantages of alternative financing methods.

Prior to obtaining financing you need to figure out how much money you will require. Your business plan can give you a general idea. Remember to factor in additional funds for unexpected expenses and underestimated revenues in case sales are not quite as brisk as you think they will be. If you are leaving a job make sure to include the lost income. If you will need childcare or will incur other expenses include those in your estimate of how much financing you will need to obtain.

A next step is to determine your comfort level with different arrangements. Do you prefer having debt or allowing others to share the equity in your company? Are you comfortable with family, friends, or business acquaintances lending you money or owning part of your company? What arrangements would you feel comfortable with? To whom would you like to be attached for the next few years?

## Necessary Documents for Obtaining Financing

Before approaching others for financing, you will want to gather the necessary documents. You will need the

> *Tip* A professional advisor, such as a CPA or Small Business Development Center (SBDC) advisor, may help you to evaluate financing options and avoid pitfalls.

> *Silicon Valley entrepreneur and venture capitalist Guy Kawasaki says starting a new business is like starting a revolution. But beware; the naysayers will try to get you down.*
>
> —*BUZZMEDIA.COM,*
> *"BOZOS KILL SMALL BUSINESS"*

following items to get financing from almost every source:

- Balance sheet or financial reports that show the worth of the company including the status of the company's assets, liabilities, and owner's equity.
- Income statements showing revenues, costs, and expenses during one accounting period. For a new company this would be a projection.
- Cash flow projections that show when the cash actually comes into and flows out of the company.
- Last two or three years of tax returns of the business, owners, and partners.
- Business plan.
- Asset appraisals and equipment leasing information.

Some institutions and individuals will require other items, especially if large amounts of money are being requested.

Obviously if you are starting a new business you will not have all of these items. A very specific and detailed business plan along with personal financial records will sometimes suffice if you have either a brilliant idea or great personal financial situation. However, usually it is more difficult to obtain financing from institutions without a business history of at least two years of being profitable. Ideas for getting financing if you do not have this history are discussed below.

## Loans and Debt

There are a number of sources for getting loans. Loans offer the advantage of not diluting your control or ownership of the company. If the business is new or has been profitable for less than two years it will probably be difficult to get loans from institutional sources. In that case you will probably have to look toward private sources, such as family or a friend, or a Small Business Administration (SBA) guaranteed loan.

### Personal Loans

If you don't have an excellent credit rating or are in a hurry for the money, you may want to get a loan from a family member, friend, or business acquaintance. This is usually easier, quicker, and less costly than other types of loans. It usually does not involve a formal approval process. However, there may be hidden costs such as potential harm to relationships or additional stressful interactions.

A lender with a personal relationship to the borrower may feel especially entitled to express opinions, critique decisions, spend time at the office, or actually take over running the business. You may disagree about the loan terms or business, especially how it should be run. Relationships can be jeopardized in the process and increase the stress for all parties involved. In addition, some of your business acquaintances may have an ulterior motive for wanting to invest in your business.

If you decide a personal loan makes sense for your business make sure that you are careful about setting the terms and expectations. Each party should have legal representation to make sure that the loan terms are fair, will pass IRS scrutiny, and are complete enough to prevent future misunderstandings. You should have a promissory note drawn up by an attorney along with a dispute-resolution agreement describing how you will resolve things should either of you default on the loan. An attorney can also help you pass IRS scrutiny. With personal loans you must make sure that the loan is at a fair interest rate and the IRS cannot consider the loan a

*E*verybody's a little different when it comes to money. Analyzing your attitudes toward money now can help you make better decisions about financing that will speed you along on the road to success.

—IDEACAFE.COM, "FINANCING YOUR BIZ"

*Tip* Without a track record, it may be difficult to get institutional loans. The SBA may be able to help. Check their programs at www.sba.gov.

gift. Also, make sure that you meet a 3 to 1 ratio of debt-to-equity to pass IRS requirements.

### Credit Cards

Cash advances on credit cards for as much as $100,000 have been used to finance a business. You can get money quickly and without needing to specify its use through a credit card. However, this is usually a very expensive way to finance a business. It should be reserved for emergencies and short-term needs for money. If you plan to use credit cards to finance your business, plan ahead. You will be more likely to get credit cards approved when you are employed or when your business has been profitable for a few years.

Make sure that you only apply for the cards you are truly interested in. Credit card companies frown on applying for too many cards so only go after the cards most beneficial for your situation. Since they all use the same credit bureaus to check applicants' records, they will know when you apply for other cards.

Make sure that the card you select fits your situation. Analyze your monetary needs and when you will be able to repay the debt. Some cards have higher interest rates but lower annual fees. Others have higher annual fees but lower interest rates. Try to match the card so that your expenses are minimized. For example, if you plan to pay off the card each month the higher interest rate card may be cheaper due to the lower annual fee. Alternatively, if you will borrow for a longer period, a higher annual fee but lower interest rate may be better.

### Institutional Loans

Loans from banks and other financial institutions are an option for businesses with a track record of at least two years of being profitable. In some cases you can

*Tip* Credit cards provide immediate but expensive financing.

W*as that a loan or an investment? If the amount of your owner's equity isn't enough to support your level of debt, the IRS may reclassify it as an equity investment. That means your interest payments won't be tax-deductible, since they'll be considered dividends to shareholders. For example, raising $1 million from investors who "lend" you $950,000 and give you $50,000 will be frowned upon. The IRS generally accepts a 3 to 1 debt-to-equity ratio at face value. Between 3 to 1 and 7 to 1 makes them nervous, while above 7 to 1 can set off their alarm bells.*

—IDEACAFE.COM,
"FINANCING YOUR BIZ"

> *Are you an S corporation, a C corporation, or an LLC? These corporate structures place limits on the number and type of investors you may have.*
>
> —IDEACAFE.COM,
> "FINANCING YOUR BIZ"

*Tip* Before you obtain equity financing, make sure that you are comfortable with others having partial ownership of your business.

use tangible assets to act as at least partial collateral for a loan in lieu of a track record. A new business will usually find it impossible to get a loan from an institution.

Loans are for a specified amount and term. The borrower is normally required to pay a fixed payment each month. The loan can be either secured, which requires that the borrower provides collateral, such as real estate or other assets that the bank collects if the borrower defaults, or unsecured involving no collateral.

A small business may be able to get help getting a loan from the Small Business Administration (SBA). The SBA has several plans designed to help new or expanding small businesses get loans by guaranteeing the loans to the lending bank or finance company. The SBA will look at your cash flow projections and the useful life of assets when considering your application. Depending on the size of the loan they will require that the owner have equity of at least 10 percent for a microloan and 30 percent for larger loans.

### Lines of Credit

Lines of credit are bank loans for a pre-specified amount that can be used for any purpose. They are similar to a cash advance on a credit card except much cheaper. Interest rates on credit lines are usually lower than for credit cards, but more expensive than a regular bank loan.

### Equity

If you are willing to share ownership of your business, getting equity investors and partners is an option. Of course they will probably want to share control of running the business. You may know people who will want to invest, or you can try to find an angel investor, a personal investor who invests "seed" or start-up money to help get your concept off the ground.

### Angel Investors

Angel investors are small, often individual investors who generally get involved in the beginning stages of a company. They usually invest one million dollars or less. Anyone with money can be an angel investor, from a rich relative to an investor you find on an Internet site. If you do not have any rich relatives and do not know anyone who might be interested in investing you can find listings of potential investors on the Internet by using a search engine and the key words, "Angel Investors." You can also find information from sites such as America's Business Funding Directory, Money Hunter, and Ideacafe. See the listing at the end of this chapter for more information.

### Strategic Partners

Forming an alliance with another company with shared goals can be an alternative for getting financing. You may have business acquaintances with other companies who might be interested in forming beneficial partnerships. Or an investment bank or corporation with similar interests may express interest in investing in your business. If so, forming strategic partnerships can be the way to obtain financing.

### Venture Capitalists

If you need a lot of money you may be able to get a venture capitalist to invest in your business. Venture capitalists are individuals or firms who are willing to provide funding for rapidly growing, profitable businesses. Venture capital firms often combine funding

> *Tip* Angel investors can be anyone. You can either choose someone you know or someone you find on the Web.

> *Some high-tech start-up companies, especially in the Internet field, have managed to go public on the strength of their concepts and business plans, even before establishing a solid track record. However, this is unusual.*
>
> —IDEACAFE.COM, "FINANCING YOUR BIZ"

> *N*otoriously impatient, they expect big and almost immediate returns on their investment. Venture capitalists don't just invest their own money; they raise funds from wealthy individuals and institutional investors (such as pension funds) who seek to allocate a portion of their holdings into potentially very-high return investments.
>
> —*IDEACAFE.COM, "FINANCING YOUR BIZ"*

*Tip* — Try to find a venture capitalist whose interests match those of your business.

from a number of investment sources so that they can invest in potentially high yielding ventures. Due to venture capitalists' investments in new, rapidly growing businesses, they incur great risk in exchange for the possibility to make lots of money. Because they take risks, they demand quick and high percentage returns on successful investments.

Venture capitalists are likely to require a large portion of ownership along with a say in the way you run your business. They often demand board and management representation and a large amount of control over the running of the business. For some this involvement can be a source of annoyance. On the other hand, their expertise can be a great help in developing a successful business.

Venture capitalist firms come in many shapes and forms. They often specialize in an industry or company stage. Some firms provide "seed money" for start-ups while others might require that a company have a proven track record. Some might focus on companies in a particular industry or marketplace like e-commerce or technology. While good for businesses needing a lot of money and those with the potential for enormous growth, venture capitalists usually want to exert a lot of control over your business. So you will want to consider the possible loss of your control in the evaluation of this funding option.

You can find venture capitalists easily on the Web by doing a search for "venture capitalists" along with your business area. This can yield listings of potential investors. Web sources are also listed at the end of this chapter. It is wise to visit investors' Web sites and learn something about them before making contacts. Get in touch with those that invest in your type of firm and business stage.

Venture capitalists will want to see strong financials prior to investing. Since they are likely to only give you a short amount of time to convince them to invest, make sure that you have a short, convincing, and memorable presentation to sell them on your ideas. A great presentation along with owner enthusiasm can be a persuasive combination.

### *Initial Public Offering (IPO)*

If you want at least $5 million and have a great track record, you may want to consider an initial public offering or sale of stock to the general public. It requires going through the Securities and Exchange Commission's (SEC) regulatory and legal processes. After an IPO your financial situation and internal operations are open to the public and SEC review. Information about going public can be found at Ideacafe.com and other sites listed at the end of this chapter.

> *The world of venture capital oscillates between greed and fear. The last three years have been a frenzy of greed, and now we have moved into a fear stage, which generates paralysis.*
>
> —MICHAEL VISARD, "VENTURE CAPITALIST IS CAUTIOUS IN ECONOMIC SLOWDOWN"

## Summary

Getting financing can be one of the biggest challenges for a new business, though once you have a track record it is usually easier. This chapter provided guidance for getting financing at any stage of your business. Table 3.1 lists potential loan sources and equity investors for different business stages.

Now that you know how to get financing it is time to develop your Web site and applications. The next chapter provides tips for designing a successful Web site.

*I*t was a fallacy for the venture community to think that at any time it was the fountainhead of innovation. The fountainhead of innovation comes from entrepreneurs. But entrepreneurs who have great ideas are few and far between. And all those entrepreneurs who have great ideas eventually find funding, venture capital or otherwise. What happened over the past few years is that with so much venture money available, anybody with a crazy or half-baked notion who could afford a pencil and a napkin could get funding.

—MICHAEL VISARD, "VENTURE CAPITALIST IS CAUTIOUS IN ECONOMIC SLOWDOWN"

**TABLE 3.1** Summary of Finance Options

| Stage/Loan Amount | Loan Sources | Equity Investors |
|---|---|---|
| Start-up or migration to the Web | Family and friends<br>Credit cards<br>SBA guaranteed loans | Business partners<br>Personal investors<br>Angel investors |
| Expansion of existing business (up to $1 million) | Credit lines<br>Bank loans<br>Business contacts<br>SBA guaranteed loans | Angel investors<br>Venture capitalists<br>Corporations<br>Strategic business partners |
| Major expansion (over $1 million) | Institutional loans<br>Business partners | IPO<br>Investment banks<br>Corporations<br><br>Strategic business partners |

## Chapter Key Points

- This chapter describes how and where you can obtain financing for starting or expanding a business.

- To determine how much you need make sure you consider all expenses and lost income related to going into a new business. Overestimate costs and underestimate revenues.

- Before getting business funding you should evaluate your level of comfort with borrowing money versus giving up ownership in the business by selling equity.

- Without a track record, initial financing can be difficult to obtain.

- Personal loans are a great source of funding.

- SBA guaranteed loans can be used to start or expand a business.

- Credit cards can also be used to fund a new business but are expensive.

- Investors are a possibility but they can take ownership and control of the business.

- Angel investors will lend "seed money" for a start-up or expanding business.

- Venture capitalists are a source of funding but want big, quick returns.

- Business partners, investment banks, and corporations can also be sources of funding.

- Initial Public Offerings (IPOs) of stock can fund millions of dollars but place your company under the scrutiny and regulatory control of the SEC.

## Web Sources for More Information

▶ **Dun & Bradstreet Inc.** (www.dnb.com) has business information and business reports.

▶ **Ideacafe** (www.ideacafe.com) features business information, links to resources, and community for the small business sector.

▶ **National Business Incubation Association** (www.nbia.org) contains information on business incubation to support entrepreneurs. Members include entrepreneurial firms, business incubators, and business assistance specialists.

▶ **Small Business Administration (SBA)** (www.sbaonline.sba.gov) provides useful information, loan guarantees, and other information for small businesses.

▶ **The Small Business Resource Center** (www.webcom.com/seaquest/sbrc) provides information on a variety of topics and links for entrepreneurs and small business people.

▶ **Yahoo! Small Business Section** (www.yahoo.com) offers listings of resources for small businesses.

# IT'S ALL IN THE DETAILS
## *Creating Web Wonders*

A GREAT WEB SITE REALLY HELPS. ◀

*T*he youngest daughter and brother decided that a Web site would be a good way to increase their flower business. They wanted the site to be both beautiful and romantic. They made several drawings and notes on what they wanted.

They thought that the initial page should feature several large photographs of flowers with a lace background and romantic music playing to help enhance their image. On the bottom half of the page, they included small photographs of a dozen floral arrangements. Clicking these small photographs would bring up a larger photograph and descriptive information. Their thinking was "a picture is worth a thousand words" and the photographs would do a good job of advertising the daughter's talents and showing the beauty of the arrangements.

The daughter and her brother met with a Web site developer and described their thoughts. The developer agreed that they would want to project a romantic image but advised against large pictures or music. He explained that these features would drastically slow down site loading, and that users were easily turned off when they waited more than a few seconds to load the site. They worked together and developed a simple but elegant site.

Your Web site is your presentation to the world. Throughout this book you will be advised to think about everything from the user's perspective. This advice is particularly important in designing your Web page, and this chapter provides guidance on how to best design a site to attract and retain customers.

## Make Your Site Easy to Use

Above all your site needs to be easy to use. Shopping cart and site abandonment are major threats to successful e-commerce. A recent Forrester Research study cited by Agentware's Business Plan said that e-commerce sites are experiencing abandonment rates as high as 67 percent. When users of your site become frustrated, they are likely to abandon the site and never return. Their business may be lost forever. To prevent abandonment, your site needs to be as easy to use as possible.

Your site also must load quickly. Make sure it does not "weigh" (Web speak for a site's size in kilobytes) too much. In other words make sure that your Web site's home page does not exceed the maximum weight of 40 to 50 kilobytes recommended by Jupiter Media Metrix, according to Dylan Tweney in "Slim Down that Homepage." A Web page that is "heavier" or larger than that will take too long to download, especially on the 56 kilobits or slower modems that many people still have. Any heavier and you may lose potential visitors who give up in frustration, refusing to wait more than the 8 to 10 seconds it takes a 50 kilobyte page to load on a 56 kilobit modem. Heavy pages are also impossible to load on current wireless technology according to Dylan Tweney.

Another reason for abandonment is that a user can't easily find things, becomes frustrated, and quits trying. Think about finding things from the user's perspective.

---

*Anybody with a Web site should submit to the following weekly exercise. First, make a list of the top five reasons your customers come to your Web site (find this out by asking them). Second, dial in from home (don't believe anyone who tells you all your customers are on high speed lines). Third, pretend to be a customer, and do the five things on your list. You might be surprised by what you find.*

—Jeffrey Graham, "E-CRM for Dummies"

*Tip*  Ease of use is more important than fancy technology.

Design the site so that information is organized in a logical, straightforward, and intuitive manner. Make the information hierarchical with a main page referring to subordinate pages.

If you have a multipage site consider including a map describing the pages and where they can be found on the site. A map can make it easier for users to find information and navigate the site.

## Projecting Your Image

Your Web site is often the first impression you give to your customers and other Web site visitors. Therefore, it is very important that your site reflect the image that you would like to project for your business. In the words of Paul Krygowski, a senior group creative director at Organic, an Internet design consulting company: "When laying out the design of a Web site, you have to understand what its underlying business objectives are. That is going to inform everything you do. Each design decision you make must be based on who your company is and who your customers are. The look should be a catalyst to drive business forward and should never hold it back."

Make sure that all words are spelled correctly and everything works before posting the site. Misspelled words and a site that doesn't work will reflect poorly on your image and may drive potential customers away forever.

Your image will be different depending on the type of business. For example, an elegant clothing retailer will want to project an elegant, sophisticated image. On the other hand, that image would probably not be appropriate for an online building product retailer. Carefully consider your desired image while designing your Web site.

> *I f you design only for design's sake, chances are you'll distract users from your products and services or, by hindering performance and usability as elaborate graphics and plug-ins take time to load, actually drive users away.*
>
> —*CADE METZ, "DESIGN PRIMER"*

## Tiffany: Keeping the Image

Tiffany has taken great pains to retain their image on the Web (www.tiffany.com). They have avoided fast, flashy, gimmicky sites. In the words of Caroline Naggiar, senior vice president for marketing at Tiffany & Co.: "Tiffany is not about being fast and expedient.... We're about graceful behavior, beauty, and quality."

The design and the quiet approach of Tiffany's site stands in contrast to most Web sites. The site is deliberately reserved with soft, subtle colors and sparse wording. It is intentionally simple and sometimes deliberately slow. The number of images appearing at one time is minimized and pictures fade onto the screen gradually. The site projects a simple sophistication and elegance associated with Tiffany's high-end image.

—*Lisa Vickery, "Keeping the Cachet,"*
*The Wall Street Journal*

## Allow for Users with Different Technologies

To get maximum usage, make sure that your site can be used by a variety of users regardless of the browser type or version. Your pages can appear differently depending on the type of browser you use. Browsers may vary in the fonts and how items are displayed. In addition, older versions of browsers cannot handle everything that a new browser can. So avoid using the latest technologies. For example, older browsers may not handle frames properly. While frames look great and can make it easier for some people, they make it impossible for those with an older browser to use your site. If the browser doesn't let users see the frame, they can't tell where they are on the site and will not be able to bookmark individual pages.

Use standard colors and fonts. You can be sure that these will be available no matter what browser is being

*Tip* Keep your customer's technology in mind while designing.

used. Bright colors and unusual fonts may be annoying to users and are more likely to load incorrectly. Also, you may want to follow the lead of many of the most customer savvy Fortune 100 companies, which use black text with a white background since this is the easiest to read and process.

## List with Popular Search Engines

Search engine rankings may be critical to your business success. Since so many people use search engines, their listings may be an important source of traffic for your Web site.

Over 90 percent of all Web users rely on search engines to find things according to About.com's "E-Commerce Tips." Therefore, to get the maximum number of visitors, you need to consider how search engines select and rank sites. Since search engines use the title words to select pages, make sure that your title properly characterizes your site and uses the words that are most descriptive of its content. Many search engines will index the words on your site to display a description in the search results. Use META tags, the title, and additional keywords to control how your site will be indexed.

You may want to evaluate the ranking your site will get by using the software, Web Position Gold (www.webpositiongold.com). This software will tell you where your site will rank with the various search engines. Due to the importance of the rankings, some companies outsource search engine optimization tasks to an expert consultant. You will find numerous experts by searching for Web developers on any of the popular search engines. A great way to find an expert is to ask

*Y*our Web site will be the cornerstone of your success online. It should look different than the "rest of the pack" and it should have a unique domain name.

—JIM DANIELS, "10 KEY COMPONENTS TO LASTING SUCCESS ON THE WEB"

*Tip* It may pay to have someone evaluate your site's position on search engines.

someone with an excellent Web site that seems to be listed high in relevant searches.

You should consider listing with all the major search engines including:

- AltaVista
- Anzwers
- AOL Net find
- Dogpile
- EuroSeek
- Excite
- Google
- Hotbot
- InfoSeek
- LookSmart
- MetaCrawler
- MSN
- MultiCrawl
- Netscape
- Northern Light
- PlanetSearch
- WebCrawler
- Yahoo!

It is not enough to list with popular engines; you must update the listings regularly as these engines drop listings frequently. Also make sure that your site and address (URL) are both listed and highly ranked. You may have to update site content, descriptive words, and tags to retain a good ranking position. Make sure that your HTML tags are all valid, as most search engines will not tolerate invalid HTML tags. You can get specific instructions on how each search engine works on their site.

*The degree to which a site will be successful depends on how professional that site is perceived to be by potential customers.*

—*ABOUT.COM, "E-COMMERCE TIPS"*

*Tip*  Make sure your site works properly and nothing is misspelled.

## Add On Features for "Stickiness"

You can build a community by including features that keep users coming back. Some ideas to increase your site's stickiness include:

- Message boards
- Chat rooms
- Free e-mail
- Syndicated content
- Site search

These features can be quickly added to your Web site with the appropriate software. Of course, the costs to do this depend on your desired level of sophistication.

One example is a message board that can be easily set up for free (i.e., Multicity.com). Or you pay a fee of $24.99 a month for 1.5GB of traffic and 10,000 messages for Infopop's sophisticated message board service, OpenTopic. A word of warning about free services: you may get what you pay for. These free message board services may appear unprofessional and not create the impression you want for your business. Free chat rooms can also be easily set up by using Multicity or, for a modest fee, Firetalk or Rooms 5.0.

Providing users with e-mail is a little more costly. The highly rated program, Bungo.com, costs between $1,000 and $5,000 for setup and $5 to $8 dollars a month per user.

By providing users with personalized content, such as news and other information that is based on their profile or preferences, you create a reason for your users to return to your site. A variety of syndicators will provide services for a range of prices based on the sophistication of service. You can add a good search engine to your site

*D id you know that approximately 90 percent of all Internet users access at least one of the major search engines to find Web sites of interest? It is critical that your Web site is ranked toward the top.*

—ABOUT.COM, "E-COMMERCE TIPS"

*Tip* Make your site is "sticky," or has features that entice users to come back.

> *If your shoestring operation means your Web site looks too pitiful to build trust, then you've cut a corner that will keep you from succeeding.*
>
> —RALPH F. WILSON, "STARTING AN E-BUSINESS ON A SHOESTRING"

*Tip* Reciprocal links are a great way to market your business.

> *Each design decision you make must be based on who your company is and who your customers are. The look should be a catalyst to drive business forward and should never hold it back.*
>
> —CADE METZ, "DESIGN PRIMER"

free and easily. Installing a search engine, like Atomz, means only adding a few lines of HTML code. When visitors cannot find information on your site, they leave and do not return. You can easily prevent this by installing search capabilities at your site. In his article "Communicating," Troy Dreier calls site search engines "among the easiest stickiness-enhancing tools a Webmaster can add."

## Linking to Other Sites

By linking to other sites and being part of affiliate programs, you can increase your Web traffic and generate revenues. In the Web environment, businesses can unite to create "win-win" opportunities for the business participating. An entire chapter is devoted to partnering with other businesses and exploring your affiliate options.

## Ensure Privacy and Security

Customers are more likely to return to your site if they feel that their communications are private and their transactions secure. Throughout this book, we provide information on how to provide customers with these features.

If users will complete sales transactions on the site, you need to make sure that the ordering process is easy and secure. More details will be provided in Chapter 19.

## Summary

This chapter showed you how to develop a Web site. Seeing things through your customer's eyes is key. Further details on designing your Web site will depend on what you want to do with your site. Remember that users may have outdated browsers or computers. You want to make sure that your site loads quickly and correctly on every computer. Since search engines are so important for visitors surfing the Net, you will want to register your site with popular search engines and make sure it ranks highly in the listings. Professional guidance can help with this. Use reciprocal links, provide services on your Web site, and make sure the site is secure.

> *Just surf the Web a while and decide what sites YOU would buy from. That will tell you volumes.*
>
> —JIM DANIELS, "10 KEY COMPONENTS TO LASTING SUCCESS ON THE WEB"

### Chapter Key Points

- When building a Web site, ease of use is key; you don't want to give visitors a reason to abandon your Web site.

- Think through the site user's eyes.

- Account for different kinds of technologies, both old and new.

- Test your page using different technologies to make sure it loads correctly.

- Register on search engines and take steps to make sure your site is highly ranked.

- You may want professional help making sure your site is ranked highly.

- Use relationship builders on your site. Discussion lists, chat rooms, and other services increase stickiness.

- Use reciprocal links to generate traffic and add value to your site.

- Make sure your site is secure and that your users know it is safe.

## Web Sources for More Information

▶ **About.com** (www.about.com) provides many useful articles and links.

▶ **B2Bmarketer.com** (www.b2bmarketer.com) is a good site for finding information on B2B marketing.

▶ **HTML Goodies** (www.htmlgoodies.com) has many good links and articles on HTML.

▶ **Quadzilla.com** (www.quadzilla.com) is a reference guide.

▶ **Stars.com** (www.stars.com) offers a lot of links and is a very good guide.

▶ **The Web Wizard.com** (www.thewebwizard.com) features tips and advice on building a Web site and how to maximize effectiveness on the Web. User ratings and reviews are also provided.

▶ **The WebMonkey** (http://hotwired.lycos.com/webmonkey/design/site_building/tutorials/tutorial1.html) is a great tutorial on building and designing Web sites with the customer in mind.

▶ **Web Position Gold** (www.webpositiongold.com) is an inexpensive software package that helps you evaluate how your site will do on search engine listings.

# SECRETS OF SUCCESS
## *Learning from Others' Mistakes*

E-COMMERCE IS BUSINESS AND THE FUNDAMENTALS APPLY. ◄

*The youngest daughter and her brother presented their proposed Web site and ideas for expanding the flower business to the rest of the family. They told the family about using the Web to sell flowers for holidays and special occasions. They also described the daughter's proposition for expanding her floral wedding arrangement designs as part of their flower business.*

*The other family members loved their ideas but were concerned about their ability to compete with the well-known, national Web-based florists. They also were not sure how they would make any money after paying for the Web site, flower delivery, and other expenses. After doing a number of projections they quickly realized that the delivery costs would be their largest expense. It became clear they could not profitably compete with the national chains selling flower arrangements for holidays and special occasions.*

*At first the daughter was devastated that she would not be able to pursue her dreams. After some thought, she realized that they could overcome some of their potential problems by specializing in floral wedding arrangements. She could use the Web site to provide pictures of her work and establish links with other wedding services. By specializing in orchid wedding packages, she would not directly compete with the large online florists. Also, delivery expenses would be cost justified by the amount they could charge for the larger orders.*

> *The most important thing to understand about e-business is that it is first and foremost about business.... E-business starts with the CEO, not the CIO.*
>
> —TREVOR R. STEWART,
> "SUCCEEDING IN E-BUSINESS"

*Tip* > Even in the "new economy" the old business rules apply.

Before building a new business take a look at those who have gone before. The well-publicized failures of e-commerce firms demonstrate the dangers of going into new business territory blindly. To avoid a similar fate and be victorious on the Internet, you need to learn from the mistakes and successes of those that have gone before.

This chapter will present the major lessons learned from e-commerce business ventures and describe steps to take in order to increase the likelihood of success. While all of these are important determinants of e-commerce success, the first three are not only important, but critical to your survival.

## Lesson #1: Always Remember that E-Commerce Is Business

Many business experts agree that many dotcoms failed due to the neglect of fundamental business principles. With all the hype and frenzy of the dotcom craze the companies forgot that e-commerce is just a technically enhanced form of business and violated fundamental principles. Many of the dotcom failures were businesses built on unprofitable business ideas. They seemed to mistake Web site popularity for profits. The focus was on generating investor funding rather than profits. They overspent on people, technology, marketing, and other areas without having the revenues to support the spending. They forgot that e-business is business.

## Lesson #2: Have a Profitable Idea

This may sound like common sense but a number of the early Web pioneers forgot that to succeed in any kind of business, including e-commerce, you need to have a potentially profitable business idea or model. Profits are

## Sigma Networks

The importance of good planning is demonstrated by the approach of Sigma Networks, a provider of broadband links between high-traffic users and the Internet backbone. John K. Peters, Sigma CEO, is taking a slow approach to growth after witnessing the mistakes of other high-speed Net access providers. His experience in the industry includes being CEO of Concentric Networks, which was sold to NextLink Communications in 2000 for $2.9 billion. He has seen providers run out of cash after blanketing metropolitan areas with their networks. He describes the change in approach as, "In the old days, the strategy was: `Build it, and they will come.' Now, you want to see the whites of their eyes before you build it."

—STEVE KAMM, "THE NEW NETREPRENEURS," BUSINESS WEEK E.BIZ

the money left after costs are subtracted from revenues. Some early pioneers spent more than they made and had no money left after their expenses were paid.

To be successful, it is critical that you have a profitable business idea or model. This means that you not only need to generate revenues, but it is also essential that you minimize your costs. Don't hire anyone or buy anything you don't absolutely need. Make sure that all investments can be cost justified and are directly related to your future profits. Chapter 6 describes current business models and how others have made money on the Net.

## Lesson #3: See Through the Customers' Eyes

Throughout this book, you will be advised to see things through your customers' eyes. To succeed you must see things as your customers do whether you are designing your Web site, advertising, performing customer service, processing orders, or delivering products. According to

In the end, an e-business is just another business.

—JEFFREY RAYPORT, "THE TRUTH ABOUT INTERNET BUSINESS"

## Keeping the Purse Strings Tight at Epinions.com

While the high profile Productopia failed late last year, Epinions.com is succeeding in the same business by keeping a tight rein over its expenses. Both depended largely on advertising revenues to support their site, listing customer reviews and ratings for products and services. The business is built on content from customers, so Epinions.com has always been dependent on users for providing product and service reviews. By enticing users through an interesting and informative site, Epinions.com has been able to reduce the rate paid for customer reviews by a factor of ten and users are continuing to provide content. Through the use of popular site features, such as the innovative "Web of Trust" that allows users rate reviews, Epinions.com has been able to efficiently outsource category management to its users. It has reduced their expenses to less than $1 million a month, a reduction of 50 percent in ten months.

—*JOE ASHBROOK NICKELL,*
*"RADAR: THE DOTCOM CLASS OF 2000 GROWS UP,"*
SMARTBUSINESSMAG.COM

Jeffrey Graham in his article "E-CRM for Dummies," the number one rule of customer relationship management is seeing your company's processes and interactions through your customers' eye. You can make your customers happy if you can view your company as they do and make changes to best fit their needs.

## Lesson #4: Relationships Are Everything

Build relationships with present and potential customers. Dana Blankenhorn in "This Week's Clue: Secrets" says, "make every customer service call an opportunity to thrill someone. That's how you build 'word-of-mouse,' and dominate larger opponents. Large companies see customer service as a cost, and an opportunity to up-sell. Don't make that mistake."

It is much cheaper to take the steps necessary to retain a current customer than to get a new one. Chapter

*Tip* Make sure you have the needed resources and are fully prepared before making major changes.

## The Wisdom of Slow Growth: Tesco.com

Tesco.com, a British online grocer, ignored criticism by analysts for their slow growth approach. Tesco.com started slowly by allowing customers to order from a single store of the Tesco chain, which is a giant British grocery retailer. Before growing larger, Tesco.com wanted to make sure that delivering groceries made sense. It experimented with processes and made sure the venture would be profitable prior to expansion.

Due to the extremely competitive nature of the grocery business, Tesco.com proceeded cautiously and perfected processes to minimize costs. They required that delivery customers only place orders on the Web. Rather than building costly warehouses as did the failed Webvan.com, pickers use handheld devices to speed order gathering in existing stores. While the additional processes add some cost, Tesco.com has found that online customers tend to be more affluent, order higher margin merchandise, and are willing to pay a delivery fee.

Through their slow, deliberate approach Tesco.com has built a successful business in a seemingly impossible one. It now has the service available in 250 stores with capacity to deliver to 91 percent of Britain's population. This year revenues are expected to be more than $450 million with a net operating margin of over $22 million. According to retail analyst David V. McCarthy of Schroder Salomon Smith Barney, "They were the only company in the world to really get it."

—*Andy Reinhardt, "Tesco Bets Small and Wins Big,"*
*BusinessWeek Online*

15 gives greater guidance on how to develop loyal customers through Customer Relationship Management (CRM) programs and issues.

## Lesson #5: Think Long-Term

Many dotcom failures were very innovative. Unfortunately for them, "first movers" are not necessarily the long-term winners. Being first requires greater risk and expenditure. The failures of innovative dotcoms show that.

*Tip* Ignoring the fundamentals can be fatal for your business.

WINNING THE NET GAME

*A brief stop at the Standard's Flop Tracker shows plenty of companies that were, at one time, the biggest dogs on the block. When I hear of one dotcom or another laying off hundreds of employees, my first reaction is always 'What the heck were those people doing anyway? Wasn't the Net supposed to breed unheard-of efficiencies?*

*Weren't we actually supposed to be able to do more with less?' Growth on investment money isn't necessarily real growth. In many cases, it might just be a major monument to major egos. Look at your growth strategy. Is it working? Do you really need all those people? How efficient are your processes? Is size merely masking the symptoms while the company rots from the core?*

*All in all, none of this stuff is rocket science.*

—SEAN CARLTON, "BUILDING A SUCCESSFUL BUSINESS IN 2001"

While the Internet provides unique opportunities for both attracting and retaining customers, Web innovators like Drkoop.com, Chemdex.com, and Pets.com prove that success is not guaranteed for a "first mover" even if the idea is brilliant. The expenditures of first movers for designing and creating everything from scratch are enormous. Often, their expenditures are much higher than those incurred by others who follow the leader. Sometimes innovators win the market, sometimes they don't. In the words of Peter Keen, it is more important to be a "first learner than a first mover."

## Lesson #6: Specialize

A great way for small businesses to thrive is to specialize by finding a niche market. The market can be something everyone wants or needs that no businesses are adequately filling. Friedman's Shoes of Atlanta, Georgia turned its business around by specializing. Friedman's was a small shoe store located in a depressed area before realizing there was a market for supplying NBA players with shoes for their very big feet. They developed a small, plain Web site but succeeded online by filling the unmet needs in an unusual niche market.

Small specialized businesses were among the survivors of the recent dotcom crashes. A new class of dotcoms, the "mini-dots," have succeeded by focusing on one specialized product or service rather than directly competing with larger businesses.

Mini-dots, like the company "Waggin Tails," that specializes in hard to find pet vitamins, have thrived as they sell products customers would otherwise have difficulty finding. They don't compete with the larger businesses, because they don't carry the same products. Waggin Tails doesn't have to be concerned with selling at the lowest possible price since almost no one else carries the products. That may account for the success of Waggin Tails while Pets.com, a much larger, heavily funded Web business that sold a large variety of products, failed.

## Lesson #7: Make Your Business Ready for E-Commerce

Make sure that your business culture is ready for e-commerce. If you are migrating from a traditional brick and mortar business to one with an e-commerce component you need to make sure that your people, technologies, and processes are ready. Do you have the technical skills and infrastructure necessary to succeed in e-commerce? Are you and other top executives willing to commit your time and resources to the project? Are you willing to provide employees with the training and education necessary to make the project a success? A new project is much more likely to succeed if your organization is prepared and willing to take it on.

## Lesson #8: Grow Slowly

Focus on slow growth rather than rapid expansion. Make sure that you don't mistake initial popularity of your site for loyal customers. A new, novel site may generate a large number of site visits. However, that initial excitement does not necessarily translate to either return customers or profits.

The lesson for us all is to grow cautiously and not to become overconfident and greedy due to initial high volume traffic and immediate success.

## Lesson #9: Run Your Business Well

Don't try to do everything yourself. Don't try to do everything internally. Outsource all items outside your

> *F*orty-four percent of companies with fewer than 10 people turn profit, while only 26 percent of companies with more than 100 turn profit on their Web sales.... Small companies whose sales increase 336 percent from 2000 to $120 billion in 2002 will outpace overall e-commerce growth of 249 percent.
>
> —ARLENE WEINTRAUB, "THE MIGHTY MINI-DOTS"

*Tip* Find a niche, one no one else is meeting, and fill the void.

*U*nlike some dotcoms with inexperienced executives, the minidots are succeeding by employing the same strategies that small-business owners have relied on for centuries: They're sticking to niches they know well. They scrimp on expenses, forgoing expensive portal deals and using Net resources, from e-mail to customer-sharing arrangements, to save money. And they're banding together on the Web, presenting a bigger face to the online world.

—ARLENE WEINTRAUB,
"THE MIGHTY MINI-DOTS"

*Tip*  Market through multiple channels to reach more potential customers.

expertise. Outsourcing allows you to improve your performance and profitability by letting you concentrate on your core, value-adding activities while reducing your investments in technology, people, and infrastructure. The decades old Peters and Waterman axiom, "stick to your knitting," applies here.

## Lesson #10: Multichannel May Be the Way

Multichanneling is the practice of using many different mediums to sell your products. Selling online is one channel, while catalog or direct mail may be another. Based on a recent study of five e-commerce industries by McKinsey & Company, they recommend that e-commerce businesses use multiple channels for sales including online, catalogs, and stores. Joanna Barsh, a director at McKinsey & Company, explains that to be successful, online retailers need to exploit other marketing channels simultaneously, such as in-store and catalog sales, as well as private labels. She points to the success of a number of apparel e-tailers that are already using multiple channels. Their study shows that multichannel players can increase their share of the wallet, as many consumers are already browsing on the Web before buying in the store.

## Lesson #11: Form Strategic Alliances

Gordon Whyte in his article "An E-Commerce Survival Guide" describes partnerships as "one of the best ways of protecting your business. This can be as simple as cross-linking with complementary (not competing) sites or more formal arrangements to promote and sell products on other companies sites."

Chapter 21 describes in greater detail how alliances and strategic partnerships can help you succeed on the Web.

## Summary

This chapter has outlined the lessons learned from e-commerce successes and failures. The most important lessons to remember are the rules for e-commerce, which are the same as for any business: profits matter, and you need to see things through your customers' eyes. Learn from the lessons of others outlined in this chapter and you will be able to achieve success.

### Chapter Key Points

-  This chapter outlined the lessons learned from e-commerce successes and failures. The first three lessons are critical to success. Failure to adhere to these can easily undermine your chances of success.

- Always remember that e-commerce is business.

- Have a profitable idea.

- See things through the customers' eyes.

- Relationships are everything.

- Make your business ready for e-commerce.

- Think long term.

- Specialize.

- Grow slowly.

*There are all sorts of specialties. There are product specialties, service specialties, and content specialties. By specializing you get depth larger rivals can't match. Even if the rival has lower prices, your knowledge of the field gives you an edge, and real market share.*

*How do you choose your niche? The key word, as with this newsletter, is passion. Ask yourself what you care about most, what you would do for nothing. That's where your specialty will lie. Your chance of success is greatest when you really enjoy what you are doing. That passion comes through online.*

*—DANA BLANKENHORN, "THIS WEEK'S CLUE: SECRETS"*

*Tip* — Stick to your knitting.

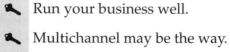

🔑 Run your business well.

🔑 Multichannel may be the way.

🔑 Form strategic alliances.

## Web Sources for More Information

▶ **About.com** (www.about.com) provides a lot of information and numerous links to information sources, vendors, and Web sites.

▶ **Brint.com** (www.brint.com) is a free membership organization that provides links to articles, information, and vendors. White pages describing aspects of B2B commerce are posted on the site.

▶ **B2B Today** (www.b2btoday.com) is a B2B vertical portal, community, and directory. It also contains a business shopping directory.

▶ **ClickZ.com** (www.clickz.com) provides community, information, resources, and links to a number of business topics.

▶ **CommunityB2B.com** (www.communityb2b.com) is a community and contains B2B white papers, articles, and news.

▶ **E-Marketer.com** (www.emarketer.com) contains statistics and analysis of the latest marketing, B2B, and e-commerce trends.

▶ **Line56** (www.line56.com) contains newsletters and research giving an analysis of B2B e-commerce. Current, as well as back-issues of these papers are available.

# MODELS FOR MONEY
## *Developing Profitable Ideas*

THE INTERNET OFFERS A VARIETY OF WAYS TO DO BUSINESS. ◄

*The widow found the Internet fascinating and believed it held the key to long-term farm stand profitability. She was beginning to find ways to save money on the Web. She joined an Internet group of farmers who pooled their purchasing power to get quantity discounts on supplies, equipment, and services. The discounts allowed the smaller farms to better compete with the large, factory farms that seemed to be swallowing up all the remaining small farms in their area.*

*The widow used an auction site to sell some equipment that they no longer were using and purchased some rare antique farming tools. When they needed a new tractor, she was able to find customer reviews and a listing of dealers and prices. Using this information she got a much better price from her local dealer. She even switched from her traditional broker to an online broker, because she loved being able to trade instantly.*

*The widow knew that the Web was huge and that she was only aware of a small part of its potential for improving farm stand viability. She wanted to learn as much as possible about the types of businesses and marketplaces on the Web.*

*The Internet and e-business provide significant opportunities for businesses of all sizes. However, like any operation, one needs a clearly defined strategy with a solid business model in order to succeed.*

*—UNIVERSITY OF SOUTH CAROLINA DARLA MOORE SCHOOL OF BUSINESS, "E-COMMERCE"*

*Tip* B2C and B2B are the most talked about forms of business but there are others. Most notable are government interactions with businesses and peer computer interactions.

Throughout this book, the emphasis has been on the need to have a successful and profitable business model. In their book, *Internet Business Models and Strategies* (McGraw-Hill), Afuah and Tucci make the point that "the first determinant of a firm's performance is its business model. This is the method by which a firm builds and uses its resources to offer its customers better value than its competitors can and make money doing so. It details how a firm makes money now and how it plans to do so in the long term. It is what, preferably, enables a firm to have a sustainable competitive advantage."

This chapter describes the e-commerce marketplace, different types of e-commerce, and a variety of e-commerce models. By learning about how others have made money on the Internet, you will have a better foundation and more ideas on how you can do it too. Subsequent chapters define how these models are implemented within the marketplace.

## E-Commerce Marketplaces

The e-commerce marketplace consists of several different types of businesses.

- Business-to-Business (B2B)
- Business-to-Customer (B2C)
- Peer-to-Peer (P2P)
- Business-to-Employee (B2E)
- Business-to-Government (B2G)
- Government-to-Business (G2B)
- Government-to-Consumers (G2C)
- Government-to-Government (G2G)

The Business-to-Customer (B2C) marketplace consists of businesses selling products, services, and information to consumers. B2C commerce contains a host of virtual stores and "e-tailers." Consumers are most familiar with this type of e-business, and there are countless examples of B2C commerce on the Web including Amazon.com, Eyewire.com, eBay.com, uBid.com, and other online B2C auction sites. Some would argue that auction sites like these are actually examples of Consumer-to-Consumer, or C2C, implementations. Because they are interacting with a business not directly with each other, they are categorized as B2C. The Business-to-Business (B2B) marketplace consists of companies exchanging products, services, and information with other companies. This is an enormous area of e-commerce. When you hear someone mention Many-to-Many commerce, they are usually talking about one type of B2B market exchange. Applications include supply chain linkages between companies and suppliers and automated procurement systems. Businesses may exchange with each other to sell to a customer or another business.

Business-to-Employee applications allow businesses to save money and time getting information to employees. They can increase employee productivity by giving easy access to information.

The Peer-to-Peer (P2P) market has been publicized due to the Napster case. P2P is personal computers and other Internet connection devices—the peer devices—interacting directly rather than through a server computer or hub. P2P computing is almost always used in conjunction with other more traditional modes of computing.

The Business-to-Government (B2G) marketplaces consist of government organizations buying services and goods from the business community, often through auction sites and other marketplaces. Government-to-Business (G2B) and Government-to-Consumer (G2C)

> *The marketplace is the place of exchange between buyer and seller. Once one rode a mule to get there; now one rides the Internet. An electronic marketplace can span two rooms in the same building or two continents. How individuals, firms, and organizations will approach and define the electronic marketplace depends on people's ability to ask the right questions now and to take advantage of the opportunities that will arise over the next few years.*
>
> —DEREK LEEBAERT, THE FUTURE OF THE ELECTRONIC MARKETPLACE

*Tip* The Web has given rise to new, innovative, and creative approaches to business.

markets are the government offering Web-based services for businesses, citizens, and consumers. Government-to-Government (G2G) commerce is government organizations forming exchanges to streamline their interactions.

## E-Commerce Business Models

Business models are the ideas that describe how the organizations make money. Michael Rappa in "Business Models on the Web" defines a business model as "the method of doing business by which a company can sustain itself—that is, generate revenue. The business model spells out how a company makes money by specifying where it is positioned in the value chain."

Usually, revenues are calculated by multiplying price by the quantity sold. From that revenue subtract your costs and expenses. To give you some idea of the potential business models explore the generic Web-based commerce models presented in this chapter. These are based largely on the taxonomy of Web business models identified by Michael Rappa, professor of e-commerce, at the University of North Carolina, Chapel Hill. He has developed a very comprehensive, often cited description of Web-based business models. He identifies the following models, each of which has several subtypes. (See his Web site for further details: http://ecommerce.ncsu.edu/business_models. html.) These models are:

- Brokerage
- Advertising
- Infomediary
- Merchant
- Manufacturer
- Affiliate

> *F*irst-generation B2B and B2C models are now morphing into "B2B2C" and "B2B2B" hybrids. These new e-commerce models are more than the sum of their organizational components. And many e-businesses see them as their corporate salvation.
>
> —CESAR BREA, "MANY-2-MANY"

*Tip* Government organizations are developing e-government applications in a big way.

- Community
- Subscription

The *Brokerage Model* represents several types of Internet brokers, which serve the same functions as traditional brokers. They bring buyers and sellers together for a fee. Rappa calls them "market makers." Brokers are a powerful force in many e-commerce realms. They can assist buyers and sellers by reducing their overall search, marketing, and procurement costs.

Under the broker category, Rappa describes a *Buy/Sell Fulfillment Model* in which brokers match buyers and sellers and charge a transaction fee.

A number of types of *Brokerage Service* cater to the B2B marketplace. *Market Exchanges* match business buyers and sellers using offers to sell and buy or auctions and bids to establish prices. *Business Trading Communities* assist in B2B exchanges by aggregating information on products, suppliers, industry news, job listings, and classified advertisements for their users. *Buyer Aggregators* help small purchasers unite so that they can get volume discounts.

*Catalog Aggregators* combine several catalogs on one site. This is an enormous area in the B2B procurement marketplace. *Distributors* connect product manufacturers with volume and retail buyers using a catalog-type operation, which in turn connects a large number of product manufacturers with volume and retail buyers. *Classifieds* charge fees for listing advertisements for items being sold or wanted for purchase.

*Virtual Malls* host a number of online merchants for a monthly charge and transaction fee. Metamediary and zShops provide more sophisticated services such as automated transaction and relationship marketing. Companies such as *Auction Brokers* charge the seller a fee to list their products, take bids, and assist with purchases.

*Tip* Most of the B2B markets are online brokers.

*J*ean-Paul Sartre once said history could be viewed as if one were looking out the back of a moving car: all the nearby scenery is a blur that starts to come into focus somewhere down the road. And so too it is with e-commerce business models—they are still blurring past us at an unprecedented speed, whilst there is not yet much further down the road on which we may focus.

—CHRIS FOX, "BUSINESS MODELS THAT HAVE SUCCEEDED AND BUSINESS MODELS THAT HAVE FAILED— INTERNATIONAL CASE STUDIES"

> *O*nline auctions are the biggest success story. Online auctions will account for $1B in sales for 1998. Fixed pricing was invented as recently as 1872. The Web has allowed large scale haggling to make a comeback. OnSale does $150M/year. eBay does $25M/month. TravelBids.com provides a reverse vacation bidding process—where travelers enter in their vacation desires and participating travel agents bid on the business.
>
> —TIGER BUFORD, "EMERGING BUSINESS MODELS ON THE WEB"

*Tip* Catalog aggregators are very important in B2B.

In *Reverse Auctions* (i.e., Priceline) buyers are told to "name-your-price" and make a bid for the product or service.

*Search Agents* use an intelligent software agent or "robot" to find a specific good or service for a buyer at the best price. An employment agency can act as a search agent broker, finding work for job-seekers or people to fill open positions listed by an employer.

*Bounty Brokers*, such as Peoplefinder.com, offer rewards for finding a person or hard to find item.

When traffic volume is large or specialized, the *Advertising Model*, posting ads on Web sites, can be successful. Generalized portals (i.e., Yahoo!) post advertisements in many areas; specialized portals only handle ads in that specialty; and personal portals allow users to personalize their Web content. Incentive sites provide users with a payment or incentive for viewing advertisements. Free sites offer "freebies" such as Web services, Internet access, hardware, or greeting cards to create a large volume for their advertisements. *Bargain Discounters* sell goods at a reduced cost and make money on advertisements.

An *Infomediary Model* collects, analyzes, and sells information to other businesses. They may provide consumers with information about Web sites. Some offer users Internet access or free hardware in exchange for buyer information. *Recommender System* sites exchange customers' opinions about products and services they purchased.

The *Merchant Model* includes the "etailers" who use the Internet to sell products to businesses and customers. *Catalog Merchants* sell using a catalog. *Virtual Merchants* are the pure-play e-tailers that only sell online. *Clicks and Bricks* (also called Clicks and Mortar or, by Rappa, Surf and Turf) are traditional stores supplemented by Web sites. *Bit Vendors* are Web sites that sell digital products.

The *Manufacturer Model* consists of manufacturers selling directly to customers, bypassing the traditional middleperson. The *Registration Model* generates data by having users register and provide information in key areas prior to using their site.

The *Affiliate Model* consists of businesses partnering to increase their individual revenues through financial incentives and programs, such as banner exchange, pay-per-click, and revenue sharing programs. The *Community Model* consists of opportunities to advertise, be an info-mediary, or form a specialized portal to loyal communities. The *Voluntary Contribution* model exists as users make voluntary contributions. *Knowledge Networks* are sites where people can consult expert volunteers and users about a variety of topics.

*Subscription Models* users pay access to the site. *Utility Models* charge users depending on the time or amount of information obtained.

> *M*anufacturer Model— This model is designed to take advantage of the Internet and allow manufacturers to reach buyers directly thereby compressing the distribution channel. The resulting cost savings can be passed on to the customer through lower prices, improved customer service, or better understanding of customer preferences.
>
> —UNIVERSITY OF SOUTH CAROLINA DARLA MOORE SCHOOL OF BUSINESS, "E-COMMERCE"

## Summary

This chapter presented an overview of the different types of marketplaces and models that exist on the Web. The next chapters will provide examples of how these types of models are implemented in B2B and B2C commerce. The descriptions of marketplaces and models should help you to further develop your business ideas so you can make money on the Internet.

> *Tip* Business partnerships and affiliate programs form a large part of Web business.

> *P*erhaps the company that best exemplifies how the Internet can change business models is Dell, whose massive online selling effort isn't about making and selling PCs as much as it is about using the Internet to meet a variety of customer needs, such as automated corporate procurement and self-service technical support.
>
> —RICHARD KARPINSKI, "THE NET CONTINUES TO TRANSFORM BUSINESS MODELS"

## Chapter Key Points

- This chapter has described different Web marketplaces and models.

- The basic marketplaces were defined: Business-to-Business (B2B), Business-to-Customer (B2C), Peer-to-Peer (P2P), Business-to-Government (B2G), Government-to-Business (G2B), Government-to-Consumers (G2C), and Government-to-Government (G2G).

- The generic models that exist within the marketplaces were also described. These are based on Rappa's taxonomy of Web business models. Future chapters will describe their implementation for B2C and B2B.

- The models are Brokerage, Advertising, Infomediary, Merchant, Manufacturer, Affiliate, Community, and Subscription.

## Web Sources for More Information

▶ **Business Models for Electronic Markets** (www.electronicmarkets.org/netacademy/publica tions.nsf/all) includes Paul Timmers' description of business models on the Web.

▶ **Business Models on the Web** (http://ecommerce.ncsu.edu/business_models.html) presents professor Michael Rappa's taxonomy of Web-based business models.

▶ **Online Business Models** (www.wired.com/wired/archive/online_business_models) defines online business models.

▶ **Portals to Profit: E-Commerce Business Models** (www.igigroup.com/st/pages/portal.html) is a market report that describes current e-commerce business models.

▶ **The Truth about Internet Business Models** (www.strategy-business.com/briefs/99301/page1.html) is an article in which Jeffrey F. Rayport explains that "in the end, an e-business is just another business."

▶ **Wharton's Value through e-Commerce Business Models** (www.ebizchronicle.com/wharton/ 18_creating_value.htm) presents another way to look at e-commerce business models.

# B2B COMMERCE
## *Exchanging for Market Share*

THERE ARE MANY OPPORTUNITIES FOR B2B COMMERCE. ◄

*T*he family was branching into a number of new businesses. The older daughter was developing her floral wedding arrangement business, the son was selling produce to local supermarkets, and the grandson was developing ideas for a delivery business. While each business seemed to be doing fairly well, the widow still worried it would not be enough.

Before he died, the widow's husband had been very involved in developing a superior line of crops through production of hybrid seeds. He competed and won awards for growing the best watermelons and tomatoes in the state. The younger daughter had loved the competition. She spent most of her time trying to perfect their produce by growing hybrid crops and developing better growing processes. Unfortunately, produce sales at the farm stand were down. People did not seem to want to drive as far for superior produce. Also, perfect produce seemed less important to the supermarkets than low price.

The younger daughter wanted to find a way to justify the time she was spending on growing superior produce. Since the farm stand was well known for its produce and had won state-wide awards, she thought that she could make money by selling seeds to other farmers. She found a B2B exchange devoted to plants and garden supplies. She began to sell her seeds but got only a few sales. She was not surprised when the exchange went out of business.

*The daughter found a site focusing on crops. It contained an auction devoted to crops and listed her seeds. She immediately began to sell more seeds. The site got a lot of traffic. It offered management and agricultural expertise, weather information, growing tips, and news.*

▲  ▲  ▲

*T*hroughout history, markets have always recreated themselves, shifting the economic fortunes of those present at the creation.

—*Peter Fingar, Harshna Kumar, and Tarun Shirma, "21st Century Markets"*

Businesses are using Web-based business-to-business (B2B) commerce to improve processes, reduce costs, and even create new ways of doing business. By 2005, the B2B marketplace is expected to trigger more than $6 trillion in trade, according to a new report by Jupiter Communications. This chapter shows you the ways businesses make money in B2B commerce. By studying how other businesses are making money on the Web, you may get some ideas about how your company could make money through B2B commerce.

## Types of Exchanges

Web-based B2B commerce consists of information exchanges between companies. These can be divided into three basic types of exchanges.

*Tip* — Small companies can use the Internet to benefit from sharing information with business partners as some large companies have done for years.

1. *One-to-one exchanges.* Individual companies sharing information and conducting electronic transactions with each other through the Internet, Extranets, and other private networks.

2. *One-to-many exchanges.* "Hub and spokes" markets in which small companies (spokes) buy from or sell to one dominant company (or in some cases a few companies), which develops and maintains the market for its benefit.

3. *Many-to-many exchanges.* Many buyers and many sellers participate in B2B marketplaces and

exchange goods, services, information, and money with many other businesses.

## One-to-One B2B Exchanges

Companies can receive great benefits by establishing one-to-one communication links with other companies. One-to-one company exchanges are not new. Large companies have been doing this for years, using electronic data interchange (EDI), which is the exchange of data and processing of transactions over private networks. For many years large buyers and suppliers within specific industries, such as automobile, aerospace, and chemical, have used EDI to exchange information to order goods, check on order and inventory status, and automate accounting. These systems sometimes evolved into automated procurement systems.

The Internet has made this type of information exchange feasible for many more companies. Using the Web for one-to-one information exchange with each other, companies are able to reduce transaction costs, minimize inventory lead-times, and enhance product quality. Throughout this book, you will read about how organizations are using information collected from their business partners to customize product design, shorten product development cycles, and improve their value chain efficiencies. The most sophisticated implementation of this trend is *collaborative commerce*.

## One-to-Many B2B Exchanges

Realizing the power of exchanges, some large companies have set up exchanges to purchase and sell products to small companies. Some large companies set up *buy-centric markets* or procurement hubs. Some were

> *O*ver the next several years, businesses will face an array of new opportunities to improve and expand their sales and procurement processes. They must invest now, even though the payoff will take some time. It will require several years to see a substantial migration from today's manual, paper-based solutions to tomorrow's Internet purchasing counter.
>
> —Chet Dembeck, *"U.S. B2B to Reach $6 Trillion by 2005"*

*Tip* ▷ Large companies have used EDI for years to exchange information. Using the Internet, small businesses can do the same.

> *A study released in June by Forrester Research says that firms must master dynamic collaboration. They must share information, not only across the enterprise but outside the enterprise, to achieve their next big B2B breakthrough.*
>
> —KOVAIR, INC., "STRATEGICALLY SPEAKING: SRM NEWS AND FACTS"

*Tip*

Large companies aggregate smaller companies in exchange for their own convenience and for service, product, and price comparisons.

formed by single large companies while others were formed by a few large buyers. Examples are K-Mart's Retail Link, K-Mart's buying hub, and Covisint, an automobile supplies procurement site founded by General Motors, Ford, and DaimlerChrysler to assist them in their purchasing. The companies have developed the markets for their own benefit. By bringing together fragmented small businesses in a common market, they are able to more easily compare products, services, and prices.

The opposite are sell-centric markets, such as Grainger.com and GE Global Exchange, that have only one or a few big sellers working together to build a marketplace for many small dispersed buyers. These sites may have one-to-many relationships with one or a few sellers interacting with many buyers. These markets have been set up for the benefit of the seller or in some cases, a few sellers. Seagate Technology uses its portal, Seagate Reseller Marketplace, to sell its products. Its Web-based order-management portal allows business buyers to purchase Seagate products, check available inventory, compare prices, and order. Seagate's portal allows registered resellers to sell their products through the site but permits Seagate to maintain control over its brand and prevent channel conflicts.

## Many-to-Many B2B Exchanges

B2B marketplaces join many buyers with many sellers to form virtual venues for exchanging goods, services, and information. Using Rappa's terminology (see Chapter 6), you can identify different types of B2B marketplaces including *Market Exchanges, Auctions, Infomediaries,* and *Community Sites.* Businesses can fall into more than one category.

When you hear discussions of B2B, often the reference is to what Rappa calls the *Market Exchanges*, B2B exchanges with many buyers and many sellers. These are neutral markets, favoring neither buyer nor seller. They add value and charge a fee, usually a transaction fee, for providing a market forum where buyers and sellers may exchange. Their survival depends on their ability to get a critical mass of buyers, sellers, and transactions.

To confuse the picture, there are many other names often used for many-to-many B2B market exchanges including vertical hubs, online exchanges, e-market, infomediaries, metamediaries, electronic markets, Internet markets, I-market, digital marketplaces, digital exchanges, net hubs, virtual store fronts, virtual marketplaces, e-hubs, butterfly markets, vortex businesses, online exchanges, private exchanges, fat butterfly, vortals, private exchanges, vertical exchange, and horizontal exchange. The terms, "butterfly markets" and "butterfly hubs," are good descriptions of what these markets look like, because they resemble a butterfly with a large number of sellers joined by the body or exchange to a large number of buyers.

Ariba.com operates one of the largest B2B exchanges focusing on the purchasing of noncapital, nonraw material items that range from office supplies to temporary help. Ariba has partnering arrangements with many Fortune 100 and other companies including Ernst & Young, Hewlett Packard, and IBM to include goods they would like to buy or sell. Ariba.com is an example of a horizontal exchange as it offers a category of products to a wide range of businesses.

Since exchanges like Ariba charge transaction fees to act as "middlepeople" or "disintermediaries" and favor neither buyers nor sellers, they can be considered to be

*C*urrently, direct channel—a model of one seller to many buyers—dominates 92 percent of the Internet B2B market," says a report by Jupiter Communications. "However, in 2005, 35 percent of the Internet B2B trade volume will be conducted via a net market, a matching up of many buyers and sellers."

—*"TRENDLINES,"* CIO MAGAZINE

*Tip* You can use your catalog to develop collaborative commerce with your buyers.

*Tip*  Infomedi-
aries col-
lect,
analyze, and sell
information on
all products,
Web habits, and
other things.

*E*xchanges will have to add collaboration to create stickiness. Simple buy/sell transactions will be almost free, like e-mail. B2B winners will establish "platforms" that link deeply with their customers—we call them "e-hubs".... Exchanges that handle complex, collaborative functions before and after the order (design, fulfillment, and coordination) can evolve into e-hubs with economics of interest to investors. In B2B margins are a function of complexity and branding, not volume."

—CESAR BREA, "MANY-2-MANY"

neutral exchanges. To succeed, neutral exchanges need a critical mass of buyers, sellers, and exchange transactions. By partnering with both large and small businesses, Ariba has reached the critical mass required to succeed as a neutral market exchange.

Some exchanges specialize in meeting the needs of specific industries or segments. *Vertical markets* provide a wide variety of products and services but are tailored to one type of business or industry segment. Rappa uses the term *Business Trading Communities* to describe these vertical markets or exchanges that aggregate information on products, suppliers, industry news, job listings, and classified advertisements for their users. PlasticsNet.com, which focuses on the needs of the plastics industry, and eSteel.com, which focuses on the needs of the steel industry, are examples of vertical markets.

On the other hand, some markets specialize in particular categories of goods and services. *Horizontal markets* specialize in a specific category of products and services for a wide variety of businesses and industries. These include Guru.com, which posts labor projects needing workers, and Tradeout, which lists surplus assets.

There are other types of many-to-many exchanges. *Buyer Aggregators,* such as BountyQuest, bring together small purchasers so that they can get volume discounts. Catalog businesses act as intermediaries between producers and potential buyers to create added value.

*Catalog Sites,* also called *Catalog Aggregators* and *Distributors,* match buyers with sellers of a variety of items, usually fixed price items from a number of businesses. This is a very common distribution method for retail companies to use for transactions with other companies. For example, Emhart Fastening Teknologies, a division of Black and

Decker, sells 10,000 types of fasteners to the automotive, aerospace, defense, domestic appliances, electronics, and telecommunications industries through digital catalogs that connect with buyers from any B2B procurement network, exchange, or marketplace. The catalog allows users to search for products meeting exact specifications, provides streaming video to help users define specifications, allows users to define and set parameters, and provides design capabilities including Computer Aided Design (CAD) so that users can immediately create their own products online. Through its catalog, Emhart automates its selling processes and, by collaborating on product specifications, is able to differentiate itself from the competition in spite of the commodity nature of its business.

Catalog applications are a huge component of B2B commerce, largely due to the high volume and repeat purchases of Maintenance Repair and Operations (MRO) procurement. Businesses repeatedly buy the same large numbers of low value nonproduction goods, such as office supplies, repair parts, cleaning and facility maintenance supplies, and related services. Businesses are focusing a lot of attention on using the Internet to reduce these costs and their particularly high order processing costs, as they account for as much as 30 percent of the total cost of doing business according to the article "21st Century Markets" by Fingar, Kumar, and Shirma.

## Auction Sites

Auction sites provide an efficient method for businesses to sell items and surpluses to other businesses. For example, Autodaq Corporation uses online auctions to match wholesale buyers and sellers of used cars. This is

> *When both sellers and buyers are fragmented a third party creates a neutral exchange. It's easy to see that an online marketplace, which mirrors the physical marketplace, will make it easier for companies to transfer information, and make financial transactions quicker and more efficient. The real point about business on the Net is that it allows completely new ways of doing business to develop.*
>
> —TIGER BUFORD, "EMERGING BUSINESS MODELS ON THE WEB"

*Tip* Auctions are a powerful force in e-commerce.

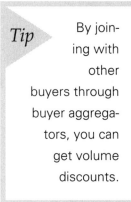

*Tip*  By joining with other buyers through buyer aggregators, you can get volume discounts.

*T*he broker aggregates supplier offerings, simplifying matching and searching for the buyer. Conversely, the broker brings an aggregation of potential buyers to the seller whose task of getting buyer attention is reduced.

—PETER FINGAR, HARSHNA KUMAR, AND TARUN SHIRMA, "21ST CENTURY MARKETS"

a major process improvement for buyers and sellers. It saves the transportation costs of moving vehicles and people to and from the auctions and also saves the time involved. Because buyers and sellers are not limited in time and space, they can interact with others from long distances away, these auctions are changing the way business is done. Com Auction is an example of an online B2B auction site. Businesses use B2B auction sites to sell off surplus inventory and equipment.

Another auction example is FreeMarkets, which is a buy-centric site, hosting auctions for purchasers of industrial parts, raw materials, commodities, and services, such as injection-molded plastic parts, commercial machining, metal, chemicals, circuit boards, corrugated packaging, and other industrial-type components. Buyers list their goods and compete to bid the lowest price; this is the opposite of a traditional auction site like eBay.com, in which the winning bid is the highest.

Since Freemarkets.com favors the buyer by attempting to obtain low purchase prices, auctions can be either buy-centric or sell-centric. However, eBay and many well-known auctions derive their revenues from transaction fees and can be considered neutral.

## Community Sites

Businesses also interact on community sites, also known as community alliances, which allow them to barter goods, services, or physical space without any money changing hands. They can also exchange ideas. They can also research information on a range of topics of interest for a specific industry and form political lobbies. For example, one company may have surplus warehouse space while another has too much of a particular raw product. Rather than selling these, the two can exchange them on a community site. Members of communities may be affiliated with a specific industry, be members of the same profession, or have shared interests. A member having a problem or needing information on something can communicate with others in the community to obtain answers. Often, members will exchange services and helpful information.

## Infomediary Model

You can collect, analyze, and sell information to other businesses with the infomediary model (i.e., ClickTheButton). They may provide consumers with information about Web sites. Some offer users Internet access (i.e., NetZero) or free hardware (i.e., eMachines.com) in exchange for buyer information. The *Recommender System* (i.e., Epinions) exchanges customers' opinions about products and services they purchased. Depending on the communities served, the implementation of the models can be either vertical or horizontal.

## The Future: Collaborative Commerce?

By many accounts, the future of B2B is collaborative commerce—the cooperation, coordination, and support of transactions and surrounding processes by people in one or multiple organizations. An example of collaborative commerce would be suppliers and purchasers collaborating on the development of both products and specifications. The collaborations could be supported by the B2B exchange through sophisticated workflow and resource management or simply though bulletin boards, chat rooms, and e-mail.

> *The future of e-commerce has less to do with selling CDs and books online to consumers, than it does with selling transformers and rivets via the Internet to other businesses.*
> —*Lori Enos, "The Biggest Myths about B2B"*

*Tip* Community sites allow you to exchange things without money changing hands.

# Summary

This chapter has described B2B commerce so you can benefit from the many opportunities available. The various relationships—one-to-one, one-to-many, and many-to–many—were explained. The Internet brings the power of EDI, something that large businesses have used to exchange information for years to small businesses.

One-to-many exchanges are usually controlled by one or a few large businesses who want to aggregate small sellers or control sales. Many-to-many B2B exchange markets are many sellers and many buyers coming together in some type of hub to exchange goods, services, information, and money. The future of B2B is enabling the market participants to engage in collaborative commerce.

## *Chapter Key Points*

🔑 This chapter defines the types of B2B models to help you see how you may be able to make money using B2B commerce.

🔑 B2B models can be divided into three types of relationships: one-to-one, one-to-many, and many-to-many.

🔑 Large businesses have used EDI to exchange information (one-to-one) with individual business partners. You can use the Internet to exchange information with your business partners.

🔑 Large companies use the Internet for their own benefit when they form one-to-many relationships by forming markets of small businesses who want to sell to or buy from them. These are also called buy-centric or sell-centric markets.

- B2B market exchanges are many-to-many markets where many buyers and many suppliers exchange money, goods, and services.

- B2B market exchanges take many forms such as auctions, aggregated catalogs, horizontal markets, vertical markets, etc.

- Collaborative commerce is changing business and B2B markets. B2B markets can enable collaborations between parties so they can work together in support of business transactions.

## Web Sources for More Information

▶ **About.com** (www.about.com) provides a lot of information and numerous links to information sources, vendors, and Web sites.

▶ **Brint.com** (www.brint.com) is a free membership organization that provides links to articles, information, and vendors. White pages describing aspects of B2B commerce are posted on the site.

▶ **B2B Today** (www.b2btoday.com) is a B2B vertical portal, community, and directory. It also contains a business shopping directory.

▶ **ClickZ.com** (www.clickz.com) offers community, information, resources, and links to a number of business topics.

▶ **CommunityB2B.com** (www.communityb2b.com) is a community and contains B2B white papers, articles, and news.

▶ **E-Marketer.com** (www.emarketer.com) contains statistics and analysis of the latest marketing, B2B, and e-commerce trends.

▶ **Line56** (www.line56.com) contains newsletters and research giving an analysis of B2B e-commerce. Current, as well as back-issues of these papers are available.

# E-TAIL AND MORE
## *Clicking with Customers*

THERE ARE MANY OPPORTUNITIES FOR B2C COMMERCE. ◀

*T*he oldest grandson had just gotten his driver's license and delivering groceries would be a great way to let him practice driving and earn money. He was disappointed when the family told him that the grocery business had only about a 1 percent profit margin so it would be very difficult to launch a successful delivery business. He wondered how he could compete with large area supermarkets while incurring the expenses for purchasing and maintaining delivery vehicles, implementing needed technologies, delivering and arranging delivery times (allowing for getting lost and people not being home as scheduled), and sorting orders.

Another idea occurred to him. He suggested that the family begin a shopping service with delivery of groceries and other items to the farm stand for customer pickup. He would charge an annual fee for the service. They had some storage space and he could use the farm stand truck for now. If enough customers signed up, the fee would pay for additional space and a larger vehicle. He would include groceries and other potentially higher margin items in the service. He was sure the dry cleaner, pharmacist, and other businesses would pay him a small percentage for this service.

The grandson decided to use an easily implemented e-mail ordering system. He sent an electronic form to customers as an e-mail and instructed customers to simply cut and paste the form into a new e-mail, fill it in, and return it to him as *their order. He was pleased with his concept. He had thought of a way to do some driving, help his customers, and eliminate many of the logistical problems of online grocery services.*

▲ ▲ ▲

The business to consumer (B2C) marketplace consists of businesses selling products, services, and information to consumers. The Web opens up a number of profitable options that weren't possible in traditional retail settings. Not only can the Web be used for promotion and sales, it allows businesses to better meet customer needs, automating the entire process from sale to product delivery. B2C commerce is synonymous with "e-tailing." Consumers are most familiar with this type of e-business.

While the media has tended to focus on dotcom failures, B2C commerce is growing worldwide. In the recent Ernst and Young's study of online commerce in 12 countries, two-thirds of the people interviewed worldwide reported making at least one online purchase during the past year. In the United States, 74 percent of the respondents reported buying online while 75 percent of respondents from the United Kingdom and Germany reported buying something online during the past year. For 97 percent of the participating consumers worldwide, the number of purchases either stayed the same or increased. For 96 percent of the respondents, the amount spent online increased.

Worldwide, 97 percent of those who bought something through the Internet said they would continue to shop online in the future.

## Benefits of B2C Commerce

B2C will continue to grow as it can bring benefits for both companies and consumers. Most consumers say their

> *O*nline retailing is emerging from the shakeout of 2000 with stronger consumer demand and improved profitability.
>
> —*Melody Vargas, "The State of Online Retailing"*

*Tip*   In spite of the media's reports of gloom and doom, worldwide online sales are growing.

primary reason for shopping online is saving time. Ease of selection was mentioned by 57 percent, and 54 percent said competitive pricing was their main reason for shopping on the Web according to Ernst and Young's Global Online Retail 2001. For companies, potential benefits from B2C commerce include:

- Anytime, any place shopping
- Reduced inventory costs
- Lower capital expenditures on physical store locations
- *Disintermediation* or cutting out any intermediaries or middlemen

There are three main types of B2C businesses: (1) "pure-play" companies that do business only over the Internet; (2) catalog merchants that sell through direct mail catalogs and online; and (3) "clicks and bricks," also called "clicks and mortars," businesses that have a traditional brick and mortar business that is complemented by a thriving online business.

## Frequent Online Purchases

Consumers are purchasing a number of products on the Web. The most popular purchases were books, CDs, and computer equipment. Worldwide, 54 percent of the respondents bought books, and in the United States it was 52 percent. Worldwide, music was next popular with 48 percent. In the United States, the five most popular products for purchase were books followed by computers, music, apparel, and tickets/reservations. In non-U.S. countries the top five purchases in decreasing order of sales volume were books, CDs, computers, tickets/reservations, and videos.

> *T*he business model is first and foremost for a strategist. It leads and it is the center point. Building the model takes around 60 percent of the effort.
>
> —*EMELIE RUTHERFORD, "TO E OR NOT TO E"*

*Tip*  Most consumers report that time savings is a major reason for shopping online.

## Formula for Success in E-Tailing

According to a new study by McKinsey & Company and Salomon Smith Barney, pure-play retailers are the most vulnerable to failure. The authors found multichannel e-tailers significantly increased their chances of survival if they not only sold from the Web but also used at least one other channel to sell their goods. This is according to Beth Cox in "Is Pure Play the Wrong Play? Yes, Says New E-tail Study." Multichannel retailers have more avenues for generating revenues and were more likely to have survived the B2C shakeout.

Many online shoppers, about 30 percent in the McKinsey study, reported having a preference for shopping at sites that had physical stores. Unfortunately for the physical stores, over half of online shoppers report they actually go to the store location less frequently due to online shopping. Ernst and Young found that traditional brick and mortar retailers are losing sales to online retailers.

The McKinsey-Salomon Smith Barney report also suggested that to be profitable e-tailers should try to increase their average order size, discount item prices as infrequently as possible, and sell higher-margin items. In the words of Joanna Barsh, the leader for McKinsey & Company's e-tail practice and also a director, "The e-tail shakeout now underway doesn't mean the industry is economically unsound. Winners will be those who focus on making their current transactions profitable while stopping the suicidal race to acquire unprofitable customers at any cost."

The McKinsey-Salomon Smith Barney e-tail economic study found that due to low Internet margins, e-tailers were often forced to spend more than they made on orders, ranging from $2 to $12 per order. They found that frequency and size of orders was more of a factor in profitability than the number of customers.

> *Consumers are demanding an online option, and it has become a competitive necessity. If you're not selling online, shoppers will look elsewhere to make online purchases.*
>
> —ERNST AND YOUNG, "GLOBAL ONLINE: RETAILING: 2001"

*Tip* Some say pure-play is the wrong play.

## The Look of the E-Tail Marketplace

Using Rappa's categories, look at the different types of B2C businesses. B2C businesses can be placed into Rappa's model major categories of Merchant, Brokerage, Advertising, Infomediary, Subscription, Affiliate, and Community models. Subcategories include Search Agent, Bounty Broker, Virtual Mall, and the Registration model.

### *Merchant Model*

Most B2C businesses fall under the merchant category. These include pure-play virtual merchants, catalog merchants, and click and brick merchants. When people think of e-commerce, they usually think of businesses in the merchant category. E-tailers such as CDNow.com and Drugstore.com fall into this category. These are pure-play merchants, virtual merchants that do business only on the Internet. We can also think of numerous high profile dotcoms in this category that did not survive the B2C shakeout including eToys.com and Pets.com. This is not surprising given the McKinsey study. Even Amazon.com, the favorite Web site of 29 percent of the people interviewed in the Ernst and Young study, made its first profit in late 2001. Catalog sites or distributors are those that sell on the Internet and through a catalog. Web catalogs give users power to do things impossible with paper catalogs. For example, the Lands' End online catalog allows you to shop virtually with a friend, dress an online model of yourself so that you can see how items will look on you, and use a personal shopper to advise you on fashion and dressing.

Clicks and bricks merchants are those that have at least one traditional location in addition to selling through the Web. They include specialty stores, discount

*Tip* A multi-channel approach, larger orders, and frequent orders are key.

*As online retailers gather more experience and develop more sophisticated techniques, the potential is there to delight consumers in new and interesting ways."*

—BETH COX, "IS PURE PLAY THE WRONG PLAY?"

*Tip* Many traditional retailers are getting Web sites.

*C*lick and brick merchants include department stores like Federated Department Stores, J. C. Penney Company, May Department Stores Company, Sears, Roebuck and Co., Target Corporation, Wal-Mart Stores, Gap.com, Costco Online, REI.com, and many others.

*Tip* Auctions are changing the way business is done and are creating opportunities for small business.

stores, hypermart and department stores, and retail mass merchants (discount store and department store operators). Recent studies have shown that merchants with a physical location and those using multiple channels for sales, distribution, and advertising are more successful than pure-play merchants. There are many examples of clicks and bricks merchants including traditional department stores, bookstores, toy stores, pharmacies, hobby/craft stores, and others.

### Auction Sites

Auction sites are changing the way we do business and creating profitable venues for small businesses that might otherwise not be able to find them. For example, on the traditional sites, uBid, eBay, and Onsale, buyers compete and thus, drive up the price. The opposite happens on sites where aggregate buyers end up reducing prices. For example, Mercata uses We-Commerce™ to reduce prices as more people purchase a particular product or service. Reverse auctions let people submit the lowest possible bid and then see if their bid is accepted. For example, Priceline.com sells airline tickets, hotel rooms, and other items through the reverse bidding process. Through Priceline's "name your own price," customers state the price they are willing to pay for items, and Priceline lets them know whether or not the price was accepted.

### Advertising Model

When traffic volume is large or specialized, the advertising model of charging fees for posting ads on your Web site can be successful. Generalized portals (i.e., Yahoo!) post advertisements in many areas specialized portals (i.e., 1st Search) only handle ads in that specialty; and personal portals (i.e., myYahoo!) allow users to personalize their Web content.

Some incentive programs give Web site users a payment or incentive for viewing advertisements. Others, such as those using the free model (i.e., BlueMountain), offer freebies such as Web services, Internet access, hardware, or greeting cards, to create a large volume for their advertisements. Bargain discounters (i.e., Buy.com) are able to reduce the cost of goods and make money on advertisements.

Many businesses use the advertising model to supplement another type of business. Businesses with another dominant business can also derive a substantial portion of their income from advertising. These include a range of horizontal, vertical, and personalized portals

*Web catalogs/orders include Chadwicks of Boston, Coldwater Creek, Concepts Direct, Great Universal Stores PLC, Hanover Direct, J.C. Penney, Lands' End, Lillian Vernon, Rivertown, SkyMall, and the Spiegel Group.*

# Reflect.com

Reflect.com, a beauty products retailer, provides a customized, interactive experience for site visitors. Hannelore Schmidt's title, "director of consumer delight and loyalty" is an indication of how determined the company is to excel at customer service. They aim to duplicate "Nordstrom's model of customer service, which is based on the theory of surprise and delight."

To achieve customer loyalty, the company collects and analyzes information about customers and site visitors. The company asks customers to complete a lengthy questionnaire about preferences regarding cosmetics.

Reflect.com uses the information collected to generate personalized e-mail, develop customized products for each customer, analyze visitor information, and create custom Web pages on the fly. They can quickly change their Web site to include promotions on specific products in reaction to weather conditions and other environmental factors.

—Lisa Napell Dicksteen, "Beauty site gets personal with Oracle, WebSphere, E.piphany," TechUpdate

Tip Infomediaries provide information about Web sites and consumers.

*Web sellers of books, videos, and music are Barnes & Noble, Blockbuster, Books-A-Million, Borders Group, Chapters, Family Christian Stores, Hollywood Video, Musicland, and Textbook Retailers.*

Tip Selling Web advertising is frequently used to supplement revenues.

and other sites including Yahoo!, AltaVista.com, MSN, Excite@Home, and Amazon.com, which derive much of their revenue from selling the advertisements that appear on their site. Yahoo!, for example, sells banner advertisements that appear on each of their pages and also banner advertisements that appear only when certain key words are the basis of a search.

## Infomediary Model

Businesses using the infomediary model collect, analyze, and sell information to other businesses. For example, Clickthebutton.com provides consumers with price, feature, and service comparisons for millions of consumer items. Some infomediaries offer users Internet access (i.e., NetZero) or free hardware (i.e., eMachines.com) in exchange for information about you as a consumer. The Recommender System (i.e., Epinions) exchanges customers' opinions about products and services they have purchased.

## Search Agents

Search agents use an intelligent software agent or "robot" to find a specific good or service for a buyer at the best price. For example, MySimon.com will search the Web for retailers that sell a particular product or service. Sites in this category will provide information on price, product and merchant evaluations, customer ratings, and other information that will help a customer make purchase decisions. An employment agency type search agent finds work for job-seekers and people to fill open positions that are listed by an employer.

### Bounty Brokers

Bounty brokers, such as Bountyquest, offer rewards for finding a person or hard to find item. There are several services, such as USPublicinfo.com and PeopleFinder.com, that offer to find people you went to high school with, ancestors, and others, as well as people's criminal and other records you are willing to pay for.

### Virtual Malls

Virtual malls, such as ChoiceMall, host a number of online merchants for a monthly charge and transaction fee. Metamediary, Yahoo! stores, and zShops provide special features such as shopping carts, credit card processing, relationship marketing, and other automated transaction services.

### Manufacturer Model

The manufacturer model (i.e., Intel) consists of manufacturers selling directly to customers, bypassing the traditional middleman. These manufacturers lower costs through disintermediation and pass savings on through lower prices, improved customer service, or better understanding of customer preferences. Dell computer is an example of this model at its best. It uses the Web to allow customers to individualize their computer configurations. Since Dell only builds the computers after they are ordered, they save costs through disintermediation and reduced inventory and related expenses.

### Registration Model

The registration model generates data by having users register and provide information in key areas prior to

*Toy sellers on the Web include FAO Schwarz, KB Toys, and Toys "R" Us.*

*Tip* You can pay to find almost anyone or anything on the Web.

*Direct to consumer merchants include Amway, Avon, Creative Memories, Kirby, Longaberger, Mary Kay, Shaklee, and Tupperware.*

## Southtrust Bank: E-Travel

Two years ago Southtrust Bank switched to a Web-based booking system for its 14,000 employees. Company-wide employees are encouraged to use the online booking system for their travel arrangements. The company still uses travel agents for special or unusual bookings or last minute trips requiring the skills of a booking expert.

Karen Bearden, travel manager for Southtrust Bank, estimates "Southtrust has saved tens of thousands of dollars so far from using Web-based bookings." Much of the savings comes from the system's built-in travel policies that only allow employees to make selections that comply with company travel guidelines and take advantage of lower fares. Productivity is also increased as employees are freed from "playing phone tag" with travel agents trying to book their flights.

—*Renuka Rayasam, "Time Travel Expenses,"*
*Smart Business Magazine*

using their site. These sites require you to register as a member and provide your e-mail address and other information. They can then use that information to market to you or sell the information to others who will use the information to better target marketing efforts.

### Voluntary Contribution Model

The voluntary contribution model exists as users make voluntary contributions. For example, knowledge networks (i.e., Abuzz) are sites where people volunteer expertise to a community to benefit others.

### Subscription Model

Subscription models (i.e., *The Wall Street Journal, Consumer Reports*) users pay to access the site. Utility models (i.e., FatBrain) charge users depending on the time or information obtained.

*Tip* You can save money bypassing traditional distribution methods.

## Summary

This chapter has described the many forms that businesses use to sell to consumers. The descriptions of marketplaces and models will help you to further develop your business ideas so that you can make money on the Internet. The next chapter touches on one of the most important parts of e-commerce, building relationships with your customers.

*E*vidence is mounting that multichannel retailing is a compelling premise for every type of store operator in every product classification.

—*Ernst and Young,*
*"Global Online: Retailing: 2001"*

### Chapter Key Points

🔧 In spite of well-publicized B2C failures, online shopping is growing worldwide.

🔧 There are many ways for businesses to sell to consumers online.

🔧 There are three kinds of B2C commerce:
- *Pure-plays*. Companies who only do business online.
- *Catalog merchants*. These companies sell through direct mail catalogs and online.
- *Clicks and bricks*. Companies that have a physical store and conduct business online.

🔧 Brokerage sites use traditional, reverse, and innovative forms of auctions to sell products.

🔧 Manufacturers can use the Web to bypass traditional middlemen.

*Tip*    Information is a valuable commodity for which Web sites will exchange services.

*A*s the Internet adds to an already complex business environment, multichannel retailers can't expect to meet their corporate objectives if they go it alone...Alliances offer viable solutions when partners complement each other...Trend is toward short alliances.

—*Ernst and Young,*
*"Global Online: Retailing: 2001"*

## Web Sources for More Information

▶ **About.com** (www.about.com) provides a lot of information and numerous links to sources, vendors, and Web sites.

▶ **Brint.com** (www.brint.com) is a free membership organization that provides links to articles, information, and vendors. White pages describing aspects of B2C commerce are posted on the site.

▶ **ClickZ.com** (www.clickz.com) provides community, information, resources, and links to a number of business topics.

▶ **CommunityB2B.com** (www.communityb2b.com) is a community and contains B2B white papers, articles, and news.

▶ **E-Marketer.com** (www.emarketer.com) contains statistics and analysis of the latest marketing and e-commerce trends.

▶ **Line56** (www.line56.com) contains newsletters and research giving an analysis of B2C e-commerce. Current, as well as back-issues of these papers are available.

*Tip* — Being online is becoming a requirement for retailers.

# E-GOVERNMENT AND NONPROFIT E-COMMERCE
## *Gaining New Opportunities*

GOVERNMENTS ARE DISCOVERING THE POWER OF THE INTERNET.

*The grandson began his business taking grocery orders using e-mail, facsimile, and phone, and then shopped for customers and brought orders to the farm stand. Enough customers had paid the annual fee for him to purchase a freezer, refrigerator, and a small used trailer for temporary storage of the groceries and other items. His customers were pleased with the service and tipped generously. He wanted to find ways to expand the business.*

*Unfortunately, the logistics of home delivery made it unprofitable. Searching the Web one day he came across a B2G portal site that was requesting bids for grocery delivery to the state youth correctional facility, located a few miles from the farm stand. The grandson thought that delivering food to the facility for the 50 facility residents would be a natural expansion of his business. It would allow him to practice his driving skills and buy himself a new, larger truck he had long been eyeing.*

*The grandson used calculations from his present grocery pickup service to determine how much he would have to charge for the business. He was hoping that they would eventually want to expand to higher margin purchases but thought that there would be little demand by facility residents for higher margin items such as dry cleaning and flowers. On the other hand, he had been able to obtain a promise for a government discount from the primary supermarket where he purchased goods. He put together an estimate of his costs, and submitted a bid on the B2G portal.*

Government and nonprofit organizations are increasingly using the Web to perform business. Their growing use of the Web has created many opportunities for small business. First, small businesses can sell products and services to the government and nonprofit organizations. They can sell services to help these organizations successfully develop their Web businesses. They can benefit from participation in the new markets developed by these organizations. Finally, they can form alliances with government agencies and nonprofits to enter new Web markets.

Most government organizations have been slow to fully commit to e-government but are gradually becoming more involved. In Rachel Konrad's "Will B2G Become the Next Big Thing?," she predicts that government e-commerce is a potentially very large market, although it isn't likely to eclipse the overall size of the B2B market, which is estimated to be anywhere from $3 trillion to $50 trillion annually by 2005. According to the Gartner Group, government e-commerce, also called e-government, is expected to grow from $1.5 billion in 2000 to $6.2 billion in 2005. Recent legislative efforts are likely to make e-government even larger. They have established hundreds of millions of dollars annually in funding, an e-government portal, and the addition of a federal CIO responsible for implementing information policy, overseeing procurement, facilitating program coordination of e-government ventures across federal agencies, and setting standards and protocols.

## E-Government Opportunities

The Internet offers new opportunities for small business to participate in government offerings. E-government consists of four types of commerce:

---

*A*t its ITexpo 2000 symposium in San Diego, technology analysis firm Gartner Group predicted the dollar value of e-government, including hardware, software, and internal and external services, will grow from $1.5 billion in 2000 to $6.2 billion in 2005.

—MARY MITCHELL IN FRANCISCO QUINTANILLA'S "B2G COMMERCE WILL BE BIG BUSINESS"

---

*Tip* Government and nonprofit organizations are finding value in the Web.

- Business-to-Government (B2G)
- Government-to-Business (G2B)
- Government-to-Consumer or citizen (G2C)
- Government-to-Government (G2G)

There are numerous opportunities for small businesses to benefit from each of these realms of commerce.

## B2G

Opportunities for small businesses to benefit in B2G commerce include:

- Being able to compete in requests for proposals
- Selling through government e-procurement
- Offering software and programming services
- Partnering with other firms and government organizations

### Request for Proposals (RFP)

In the past, it was difficult for many small businesses to learn about government needs, and even harder to successfully compete for a RFP. The Internet allows government organizations to reach out to more businesses by posting needs and request for proposal announcements on B2G portals accessible to anyone with Web access. The Web also makes it possible for a small business to easily contact other businesses so that they can join forces to fill RFPs.

### Selling Products and Services

Government purchases are an enormous source of revenue for traditional businesses. Through B2G procurement sites, small businesses can sell goods and services to government entities. There are a number of B2G

*Even with growth projected at more than 400 percent over the next five years, B2G will continue to be a small part of Internet business compared to the $6 trillion in B2B transactions recently projected for 2005 by Internet commerce research firm Jupiter Communications.*

*—Francisco Quintanilla, "B2G Commerce Will Be Big Business"*

*Tip* There are numerous activities for small businesses in B2G, G2B, G2C, G2C, and nonprofit Web commerce.

*O*ne valuable aspect of developing B2G expertise lies in the fact that even with the potential in the United States, still more opportunities await overseas as all governments succumb to the online itch.

—*JOHN FURTH,*
*"UNCLE SAM WANTS B2G"*

*Tip* ▸ The Web allows small businesses to sell goods and services to government agencies.

portals, such as BidNet, B2Gfree, and 8amall.com that make it easy for small businesses to sell products to government agencies.

Andrew Whinston, head of the Department of Management Science and Information Systems at the University of Texas at Austin, sees enormous potential for B2G procurement. He predicts that "you could have contractors having auctions online, product development and delivery, and tie-ins between the aerospace industry and the Defense Department. You could be talking about the largest e-commerce market in the world."

The Web provides a forum for businesses and government to share the information needed to open the process to greater small business participation.

In addition to B2G e-procurement services, some sites also support a virtual workplace allowing businesses and agencies to manage projects, coordinate work, hold online meetings, and manage projects. They also may include rentals of online applications and databases according to Whatis.com.

### Offering Web and Programming Services

There is enormous potential for small businesses offering Web and other services designed to help the government catch up with the private sector. Most government agencies currently lack the expertise, procedures, and technologies to efficiently conduct e-business. The government's ineffective use of Web e-mail is indicative of their need for outside help. In April 2000, Jupiter Benchmarking Report found that government agencies returned e-mail from their Web sites only 52 percent of the time, often with form e-mail that didn't address a person's original concerns. Less than 1 percent of all government sites were available in any language other than English. Also, the majority of sites required people to have high-end computers or take special measures to view all available information. Many of the agencies would benefit from small business expertise with these problems.

Dotcoms have already been involved in helping federal, state, and local governments to develop Web applications. GovConnect developed applications for 34 states to allow citizens to pay state taxes and child support, and apply for unemployment benefits online. State and local citizens are able to use solutions from Ezgov.com such as ezProperty, which allows them to review property records and pay property taxes online using a credit card or bank draft, and EzTicket, which collects penalties for parking and speeding tickets. Link2Gov applications let citizens renew driver's licenses and tag registrations or update professional banking and real estate licenses online as featured in "Dotcoms Pitch Public Service" by Heather B. Hayes.

A number of dotcoms such as Ezgov.com Inc., GovConnect Inc., NIC Commerce, and Carta Inc. have developed "install-and-go" software packages to service public-sector transactions. These are hosting applications, providing integration, and helping with re-engineering.

### Partnering with other Firms and Government Organizations

Partnering with other firms already established in the IT government market, can help small businesses to enter the federal market with its complex applications, need for more integration, and scalability. Also, they can use partners with government track records to help them address security and reliability concerns. For example, to

> *Look for and partner with individual leaders. Often, one or two champions within the government are able to pull a solution through the bureaucracy. Find those champions, and win them over to your cause. Take advantage of the current political tide. Political figures are eager to have their name associated with e-commerce ventures, and projected savings to the taxpayer from e-government initiatives are getting significant political mileage."*
>
> —JOHN FURTH,
> "UNCLE SAM WANTS B2G"

*Tip* The Web allows small businesses to compete for requests for proposals (RFPs).

succeed in the federal market Ezgov.com has partnered with IBM and Carta Inc. with Microsoft.

## G2B, G2C, and G2G

Small businesses can provide help to government agencies developing G2B, G2G, and G2C applications. G2B is the government providing services and selling to businesses. G2G is government agencies streamlining interactions between them. There are essentially two types of G2C: 1) the government selling to consumers and 2) the government servicing citizens, making it easier for people to obtain information and complete transactions with the government. Due to the huge potential of these areas to increase revenues, decrease expenditures, and improve services, government organizations have great incentives to develop these applications. On the other hand, most do not have the necessary expertise in-house. There are enormous opportunities for small businesses to help in these areas.

Government selling to businesses and consumers can generate huge revenues. In 2000 the Treasury Department's Web site alone made $3.3 billion dollars of its total retail sales of $15.6 billion of U.S. savings bonds, Treasury bills, and notes over the Web. Treasury Web sales were $800 million higher than the revenue of the Internet's largest retailer, Amazon.com.

The second type of G2C sites, those servicing citizens, will allow citizens to pay taxes and register vehicles online, reducing the government's need for paper pushers and possibly generating revenues for companies that build and host the government sites and charge user fees. These sites can offer forms and allow users to fill out forms, provide payments, ask questions, etc. Many state and local governments have used the Web to improve services to their citizens.

*T*o succeed in e-government: Begin at the grass-roots level. Regional governing bodies are demonstrably more flexible and open in their thinking. Build on those relationships before you think about tackling state or federal efforts.

—JOHN FURTH, "UNCLE SAM WANTS B2G"

*Tip* Programming firms have worked with the government and developed "install and go" software.

The federal government has seen the potential of G2C and G2B services to citizens and businesses to increase effectiveness and reduce expenditures. The federal Election Commission hired NIC Commerce to help it with an application that enables citizens to search for information about the source and amount of individual campaign contributions. The Census Bureau is trying to find potential partners to help it put reams of census 2000 data online for citizen queries and perusal.

In spite of these benefits, the federal government has been slow to develop G2C applications. However, federal government G2C applications will grow more in the future, especially in light of recent legislation. Larry Bradley, federal e-business solutions manager for IBM Corporation explains, "For a number of reasons, the federal government has really been focusing its time and money first on internal processes and then business-to-government connections. Now I think they're finally starting to really look at providing more Web-based government-to-citizen transactions."

Federal agencies can benefit from hiring third parties to develop applications. Enrique Gomez, program manager for the Census Bureau's Data Analysis and Dissemination System says, "The truth is, we have huge requirements to get this data out to the public, and we just don't have enough time, hardware, and expertise to do it. By going to an outside source and partnering with them, we're able to deliver our data to the public in the most cost-effective way and reach more people in the same amount of time."

## Challenges to Partnering with Government

Two major stumbling blocks for further development of government e-commerce are the additional security and trust issues in the federal government. In "B2G

*Tip* G2C and G2B sales are huge. The Treasury Department alone sold $3.3 billion on the Web in 2000.

*T*hrough an innovative Citizen-to-Government (C2G) Web portal, more than eight million people in the state of North Carolina can now go online instead of standing in line.

—ACCENTURE.COM, "STATE GOVERNMENT PORTALS CREATE ONE-STOP SHOPS FOR CITIZENS"

*Tip* Federal applications have been slow to develop but should increase with recent legislation.

> *T*he items for sale by the U.S. government can be unusual. For example, the Bureau of Land Management sells wild mustangs and burros, the Minerals Management Service sells oil leases by the Bureau of Land Management, the Minerals Management Service sells oil drilling leases in the Gulf of Mexico, and the U.S. General Services Administration (GSA) sells a wide variety of items including a light-keeper's house in Sault Sainte Marie, Michigan and a mothballed Coast Guard cutter.
>
> —ERIC YOUNG, "IN E-COMMERCE U.S. AGENCIES TRUST"

*Tip* ▸ Privacy and security concerns need to be addressed before you can partner with government.

Commerce Will Be Big Business" Francisco Quintanilla observes: "The technology is here and works, but the policy rules of engagement for security and practice still need to be worked out."

Rich Phillips, director of communications for NIC Commerce, concurs that partnering with the federal government is challenging due to the priority of citizen privacy and higher levels of public trust. He says that if the government is "going to partner with the private sector, agencies absolutely have to find a partner that understands that government is different and that it requires a much higher standard of privacy and control."

## Nonprofits

The Web has become an essential source for nonprofits that can gain great benefits through posting information on the Internet. They use the Web for publicity, public education, fundraising, volunteer recruitment, service delivery , advocacy, research, and communication. Again, numerous software firms and independent profit and nonprofit organizations have sprung up to serve this market. For example, Idealist.org aggregates job listings and information, posts job openings, and finds resources and volunteers.

Charities, such as Goodwill and the Salvation Army, use their Web sites to publicize news, auction items, advertise jobs, describe services, tell people how to make donations, and purchase goods. Museums like the Metropolitan Museum of Art use their Web sites to publish news, information about collections and exhibitions, a listing of events and programs, and a calendar of events. They may also have online retail stores selling art, gifts, and accessories. Libraries publish online catalogs and allow card holders to check book status, reserve books, and make other inquiries. As with government commerce, there are many opportunities for small businesses to provide services or partner with other organizations to help nonprofits excel at e-commerce.

## Summary

The use of the Web by public and nonprofit organizations offers ample opportunities for small business. Business-to-government (B2G), government to business (G2B), government-to-consumer or citizen (G2C), and government-to-government (G2G) commerce are rapidly expanding areas that could all use help from the business community. Businesses can sell products and services, fill requests for proposals, partner with both public and private organizations, and provide Web and programming services for these growing markets. This chapter described what is going on in these areas and showed examples. Further information on the expanding opportunities can be found on the Web sites at the end of this chapter.

### *Chapter Key Points*

🔑 There are many opportunities for small businesses to earn money through B2G, G2B, G2G, G2C, and nonprofits on the Web.

🔑 Business-to-government commerce is businesses responding to requests for proposals, selling to government, performing services, and entering partnerships with other businesses and government organizations.

🔑 Government-to-business commerce and government-to-consumer commerce are governments selling to businesses and providing services to consumers and citizens.

*Tip* Non-profits gain great benefits from Web communications.

*T*here are three overlapping stages of e-government emerging. The first stage, government-to-consumer, has been a decentralized and uncoordinated effort of communication from government to citizens, along with basic transaction services (i.e., the paying of fines and renewal of licenses). The second stage, the emergence of e-procurement at the state and local levels, engages regional governments for the first time in B2G transactions. The third stage, the participation of the federal government in the e-procurement space, will complete the e-procurement movement online."

—*JOHN FURTH,*
*"UNCLE SAM WANTS B2G"*

🔑 Government-to-government is commerce government agencies working together to streamline their dealings.

🔑 Nonprofits use the Web for publicity, public education, fundraising, volunteer recruitment, service delivery, advocacy, research, and communication.

## Web Sources for More Information

▶ **Bid4Assets.com** (www.bid4assets.com) contains an auction marketplace for buying and selling distressed assets from financial institutions, governments, bankruptcies, and private industry.

▶ **Bidmain** (www.bidmain.com) lists bids and RFP opportunities from federal, state, local, and international governments. It also provides contracts from CBD and FedBizOpps.

▶ **BidNet** (www.bidnet.com) offers information to vendors interested in bidding on state and local government procurement opportunities.

▶ **B2GFree** (www.b2gfree.com) provides free information on bid and proposal opportunities posted by international, federal, state, city, and county governments, along with universities, school districts, and large companies.

▶ **B2Gplace** (www.b2gplace.com) is a global procurement marketplace for the international supply industry. It offers tender notices, government contracts, bids, and project opportunities.

▶ **Business.com** (www.business.com) provides B2G information and referrals to other sites.

▶ **Buyers.gov** (www.buy.gov) is an e-government business and auction exchange that implements aggregation capabilities within the government.

▶ **Buysense** (amsinc.com/buysense/default.htm) is a Web-based marketplace for public-sector purchasing processes, provided by American Management Systems. (AMS).

▶ **EasyStreet.com** (www.easystreet.com) supports local charitable nonprofit corporations and encourages them to use the Internet to extend their reach within the community.

▶ **eFederal.com** (www.efederal.com) provides products, services, and information for government buyers.

▶ **8aMall.com** (www.8amall.com ) is the SmallBIZMall.Gov portal, developed for the General Services Administration, Federal Technology Service, and Federal Acquisition Services for Technology.

▶ **Idealist.org** (www.idealist.org) is a global network of individuals and nonprofit organizations.

### CHAPTER 10

# UNDERSTANDING PEER-TO-PEER COMPUTING
## *The Future*

SHARING RESOURCES THROUGH PEER-TO-PEER CAN BRING SAVINGS.

*The family had been receiving orders from local supermarkets and providing produce. Due to the perishable nature of the produce, they had been working on ways to obtain, input, and deliver items as quickly as possible. They had relied on e-mail messages, fax transmissions, and the telephone for orders. Unfortunately, messages often requested items that were unavailable due to their seasonal nature or were simply sold out. When deliveries did not include these items, their customers complained.*

*The family began to notify customers daily on the availability of items. This was a great deal of work as the process had to be repeated for customers using telephones, faxes, and e-mail. Customers did not always receive the messages. Some were annoyed by the frequent contacts. The family posted notices on their Web site but were concerned about the lack of privacy.*

*A peer-to-peer computing system provided a solution requiring no additional computer hardware resources. When customers ordered a product, the system automatically checked both the farm stand's inventory and the supplier's databases for availability. If an item was unavailable and could not be ordered in time from a supplier the customer was informed during the ordering process. If an item could be obtained, it was immediately reserved and taken out of available inventory so customers always got the requested items. Since the peer-to-peer network used existing computing resources, it gave the farm stand and its customers access to the latest information without additional hardware cost for the farm stand.*

> *P*2P, a.k.a. peer-to-peer, is the latest juice since rock and roll. If you're looking for a strict definition of what exactly is being reinvented this time around, forget it.
>
> —KAREN SOLOMON,
> "PEERING IS YOUR FUTURE"

*Tip* Napster is not an example of pure P2P as it retained central file distribution.

Some say that peer-to-peer (P2P) computing is the future of the Internet, while others say it died with the Napster court decision. Part of the confusion over the future of P2P lies in the disagreement on what P2P computing is. Much of the media has identified P2P with the Napster's model, so many may think that the two are the same. Others like Lee Gomes in "Peer to Peer Party" point out that Napster's model for music sharing is not even an implementation of pure P2P computing. He says, "One of the difficulties in assessing the state of P2P is semantic. Most people define the term as a computing scheme in which information is stored on many PCs, reducing or eliminating the need for a central repository like a Web server. In the market, however, the phrase has come to describe at least three entirely distinct categories of technologies and companies."

## What Is P2P Computing?

P2P computing is basically a new form of an old computer concept, distributed computing, which involved the networking of small computers so they can share resources. Pure P2P computing is the sharing of hardware, programs, and files by individual personal computers and Internet connection devices directly with each other without first going through a centralized computer.

P2P computing is different from the way things usually work on the Web. The current model of most Internet applications is "hub and spoke" in which the clients, personal computers, and other Internet connection devices are the spokes connected to a central hub or *server*. In this model, server computers distribute mail, files, and other resources to the client computers. In the pure P2P model all nodes can share resources directly with each other without the help of a central computer.

Thus, while Napster is based on P2P sharing concepts, it is not an example of pure P2P computing according to Mark Hachman in "Peer-to-Peer Companies Discuss Napster Ruling." He describes Napster's architecture as one that "only permits files to be shared, from one centralized server; true P2P computing can either share files or computing resources, and isn't organized around any one centralized node or machine."

On the other hand, Napster is a good example of how many companies use P2P computing now and will probably increasingly use P2P in the future. Most companies do not use pure P2P implementations; instead, they include peer-to-peer concepts for aspects of their computing combined with traditional approaches. "P2P is going to be used very broadly, but by itself, it's not going to create new companies," says Michael Tanne, chief executive of Xdegrees Inc., a start-up company that uses P2P concepts as part of a way to more easily locate files on the Web. "It's a technology. But the companies that will become successful are those that solve a problem."

Thus, while pure forms are not likely to be the future of the Internet, we will probably increasingly see some forms of P2P used in conjunction with more traditional computing.

*P2P computing isn't exactly new. As many as 30 years ago, companies were working on architectures that would now be labeled P2P. But today, several factors have lit a fire under the P2P movement: inexpensive computing power, bandwidth, and storage.*

*—MARK HACHMAN, "PEER-TO-PEER COMPANIES DISCUSS NAPSTER RULING"*

## P2P Applications

P2P can help businesses with large-scale computing needs. There is an enormous base of idle computing power out there and putting it to use makes sense. These organizations can use the disk space or processing power of idle computers according to Whatis.com. The site describes how "using a network of computers, P2P technology can use idle CPU, MIPS, and disk space allowing businesses to distribute large computational jobs across

*Tip*   Peer-to-peer computing is a new take on distributed computing.

*T*he term P2P computing has become a buzzword, much like "Internet" or "dot-com," panelists said, and its true meaning is often lost on the average consumer.

—MARK HACHMAN, "PEER-TO-PEER COMPANIES DISCUSS NAPSTER RULING"

*Tip*

Peer-to-peer appears most useful when combined with traditional approaches.

multiple computers. In addition, results can be shared directly between participating peers. The combined power of previously untapped computational resources can easily surpass the normal available power of an enterprise system without distributed computing. The results are faster completion times and lower cost because the technology takes advantage of power available on client systems."

Napster's use of P2P falls in this category. The company used the disk space on individual computers to store music files. Napster's computers at a central location knew where the files were stored and controlled access to files. The file distribution on individual "peer" computers was an implementation of P2P computing. The central control at Napster by the computers is representative of the traditional Internet hub and spoke model.

Another implementation of P2P technology is Intel's Virtual Private Networks (VPNs), consisting of groups of employees, family members, friends, or any groups that want to share information, possibly across firewalls. According to a spokesman from Intel, "Now applications [using P2P] can grow more rapidly because you don't have to build out server infrastructure." Intel sees great potential for these applications in the workplace, including distributed file-sharing and distributed computing applications that make use of spare processing power found across a network, according to John Spooner in "Intel Likes What It Hears in Napster." In the retail arena, Intel predicts that friends and families will communicate and share pictures, videos, and other files over VPNs.

Intel is also sponsoring a P2P network that provides computing power to medical researchers. The network is designed to link millions of personal computers together to create a "virtual supercomputer." This supercomputer, composed of shared power from personal computers, will be available for medical research.

Another powerful implementation of P2P computing is for collaboration between individuals and teams. P2P computing allows people working in remote locations to create and work together on projects using the Internet, Extranets, Intranets, or other networks. People can share files and therefore always have the most recent files and data. It decreases the need for e-mail exchanges and redundant storage of shared files. Ford Motor Company plans to implement P2P computing to enable collaboration between people located at different sites and using different operating systems and applications. They anticipate that using the P2P technology will save them $5 to $15 million per vehicle design program, according to John Goodman, fuel economy implementation manager at Ford. Combining P2P computing with intelligent agents can enhance collaborative work. Agents can travel between peer computers to perform tasks such as prioritizing things to be done, directing traffic flow, and detecting viruses and other anomalous behavior.

Another implementation is using P2P for more efficient storage and delivery to geographically dispersed locations. Data and programs are housed closer to the location where they are consumed. This allows faster and less costly delivery. A good example is a multi-national company wanting to distribute a new training program. Rather than streaming the database for the training session on one central server located at the main site, the company can store the video on dispersed computers, or clients, which act essentially as local database servers. Not only does it speed up the streaming due to local

> *P2P is something along the lines of one electronic device talking to another electronic device, whether it be a PC to a cell phone, a BlackBerry to a Palm, a Newton to a Game Boy, or a TiVo to a vacuum cleaner.... P2P is one-to-one, one-to-many, many-to-one, or many-to-many. The types of messages sent and the number of devices in the mix are as yet unknown children of a technology barely out of diapers.*
>
> —KAREN SOLOMON, *"PEERING IS YOUR FUTURE"*

Tip ▸ Virtual private networks are P2P networks for groups.

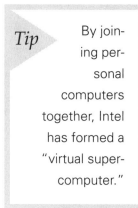

*Tip* By joining personal computers together, Intel has formed a "virtual supercomputer."

*Distributed computing certainly makes sense if you want to create a low-cost supercomputer on the fly. It may offer an even more compelling method for determining just how well a site performs under real-world conditions.*

*—Peertopeercentral.com, "What's Really Happening in Net User Land?"*

transmission but it also more effectively uses existing storage.

There are also a number of problems with P2P. First, according to Lee Gomes in "Peer to Peer Party," no one is quite sure if it will "really work, at least in the way some theorists are proposing." Security can be a problem. P2P networks need to be able to authenticate users. They also need to set the level of access any given user has to another P2P user's personal computer. Nelson Minar, CTO for the now defunct Popular Power, warns that while firewalls work in a client-server environment, in P2P these will not necessarily solve security problems. He suggests that security experts will be in demand and that intrusion detection systems, SSL, and Intel's P2P Trusted Library (PTPTL) will be needed.

Writing software applications that can take advantage of a distributed computing infrastructure is difficult. Another concern is that P2P implementations often allow too much information to be traded anonymously. Napster spin-offs, Gnutella and Freenet, allow people to exchange files without being traced. Thus, there is the potential for criminal activities, such as illegal trading of weapons and some forms of pornography.

Can companies make money by using excess capacity as theorized by P2P proponents? Several failures cast doubt on its profitability. The founders of InfraSearch Inc., a widely publicized Web-search company, sold it at a much reduced price and then folded. They predicted that P2P would be as big a business as the telephone. Popular Power Inc., another P2P company, shut down due to lack of funds. Says Bill Burnham, a venture capitalist with Softbank Venture Capital, "The whole P2P hoopla is emblematic of the mad rush to find the next big thing in technology."

According to Edward Jung, a former top software architect at Microsoft Corp., "P2P boosters were trying to recreate the excitement of Napster by simply transferring Napster-style technology to other areas. But since Napster is more of a social than a technical phenomenon, a lot of people were led down the primrose path."

## P2P Uses

P2P may have some applications for your business. Do you have extra capacity on another computer? Do you have any computers that sit idle part of the time? If so you may be a candidate for P2P computing.

Prior to upgrading your computer or adding hardware components and more disk capacity, look into the potential of P2P computing. If your computers are regularly idle for part of the day or night you may be able to sell your excess capacity to another company. You may also find applications for Virtual Private Networks like those being developed by Intel.

*P*ut simply, P2P computing is the sharing of computer resources and services by direct exchange between systems. These resources and services include the exchange of information, processing cycles, cache storage, and disk storage for files. P2P computing takes advantage of existing desktop computing power and networking connectivity, allowing economical clients to leverage their collective power to benefit the entire enterprise.

—MARK HACHMAN, "PEER-TO-PEER COMPANIES DISCUSS NAPSTER RULING"

## Summary

This chapter attempts to seek the truth about P2P computing and to shed some light on its true potential. Since P2P computing allows sharing of hardware, programs, and files by individual personal computers and Internet connection devices directly with each other without first going through a centralized computer, it can be used to share computing resources and to distribute information and technologies more efficiently. It may therefore be used more in the future as problems with security, anonymity, and implementation are resolved.

*Tip*

P2P means shared resources can be more easily located where they will be used.

*F*urther underscoring the notion that P2P technologies are here to stay, research labs backed by the likes of Microsoft and IBM are quietly developing serverless and decentralized redundant-storage computer systems that play to peer to peer computing's strengths."

—MARC RAPPORT, "MICROSOFT, IBM RESEARCHERS DEVELOP P2P NETWORKING TECHNOLOGY"

## Chapter Key Points

🔑 P2P computing is the sharing of hardware, programs, and files by individual personal computers and Internet connection devices directly with each other without first going through a centralized computer.

🔑 P2P computing differs from the traditional hub and spoke model of most Internet applications that use client server architecture.

🔑 Napster uses P2P technology but is not a good example of a pure P2P computing application.

🔑 Like Napster, most companies will use P2P in combination with traditional computing models.

🔑 P2P computing can be used for distributing computing resources, team and individual collaborations, and storing on remote locations.

🔑 Security concerns and failures of P2P computing have caused some to doubt its future.

🔑 In spite of these difficulties, the future of P2P looks bright.

## Web Sources for More Information

▶ **Infoworld** (www.infoworld.com) publishes articles on P2P computing.

▶ **Oreilly.com** (www.oreilly.com) lists books and published information on P2P computing.

▶ **P2P Central** (www.peertopeercentral.com) provides research, links to venture capital, and information on P2P computing.

▶ **Peer-to-Peer.com** (www.p2p.com) lists computing books written by industry experts.

▶ **The P2pwg.com** (www.p2p.org) is a working group organized to facilitate and accelerate the advancement of the infrastructure of best-known practices for P2P computing.

# SUPPLIES AND MORE AT THE SPEED OF LIGHT
## *Maximizing Your Value Chain*

VALUE CHAINS CAN BE WORTH THEIR WEIGHT IN GOLD. ◀

*As the farm stand began to distribute their produce to area markets they realized that one of their main competitive advantages was their ability to ship products quickly. It was ironic that the previously dreaded highway now provided a way to quickly deliver their produce. Also, along the highway numerous shopping areas were springing up providing more venues for the family to sell their produce.*

*As their business grew, it became more difficult to handle the increasing volume of orders. Due to the perishable nature of their produce, they were on a short timeline. Any produce that was not sold and delivered quickly was given away. The family realized that they needed to find better ways to process orders, organize products, ship orders, and plan future crop plantings.*

*The family looked to the Internet for solutions. They had reaped a number of benefits from the B2B exchanges they joined. They were seeing that sharing information with other organizations provided substantial benefits to all. They decided to join a "collaborative value chain," a B2B exchange designed to help business partners share information. The family and their business partners were able to increase efficiency by using the information shared with each other.*

*As the amount of information held jointly by the business partners increased the family realized that they had another problem. Many of the remaining inefficiencies resulted from failure to communicate internally. The family decided that they also needed to communicate better within the family and internally integrate their value chain.*

▲    ▲    ▲

*I*f you're not managing your value chain, you're not managing your business. That is the warning of industry leaders who predict that tomorrow's top companies will succeed based on the strength of the relationships they establish, from their raw-material suppliers, through manufacturing and distribution, and ultimately to their customers.

—DAVID DRICKHAMER,
"PEAK PERFORMANCE"

*Tip*  It makes good sense to share information with everyone on your value chain whether they are internal or external participants.

The communication links provided by the World Wide Web can be used to improve all aspects of your value chain. Both large and small businesses have been able to achieve a competitive advantage by linking internally and externally with business partners including suppliers, competitors, partners, regulators, and customers. From receipt of an order to delivery to the customer, using Internet links, Extranets, and Intranets to automate and integrate your value chain helps you to improve all of the processes related to the production of goods and services. Integration of the value chain benefits all business partners by allowing information sharing. Major benefits of this integration include better anticipation and meeting customer needs, developing closer relationships with customers, and reducing inventory costs. Value chain automation compresses the time for all aspects of the value chain from the supply of raw materials to customer receipt of goods. Customer demands are more quickly turned into product choices and the company can gain the flexibility to change products quickly and adapt to customer needs. C-commerce, or collaborative commerce, and collaborative value chains are resulting in even more substantial gains for companies who have implemented them.

## What Is the Value Chain?

The value chain consists of a series of stages, from purchase of raw products to sale to customer, during which the company adds value. The stages of a value chain are:

- Developing the product
- Planning the production
- Acquiring the needed supplies
- Making the product
- Selling the product
- Delivering the product

Improving both internal and external information exchange and processing at each of these stages can help you reduce costs, improve efficiency, and better anticipate and meet customer needs. This section will explain how automation of the value chain can result in these benefits.

## Meeting Customer Needs

Traditionally, a business uses past customer information to develop the products and services it will sell. By electronically sharing information with customers and suppliers, you can develop closer relationships with your customers and use the more up-to-date information to design products to meet customer needs. For example, BMG Entertainment uses its Web sites to gather information from customers, better understand their buyers, and increase their sales. The information helps them make decisions about how to market CDs and time new releases.

Elf Atochem North America Inc., a seller of agricultural chemicals, accepts e-mail and online orders and provides material data sheets online. They use the Internet to make sure their customers have the information they want in the form that they want it. According to Elf Atochem CIO Bob Rubin, the information "allows us to take commodities and treat them like specialties by adding a service component." Through information

> *E*fficiencies will be derived from sharing and using Internet technologies to improve logistics, automate transactions, allow companies to share and provide real-time data (such as prices or the location of inventory), and facilitate real-time collaboration (such as product design).
>
> —PETER KEEN, "IT'S VALUE IN THE CHAIN"

*Tip* Information sharing allows you to form a closer relationship with customers.

*T*o succeed in this new environment, many companies have aggressively reinvented their business strategies, beginning with a new value chain: customer needs, integrated channels, customizable offerings, flexible processes, and outsource/in-house parsing of competencies.

—GEOFFREY RAMSEY IN PETER FINGAR, HARSHNA KUMAR, AND TARUN SHIRMA'S "21ST CENTURY MARKETS"

*Tip* You can differentiate commodities through Internet-based service.

sharing, Elf Atochem is able to better compete in the marketplace, develop close ties with customers, and add value through information sharing.

Value chain integration allows you to develop products that more closely fit the customers' needs. By using shared information you can personalize relationships, products, and services to better fit the needs of your customers. Through integration of your value chain, you add value to your offerings, better anticipate future needs, and gain a competitive advantage in the marketplace.

## Reducing Production Costs and Time

The costs and time required for production can be dramatically decreased through automation and integration of value chain logistics. In the words of Peter Keen, a leading IT expert, "Internet-based logistics has transformed the economics of business more than any other factor in the past decade." Honda's experience shows the benefits of value chain integration and data sharing. Honda Motor Company has used its supply chain to cut lead-times and inventory. In the mid-1990s, Honda managers essentially made educated guesses about which cars to manufacture and ship to their dealers. If a dealer wanted a car other than the ones received, it took four months for their order to be filled. In 1996, Dan Bonawitz, a vice president at American Honda, decided to use the computer to reduce costs. Honda linked all 1,300 of its U.S. Honda dealerships to Honda headquarters so that they could place orders and check on order status directly. Each month the system would use the data to determine what to produce and send the list of suggested car orders to each dealer who could change the proposed orders based on their anticipated needs. The orders were then sent to Honda's production plants based on the system's determination of the most efficient way to distribute the manufacturing load. The system dropped load time from 120 days to between 30 and 60 days and has reduced inventories at both the factories and dealerships by 50 percent.

## Internal Value Chain Integration

Many firms are losing out on potential value chain savings due to an internal lack of communication. In "IT's Value in the Chain," Peter Keen says: "responsibilities are scattered around many functions, such as purchasing, accounting, sales administration, distribution, and credit. Units that handle their own tasks aren't familiar with the wider picture of online integration, coordination, and supply-chain collaboration. Senior management teams don't know the scale of the proven payoff and don't think of logistics as strategic. And people on the business side are unlikely to be familiar with what's happening in the business-to-business Internet space." As Keen suggests, businesses need to internally coordinate value chain components and link managers, customers, and key suppliers.

As described earlier, Honda saved time and money through internal communications along its value chain. Internal value chain integration can also be used to better meet customer needs. In Honda's case it allows them to turn customer demands into cars more quickly. Honda's goal is to sell cars the way Michael Dell sells computers: by building them when they're ordered.

Johnson Controls Inc., a supplier of interior automobile components that includes seats, has instituted a uniquue process. If a customer puts in a request for a product, their engineers, even if located in Japan, Germany, or the United States, search the database to determine if the company has

> *With differentiators such as customer satisfaction equating into direct market share, the race to integrate further up and down the value chain becomes even more critical. The ability to control the customers' total experience will likely result in higher levels of customer satisfaction; which can equate into customer retention, new customers, and bottom line results.*
>
> —WAYNE P. HAUGHLEY, "THE OBJECT MANAGEMENT GROUP'S STRATEGIC APPROACH TO VALUE CHAIN INTEGRATION"

*Tip*
You can reduce production times and costs through value chain integration.

> *M*cKinsey & Co. reports that two-thirds of a B2B customer's buying decision rests on nonprice factors including product/service quality, client service, and speed of delivery. They believe that buyers will be eager to join these chains because they will be able to reduce transaction costs without compromising (and probably enhancing) product and service quality.
>
> —COMMUNITY B2B, "B2B FUNDAMENTALS"

already developed a similar product. If a similar product exists and has passed the safety requirements, the company can save the customer as much as 30 percent of the approximately $20 million required to develop a new product. Instead of having to tool the seat frames from scratch, more time can be invested in adding value-added features and design improvements.

Ideally, the customer drives the entire value chain. "The 'customer is king' era is leading to a new model called 'postponement' in which companies design and build products only after they are sold," says Manufacturingnews.com. Dell computer comes close to this ideal. The customer order is the impetus of the manufacturing process. Both external and internal value chain integration will make this a reality.

## Using Chain Integration to Get Supplies

By linking with your suppliers you can reduce costs. Rusty Weston's article "Business Value in Communication" describes the benefits reported by 200 managers who used an electronic supply chain or value chain.

- Cost savings 78 percent
- Shorter product cycles and faster delivery times 72 percent
- Improved order speed and delivery 70 percent
- Better customer service 65 percent
- Lower order processing costs 60 percent
- Better alignment of business and IT goals 50 percent
- Better inventory management 43 percent
- More accurate sales forecast 32 percent
- Better product availability 45 percent

Companies can use automating the value chain to approach "just-in-time" inventory. Since the company and suppliers exchange electronic transactions, the supplier is notified when an order is placed and proceeds with the supply process. Therefore, lead-time is reduced. Events can trigger processes in their suppliers and/or customers. For example, if an order exceeds inventory of a particular item or part, it triggers the supply ordering process, which in turn contacts the supplier to order the part.

## Inbound and Outbound Logistics

Collaboration of transportation allows better planning and cost reductions as deliveries and shipments can be coordinated to take advantage of similar movements. Better organizing, planning, and tracking of shipments of supplies and outgoing orders can decrease costs, reduce the time from customer order to receipt, and decrease losses. Companies like Federal Express and UPS have invested millions to coordinate shipments, track packages, and minimize lost shipments. Their success in these areas adds value to their customers and gives them a competitive advantage.

## Collaborative Commerce

Value chain automation is increasingly becoming collaborative with business partners, employees, and customers sharing information and participating in value chain processes, says Philip Say in his article, "The Buzz on C-Commerce."

He predicts that "as supply-chain technology continues to become a core element of the corporate IT landscape, collaboration will naturally become more widely adopted. The benefits are too obvious, and competitive forces will drive greater interaction of all supply-chain participants."

*Tip*   Chain integration is becoming more collaborative.

> *Although the focus for B2B e-commerce has been on expediting procurement processes, many companies are discovering that collaboration across all parties associated with the supply chain is as important as the cost savings associated with corporate purchasing.*
>
> —*PHILIP SAY,*
> *"THE BUZZ ON C-COMMERCE"*

*T*he use of the Internet to facilitate product planning will continue to have a profound impact on marketers.... Here is a simple example: A consumer electronics retailer can signal to Nintendo when production should be curtailed or terminated due to shifts in consumer behavior or the impact a competing product, such as PlayStation 2, has on sales.

—CLICKZ.COM, "FIVE IMPORTANT B2B MARKETING CONCEPTS FOR 2001"

*Tip* Shipping companies use their automated logistics as a competitive advantage.

Philip Say goes on to explain that more than 75 percent of the respondents, in a recent survey by Forrester Research of manufacturers, reported that they use Internet-based collaboration technology to speed product development and reduce errors in the manufacturing process. The experience of Taiwan Semiconductor Manufacturing Company (TSMC) shows why they are so readily adopting collaborative commerce. TSMC, a contract manufacturer of integrated circuits, and similar companies share data and design information with customers by using the Internet. Prior to implementation of a collaborative solution, they were experiencing long delays in their supply chain due to the limitations of using electronic communications such as standalone Web sites, fax, e-mail, FTP, and EDI. TSMC uses shared data to improve a number of processes with both customers and suppliers, including forecasting, engineering, order management, updates on work-in-progress (WIP), and shipment notifications. The benefits for TSMC include a 25 percent reduction in lead times, reduced WIP carry costs, and improved capacity planning due to elimination of manual processes. Within the first three years of operation, they expect a 14-fold return on their investment, reports Philip Say.

## Using the Value Chain to Your Advantage

There are basically three ways to automate your value chain.

1. Enterprise Resource Planning (ERP) systems, such as those offered by Oracle, SAP, PeopleSoft, and J.D. Edwards.
2. Traditional supply chain software venders including i2, Manugistics, and Logility.

3. Collaborative value chains and B2B exchange.

Selecting which type of product to purchase can be difficult. You will make the best purchase by deciding what you need, then finding the product that best meets that need.

While some see B2B exchanges as the wave of the future, Gartner forecasts that ERP vendors will account for about 60 percent of the supply chain software market by 2004. Ideally, you should be able to use the ERP products to automate forecasting, purchasing, warehousing, information sharing among business partners, and inventory functions. These products may allow interaction between the ordering company, supplier's inventory, and catalog applications, directing data into the inventory management and manufacturing systems. They may input data into the purchasing and accounting systems, making the entire procurement process easier.

Products with Internet access let supply chain members, including employees, customers, and trading partners collaborate to optimize plans and ensure timely delivery of supplies and products. Since the offerings are continually evolving, you will want to check to make sure that a product has the features you have determined you need and is compatible with the systems used by both you and your business partners.

> *M*ost B2B marketplaces fail to provide the kinds of sophisticated supply-chain capabilities, including collaborative planning and forecasting, that customers will ultimately require. In a recent study by AMR Research, only 100 of 600 exchanges provided any integration to connect disparate supply-chain partners to the exchange.
>
> —KEVIN P. O'BRIEN, "VALUE-CHAIN REPORT—EVALUATING THE FUNCTIONALITY OF B2B MARKETPLACES"

*Tip* ▸ Supply chain integration allows you to get supplies more quickly and reduce inventory costs.

## Summary

Companies are using value chain automation to reduce costs and reap many benefits including shorter production cycles, lower inventory costs, shorter product cycles from order to delivery, better customer service, lower order processing costs, and more accurate forecasts.

*According to a 1997 study, companies with leading supply-chain management have 50 percent to 80 percent lower inventories. Managers report that automating their value chain resulted in substantial cost savings, shorter product cycles from order to delivery, shorter product development cycles, better customer service, lower order processing costs, reduced costs for inventory, and more accurate forecasts.*

*—PETER KEEN, "IT's VALUE IN THE CHAIN"*

**Tip** Value chain automation can be used to improve both inbound and outbound logistics.

Companies are also reaping benefits through improved internal value chain integration, supply ordering, and inbound/outbound logistics. Collaborative commerce and collaborative value chains, and sharing of information among all parties in the value chain, are becoming more common as their benefits become obvious.

## Chapter Key Points

- Value chain automation can help at every stage of the value chain:
  - Developing the product
  - Planning the production
  - Acquiring the needed supplies
  - Making the product
  - Selling the product
  - Delivering the product

- Companies are automating their value and supply chains to achieve a number of benefits and cost savings including shorter production cycles, lower inventory costs, shorter product cycles from order to delivery, better customer service, lower order processing costs, and more accurate forecasts.

- Internal communication within an organization produces many benefits.

- Benefits are achieved by automating supply ordering and inbound/outbound logistics.

- Options for implementing value chain applications include traditional supply chain software vendors, ERP systems, and collaborative software packages.

🔑 Collaborative commerce and collaborative value chains, and sharing of information among all parties in the value chain, are becoming more common as their benefits become obvious.

## Web Sources for More Information

▶ **ClickZ.com** (www.clickz.com) has many articles on supply chain management. A great article on collaborative commerce is "The Buzz on Collaborative Commerce" (www.clickz.com/article/cz.38 27.html).

▶ **CNet's Library** (www.cnet.researchlibrary.enterprise.cnet.com) has numerous supply chain resources.

▶ **Computerworld IT Reports**: Supply Chain Integration (http://itreports.computerworld.com/data) reports on supply chain integration.

▶ **ECompany Now** (www.ecompany.com/webguide) has a Web guide to Business 2.0 sources on supply chain management and integration.

▶ **Network Computing Tech Library**: Supply Chain Integration (http://techlibrary.networkcomputing. com/ data/rlist) provides access to many resources on supply chain integration.

▶ **ZDNet's Research Center**: Supply Chain Integration (http://researchcenter.zdnet.com) features analyst reports, research, and white papers on supply chain integration.

# PROCUREMENT POWER
*Flexing Purchasing Muscle*

PURCHASING ON THE WEB CAN HAVE BENEFITS FOR ALL. ◀

*The widow realized that they were spending a lot of money on supplies and equipment. While she knew that some of the purchases were necessary, she was annoyed about the new tractor they had recently purchased. The tractor had been very expensive. From talking to neighbors, she realized that they had paid much more for the same tractor than others had. She was very frustrated about it.*

*In addition, the widow found out that they were paying much more for agricultural supplies than the larger factory farms in the area. It was hard enough to compete when they could not grow a large volume of produce like the factory farms. Adding the increased costs for supplies that resulted from their buying in smaller quantities made it almost impossible for them to compete. For years, she had been trying to form a group of small farmers to unite and purchase supplies in higher volumes, but none of her neighbors seemed interested. From what she had read about e-procurement systems she did not think the cost of such a system would be justified. She knew she would have to find other ways to use the Web to reduce supply costs.*

*The widow searched the Web for information on farm supply costs and found several helpful sites that provided discounts, product reviews, and links to other sites. To her delight, one link was to a farm buying group: a buyer aggregator. Not only did the site provide quantity discounts for the buying group, but their*

*Web site posted member comments, feedback, and product evaluations.*

▲   ▲   ▲

> *I*n most companies, the purchasing process hasn't changed in decades. The majority of businesses still employ a largely paper-based process—inefficient and error-prone.
>
> —*SAP, "SAP SOLUTIONS: E-PROCUREMENT"*

## Benefits of Web Procurement

Online procurement is growing rapidly. B2B buying and selling online is expected to grow from 3 percent to 42 percent of total B2B domestic trade over the next five years, says Anne Knowles in "B2B: Bonanza or Bust." The market for e-procurement tools is estimated to grow from under $200 million in 1998 to $8.5 billion by 2003. Early articles on Internet-based procurement, such as Dennis P. Geller and Bradley L. Hecht's "Electronic Procurement, the Extranet, and You," have raved about the potential cost savings and benefits resulting from e-procurement systems. They say that "the whys of electronic procurement are obvious. Organizations look to e-procurement to reduce administrative costs and improve turnaround, and to help them exercise control over inventory and spending. E-procurement systems also provide new sources of supply and can lead to lower prices for the goods being procured."

Web-based procurement can be used for:

- price comparison
- product and company comparison
- forming purchasing groups to realize volume discounts
- e-procurement systems

There are several ways you can use the Web to reduce procurement costs. You can use it to search for prices and form alliances. For example, you can join

*Tip*   There are many benefits of using the Web for procurement.

purchasing groups on buyer aggregator sites or you can consult search agents for price, product, and service information. One of the most powerful tools is the ability to compare prices among countless vendors of particular products. Numerous sites will check the Web for price and show a buyer where they can purchase a product for the lowest price. Sites can have a general focus, specialize in a type of product (horizontal focus), or focus on the needs of a particular type of business or category (vertical focus). In addition to showing price information, many of these sites provide customer evaluations of sellers.

Another type of service for aiding purchases are sites that publish customer discussion boards, comments, ratings, and feedback. These boards can help consumers make better choices by providing information that may help them avoid the mistakes of others. They are then better able to purchase high rated products and services.

Alternatively, you can implement large e-procurement systems. Through automated Web-based procurement, businesses can order from online catalogs, consolidate purchasing to get volume discounts, invite bids for needed products, and expedite the purchase requisition process.

The potential benefits of e-procurement are undeniable. They include reductions of paperwork, the ability to establish a catalog of needed supplies, reduced administrative costs, reduced inventory costs, improved turnaround, development of new sources of supply, and the ability to take advantage of lower price offerings. These systems can be used to improve inventory management and reduce the need to keep excess inventory as the lead time from ordering to receipt is reduced. Other benefits of automated procurement include the

> *Indeed, the worldwide market for indirect procurement applications grew 67 percent last year, according to AMR Research, reaching $259 million in sales. AMR projects 130 percent growth this year to $583 million in sales.*
>
> —ALORIE GILBERT, "PROBLEMS BEHIND THE PROMISE"

ability to combine requests so that organizations can receive volume discounts and eliminate the paper work of extra requisitions. Due to these benefits, according to a survey conducted by *Purchasing* magazine, 90 percent of purchasing professionals expect to be buying online by the year 2002.

## Current E-Procurement Benefits Volume Purchasers

Unfortunately, due to high up-front costs for e-procurement solutions, it is uncertain that most companies will benefit from spending large sums on e-procurement systems. Most systems still cost millions to implement. In spite of a lot of hype and some good results by large businesses, the return on investment (ROI) from these systems is not well documented for many businesses. After looking at how early adopters of e-procurement are faring, Laurie Orlov reported in "Wringing ROI out of e-Procurement" that "businesses expect to save money and realize a return on investment (ROI) from e-procurement—but they have not figured out what that return should be or how to measure it. ... With the value of e-procurement so uncertain among businesses, e-procurement users should proceed cautiously—and e-procurement software firms must go back to the drawing board and hone their pricing and ability to deliver real, measurable results."

E-procurement savings for large, powerful firms are well-documented and appear to be the most significant cost savings resulting from business on the Web. In the area of maintenance repair operations (MRO) alone, savings are potentially enormous. MRO supplies and services form a market of $1.4 trillion in the United States. That

> *M*uch of the future growth is expected to involve small and medium sized firms that were not able to participate in e-commerce prior to the availability of the low cost, highly accessible Internet.
>
> —PETER FINGAR, HARSHNA KUMAR, AND TARUN SHIRMA, "21ST CENTURY MARKETS"

can be as much as 60 percent of the expenses of an organization. Grainger Consulting Services found that businesses can achieve an annual return on investment of 339 percent from the implementation of B2B procurement solutions. Automated Web-based procurement systems can reduce the costs by approximately 35 percent. Leading IT expert, Peter Keen has listed examples of firms gaining benefits from online systems.

Through online trading hubs, General Electric has reduced the prices paid for goods put out for bid by 3 to 5 percent, and IBM has reduced prices by 9 percent.

Approximately 20 percent of all orders and invoices contain at least one error in the best run companies. Online logistics can reduce the percent of orders and invoices containing errors from the current 20 percent for the best run companies to less than 1 percent. Also, lead times on procurement and distribution typically drop from weeks to days.

B2B Internet portal Ariba typically reduces the total supply-chain cost of operating resources, such as office equipment, supplies and cleaning services, which amounts to around 30 percent of any company's operating budget, by 20 percent to 30 percent.

By using e-procurement IBM saved over $2 million in 1999, and GE is currently building a multimillion dollar system that is expected to save them millions of dollars annually. General Motors, Hewlett Packard, and scores of other large corporations also have saved millions by implementing e-procurement systems. If you are a volume purchaser, these systems may provide you with similar cost savings. However, the cost savings for companies with lower volume purchasing requirements do not often justify the current costs of these systems.

> *The key shift in focus from addressing the business-to-consumer market to the business-to-business market is one from shopping to procurement.*
>
> —PETER FINGAR, HARSHNA KUMAR, AND TARUN SHIRMA, "21ST CENTURY MARKETS"

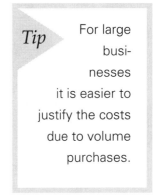

*Tip* For large businesses it is easier to justify the costs due to volume purchases.

## Digital Insight

Digital Insight, a financial services provider, uses a service provider, Core-Harbor, in conjunction with the e-procurement system, Ariba Buyer (www.ariba.com), to streamline and automate their purchasing process. Through Ariba Buyer, they can automate procurement of indirect goods, resulting in a more efficient and less costly process for repetitive purchases.

Through wireless technologies and the services of Core-Harbor, Digital Insight is able to reap further time savings from e-procurement. They use Core-Harbor's wireless connection to Ariba Buyer to let their employees have access to the system from mobile phones, pagers, and handhelds. Thus, managers can get purchase confirmation from any place at any time.

## Problems with E-Procurement

The main problem with e-procurement systems in their present form is their high cost. The Forrester report concluded that "software firms must come to the table with better options for purchasing their software. Million-dollar price tags to buy and integrate software will not mesh with uncertain expectations. This is sticker shock for companies that aren't sure they can ever get all employees and suppliers online. So vendors must slash prices with rapid deployment-hosted offers, or bite-sized subscriptions and licensing."

*But many companies sign on for e-procurement without anticipating the long road ahead. They dive into projects only to learn that e-procurement applications are limited in the types and scope of purchasing activity they address.*

*—ALORIE GILBERT, "PROBLEMS BEHIND THE PROMISE"*

Also, due to problems with suppliers, companies are unable to get maximum benefit from e-procurement. In his article, "Does E-Procurement Deliver ROI?," Larry Seban, includes Laurie M. Orlov's description of how only one of the 15 early adopters of e-procurement completed its roll-out without problems. Most companies had problems with suppliers. Orlov provides evidence of the problems caused by suppliers by pointing to a recent Forrester study for the National Association of Purchasing Managers. The study reported that 36.6 percent of surveyed purchasing managers viewed their suppliers' online capabilities as bad or poor and proof that suppliers are a major glitch.

Companies have also reported that e-procurement applications are limited, integration troublesome, and managing catalogs difficult with current offerings.

## What Should Smaller Companies Do?

For now, small businesses should proceed with caution when it comes to e-procurement systems. While using the Web for price, product, and service comparisons is wise, implementation of a complex e-procurement system might be unwise. Prior to implementing such a system, small businesses should make sure that the benefits and cost savings are well documented and will exceed the cost of such a system.

In regard to an e-procurement system, the Forrester report recommends:

- limiting initial deployment of e-procurement.
- being more selective about how they use e-procurement.
- making sure e-procurement has a verifiable ROI.
- connecting strategic suppliers with back-end systems to enable automatic replenishment and getting suppliers into the total e-procurement process as much as possible.

## Summary

In summary, e-procurement systems have huge benefits for large companies. Small companies can gain benefits from using the Web to compare prices, evaluate services, and form buying groups. For now, businesses should approach implementing e-procurement systems with caution. Make sure that the benefits outweigh the costs before spending enormous amounts on e-procurement.

> *The loose justifications of early e-procurement projects won't fly in today's cost-conscious technology-spending climate. Both vendors and users must refine expectations and wring short-term benefits from e-procurement projects.*
>
> —LARRY SEBAN, "DOES E-PROCUREMENT DELIVER ROI?"

*Tip* ▷ Problems with high system costs, suppliers, and faulty implementation hurt e-procurement.

> *It may turn out that e-procurement deployments resemble the challenge-filled enterprise resource planning implementations of the 1990s more than anyone would like. It's important for companies to realize both the risks and the rewards when they enter into such deployments.*
>
> —ALORIE GILBERT, *"PROBLEMS BEHIND THE PROMISE"*

## Chapter Key Points

🔑 E-procurement systems are said to be the biggest thing on the Web. There is a great deal of hype about how much they benefit large companies.

🔑 While the benefits to large organizations seem real, it is less certain that small businesses will gain from e-procurement.

🔑 The Web is great for comparing prices, forming buying groups, and gaining information.

🔑 Due to high implementation costs and less certain benefits, e-procurement systems may not be cost justified by many businesses.

## Web Sources for More Information

▶ **CRMDaily.com** (www.crmdaily.com) publishes articles on procurement and other issues related to customer relations management. For example, "Does E-Procurement Deliver ROI?"(www.crmdaily.com/perl/story/9821.html) gives advice on feasibility.

▶ **Ecomworld.com** (www.ecomworld.com/portals/procurement) is a portal for procurement and e-procurement vendors.

▶ **E-Procurement Advisory Committee** (www.ucop.edu/irc/nba/epro.html) is an advisory project on e-procurement.

▶ **InformationWeek.com** (www.informationweek.com) publishes articles on e-procurement and other IT topics (www.informationweek.com/813/eprocure.htm).

▶ **InternetWeek.com** (www.internetweek.com) publishes articles on the Internet and Web. E-procurement articles can be found at two sites: (www.internetweek.com/ebizapps01/ebiz020501-1.htm) and (www.internetweek.com/ebizapps01/ebiz052801).

▶ **Software vendors**: SAP.com, IBM.com, Microsoft.com, Compaq.com, and Oracle.com.

# NOT JUST NUMBERS
## *Accounting on the Web*

USING THE WEB TO AUTOMATE ACCOUNTING TRANSACTIONS IS A NATURAL. ◄

*T*he family had been using an automated accounting package for years. They used the package for all basic accounting functions including general ledger, accounts receivable, and accounts payable. Since most farm stand sales had been cash transactions, they had been able to easily do the accounting without hiring an accountant or bookkeeper.

With their expanded sales to grocery stores, they now had to bill their customers. They were considering hiring an accountant. Especially irritating to the family was having to input the same information into their system that appeared on bills sent to them and knowing that their customers were having to retype information. With all of the information being shared on the Web, it seemed ridiculous to be engaging in repetitive data entry. They wondered if they could use the Web to share information with their customers and suppliers.

They began to look at the offerings for Internet packages. While some did have the needed features, none were compatible with all of their customers' packages. In fact, switching to an Internet accounting package would mean having to abolish their current software. None of the packages allowed them to continue to use their current accounting software for internal transactions. None would allow them to easily exchange accounting information with all of their customers. Since they had been hearing about XML and the compatibility of Web data, they were a little confused by these revelations.

Automation of accounting is not just a logical step, but is necessary to efficiently conduct business on the Internet. Ideally, an order and fulfillment system should interface with an automated "back office" accounting system that includes automated invoicing, bill payment, and sharing information with key business partners. Large companies have been using electronic data interchange (EDI) to automate invoicing and payment systems for years. With the rise of the Internet and Extensible Markup Language (XML) using the Internet for sharing accounting information is becoming feasible for smaller businesses.

Computers are well suited to manipulation of numbers so accounting applications dominated the early years of computing. Businesses made the first significant computer related productivity gains by automating internal accounting functions such as payroll, accounts receivable, and accounts payable. Accounting tasks are repetitive, labor intensive, and high volume and when done manually are very vulnerable to human error. Thus, it makes sense to use the Internet for accounting transactions between organizations.

For B2B, the Internet takes accounting tasks to the next level. It allows automation of internal accounting tasks and transmissions with each other. The Web and XML potentially bring these gains to all organizations. New data formats, such as XML, are beginning to allow organizations to more easily exchange account receivable and payable data electronically. The Web will allow organizations to more easily outsource their accounting systems or develop sophisticated accounting applications interfacing with the accounting systems of key business partners.

*Ford has been using EDI to reduce costs for many years. They require that all suppliers use EDI for all financial transactions.*

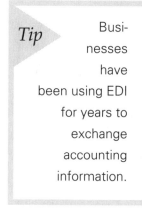

*Tip* Businesses have been using EDI for years to exchange accounting information.

Almost all small businesses use some kind of software to help with accounting. Most use stand-alone or Local Area Networks (LANs) based software. Since the accounting processes are not linked to customers, suppliers, and other business partners, these systems have a couple of limitations. Each customer, supplier, and business partner must enter the data themselves, which results in redundant data entry. They are unable to share the data with each other. These stand-alone applications are becoming outdated as Internet packages come into being.

## Capabilities of Internet Accounting Systems

The major capabilities of current Internet accounting include:

- Sending an electronic purchase order
- Receiving invoices
- Authenticating users
- Interfacing with other business systems

With these systems, small businesses should be able to send invoices, make payments, interact with bank systems to update accounts, post items on financial systems, update and be updated by inventory and supply systems, get catalogs, send purchase orders, receive invoices, and interface as needed with company systems as well as those of business partners. These systems also reduce the possibilities for human error and other costs associated with stand-alone accounting systems. In addition, these electronic transmissions speed up financial transactions and reduce interest and inventory costs.

> *When the accounting systems in various countries and languages are adapted to XML, it will make it possible for a manufacturer in Japan to automate their orders for supplies from various vendors in the U.S., Mexico, Germany, and any other country. The cost savings for industry as a whole will be enormous.*
>
> —*VERNON K. JACOBS, "E-COMMERCE ACCOUNTING SYSTEMS"*

*Tip* XML brings gains of data sharing to many more organizations.

## Cisco Systems

Cisco is using their accounting systems to provide them with a competitive advantage. They use Web-based billing, accounts payable, and order-entry to enable near-real-time financial reporting. The system allows them to stay abreast of leading indicators and future forecasting rather than being limited to a focus on lagging indicators and past events.

The up-to-date financial information provided by the system allows Cisco to make decisions quickly in response to changing conditions. While Cisco's agility is unusual for a $19 billion company, competition in the 21st century marketplace requires being able to respond rapidly to events. Thus, Cisco's quickness in adapting to their environment has become a competitive advantage. Cisco has also gained large cost savings from their virtual accounting system. It helped to save them $86 million last year alone."

—Desiree de Myer, "Speed Up Financial Reporting," SmartBusinessMag.com

Aberdeen Group cut cycle times by 25 to 30 percent and reduced prices an average of 5 to 20 percent by using the Internet to source more efficiently.... Aberdeen Group's processing costs for indirect goods (which can account for 30 to 60 percent of all company expenditures) dropped an average of $107 to $30 through use of an e-procurement system.

—Christine Greech Wendin, "Slash Purchasing Costs"

On an Internet accounting system, a company would be able to send an electronic invoice that requires authentication procedures to make sure that the customer is authentic, getting the payment from the customer, and ideally, interacting with the receiver's software so that it can be automatically updated to show the receipt of the payment. You may also want to make a payment electronically to payroll and to other individuals. You will want the system to automate as much of the procurement process as possible through interaction with inventory and catalog systems.

Unfortunately, current Web offerings may require you to switch from your present accounting software to take advantage of the Web-based system. The decision on whether or not to switch will depend on your investment and maybe your expertise in your current software compared to how much you need the new system based on your sales volume and inventory.

## Current Offerings

A few of the small business e-commerce store sites are providing some accounting capabilities. NetLedger lets you link a store and a Web-delivered accounting system. Yahoo! Store will also let you build a store to be hosted on Yahoo! and link it to NetLedger. Banks are developing e-commerce services which will be tightly integrated with their payment processing capabilities. For example, Bank of America's eStores let small merchants build and manage online stores. Wells Fargo Bank also launched its own One-Stop eStore service.

While there is still a long way to go to find the ideal accounting systems, many organizations are working on solutions. Some are trying systems that integrate other

*Tip*  Sharing accounting data means faster and more accurate payments and billing.

## Howard Building Corporation and Online Banking

Howard Building Corporation, a construction company with 75 employees in Glendale, California, monitors interest rates on company accounts and transfers money using American Business Bank's home page.

Roxanne Medina, chief financial officer at Howard Building Corporation, reports that the company uses the bank's Web page but can rely on personal service for trickier transactions. In her words, "I can pick up the phone and they will hand-carry you through the system."

In spite of increasing numbers of banks offering new online services (such as wire transfers, direct deposit for payroll, and detailed balance reporting), small business customers have been reluctant to switch from the personalized customer service. American Business Bank has convinced 20 percent of its customers to use the Web to pay bills, stop payments on checks, transfer funds, and monitor transactions. But small companies still aren't tempted. According to founder Donald P. Johnson, their success is due to the personal attention that they pay all of their customers.

—*Naveen A. Mangi, "Online Banking: The e-Perks Arrive," BusinessWeek Online*

> *I*n an automated system, when the inventory of a particular product falls below a predetermined level, an order is generated to a supplier to ship added inventory. That transaction would require an entry into the liability account for the vendor and the inventory account or an on-order temporary account. A corresponding entry needs to be made in the cost of sales account, automatically from one computer application to another. Electronic transmissions of purchase orders, invoices, and payments reduces paper work, and redundant data entry.
>
> —VERNON K. JACOBS, "E-COMMERCE ACCOUNTING SYSTEMS"

*Tip* Sharing accounting data saves inventory and personnel costs.

systems and accounting. *Ecommerce Times* reports that American Express and Ariba are developing automated electronic systems that will "pay-on-ship" or issue payments when items are shipped. The system will combine authorization, payment, and settlement into a single automated online process, based on shipment notification. Net accounting vendors (i.e., NetLedger, Yahoo! Stores, PeopleSoft, JDEdwards, and others) are working to overcome the incompatibilities that still exist on the Web.

The proliferation of several versions of XML and incompatibilities between Internet and stand-alone accounting programs also need to be overcome. The efforts of accounting system vendors and numerous Internet powerhouses should be able to surmount these problems in the not so distant future.

## Summary

Electronic systems are well suited for automating accounting. They increase accounting efficiencies and eliminate most of the mistakes due to human error. For years, large businesses have been using EDI to exchange accounting information with business partners. Accounting systems were among the first accounting applications, and the Internet can be used to take accounting systems to the next level by allowing organizations to share data. Internet accounting systems include automated invoicing, and payment and authentication systems.

## Chapter Key Points

🔑 The Internet allows small businesses to automate accounting transactions between them and business partners.

🔑 Large organizations have been using EDI for years to exchange accounting information with business partners.

🔑 Internet accounting systems include automated invoicing, payment, and authentication systems.

🔑 Internet accounting systems are being developed by accounting software companies and others.

🔑 Companies are developing systems that combine Internet accounting with other services such as storefronts and shipping systems.

🔑 Firms are working to overcome incompatibilities in software and XML versions.

*B*ig-league businesses can integrate their online operations with back-office infrastructure, including accounting systems. Small companies often don't have the resources, especially money, for such luxuries. Store-to-accounting synergy isn't out of the question, however. Some stores link with small business accounting software to automatically process sales orders, and automatically debit the purchased items from inventory.

—GREGG KEIZER, "ACCOUNT FOR ACCOUNTING"

*Tip* Web-based and other accounting systems still have compatibility problems.

## Web Sources for More Information

▶ **Brint.com** (www.brint.com) provides information on a variety of small business topics.

▶ **BusinessFinanceMag** (www.businessfinancemag.com) is a magazine that covers accounting and finance issues.

▶ **DotNetJunkies** (www.findapps.com) provides product reviews, vendor listings, and lots of other information on accounting systems.

▶ **Excite Guide: Small Business Products and Services** (www.excite.com) lists accounting software sites and programs.

# IF YOU POST IT THEY WILL COME
## *Attracting and Retaining with Information*

POST INFORMATION ON THE WEB TO SAVE TIME, REDUCE COSTS,
AND DEVELOP RELATIONSHIPS.

*T*he daughter began distributing produce to a number of local stores. Every day she called each of her customers to tell them what produce was available and how much it cost for various quantities. With a few businesses, this was no big deal. She was friendly with her contacts in each business, and they mutually enjoyed the few minutes of conversation each day.

As the business grew she found it more difficult to make all the calls. There were too many businesses for her to phone, and she felt that she was bothering her customers with daily calls. She hired an assistant to help. While the assistant saved the daughter time, he complained that many of the people he called always seemed busy and some were even rude. On the other hand, they would quickly complain if they were not informed about the daily produce and specials.

The daughter thought that posting the information on their Web site would make it accessible to the business customers. However, she was concerned that other customers would see the lower prices charged to wholesale customers. She read about providing these special customers with a password and limited access to a private Web site. She decided to investigate such a system called an Extranet. For now, she would simply provide information and still have the companies fax the orders. In the future she hoped they could automatically order and pay for produce using this system.

Your company may be able to reduce costs substantially and reap major benefits by using the Web to provide information to users. You can use your Web site to simply post information on the Internet or develop sophisticated applications available only to your employees, select customers, business partners, or the general public. By thinking about the information needs of your customers, employees, business partners, and other stakeholders you can use your Web site to build relationships and communities.

Obviously, using the Web to post information can save postage, personnel, and other administrative costs incurred with other forms of communication. Less obvious is that posting information on the Web can actually increase the level of service you are able to provide to your customers, employees, business partners, and other stakeholders. You can choose to post information publicly on the Internet, restrict information to employees and others inside the organization through an Intranet, or post the information to insiders plus select outsiders through the Extranet.

You can also provide information in a more timely manner and make it easily available. The information can be distinct for different groups of users or you can personalize it for a specific individual.

> *In today's competitive market you cannot afford to ignore personalization applications. These applications customize the Web content consumers and business users view through their desktop and mobile online interfaces.*
>
> —COLIN WHITE, "CUSTOM FIT"

**Tip** You can build relationships by supplying personalized information that meets the needs of an individual or a group.

## Posting Communications

Simply posting communications on a Web site or portal can result in significant cost savings for telephones, paper, associated processing costs (equipment, supplies), postage, and labor. In addition, by learning and anticipating customer needs, you can attract new customers and are more likely to retain present ones.

There are a number of ways that posting information can save money. Posting answers to frequently asked questions can provide customers with much needed information when customer service personnel are unavailable. This can save money by relieving personnel of answering repetitive questions. It can also reduce stress by providing answers to questions for stressed and impatient customers. For example, providing information on simple, common repairs or installation mistakes can save customers hours of frustration waiting for customer service to open or trying to figure it out themselves. Most recent information and updates can be provided in one central source, rather than having to distribute it. Thus, the information provided is more accurate and everyone has access to the same material. In addition, by providing an anywhere, anytime resource with information tailored to particular users you provide a value-added service to your customers.

Posting information of interest to your clients can both attract potential customers and keep them coming back to your site. For example, posting recipes, cleaning tips, vacation tips, money saving ideas, and other interesting items on your Web site can attract new and repeat visitors to your site.

## Intranet

Organizations can use Intranets for business-to-employee (B2E) applications such as allowing employees to gain access to self-service human resource applications (health care, pension plans, vacation time) and providing them with the capability to collaborate and communicate more effectively. These have been found to be low in cost relative to their benefits. In the words of Mel Duvall of

*Tip* Remember to consider both tangible and intangible benefits. Sometimes, the intangible ones are priceless.

*It is not only the removal of paper that leads to organizational benefit. What is done with that information in this new Web-enabled environment has a huge impact. Intranets allow an organization to spend less time on things that bring no value such as chasing down the right information to solve a problem.*

—OpenConsult, Inc.,
"Intranet Road Map"

*Interactive Week,* "What they have in common is a relatively low cost of implementation and a high return on investment." Other benefits include:

- Cost savings from decreased personnel, paper, delivery, and administrative expenses
- More accurate, up-to-date information
- Consistent company-wide information
- Convenient access to information from anywhere with a connection to the World Wide Web 24 hours a day, 7 days a week
- Improved company morale and feelings of community

In the article, "Intranet Road Map" OpenConsult, Inc. has listed both the tangible and intangible benefits of using Intranets.

*Tangible Benefits*

- Inexpensive to implement
- Easy to use, just point and click
- Saves time and money, better information faster
- Based on open standards
- Scalable and flexible
- Connects across disparate platforms
- Puts users in control of their data

*Intangible Benefits*

- Improved decision making
- Empowered users
- Builds a culture of sharing and collaboration
- Facilitates organizational learning
- Breaks down bureaucracy
- Improved quality of life at work
- Improved productivity

> *T*he Intranet is not only a powerful communication medium but also a knowledge base.
>
> —STEVEN L. TELLEEN, "INTRANETS AS KNOWLEDGE MANAGEMENT SYSTEMS"

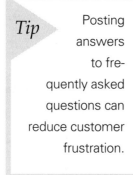

*Tip* Posting answers to frequently asked questions can reduce customer frustration.

These networks save your company the printing, distribution, and personnel costs for production of paper documents, and provide the latest information at any time from anywhere with an Internet connection. Cost savings can be substantial in these areas. The one-inch employee handbooks many corporations distribute annually can cost between $15 and $20 per employee. Policy and procedure manuals, corporate directories, and other company materials are also costly to distribute.

Although you can use an Intranet to post any information you can post on the Internet, most use it to post information that they would like to keep more private. For example, Emory University provides information about human resource policies and needed human resource forms with instructions on its Intranet site.

Intangible benefits can result from Intranets. Watson Wyatt Worldwide found that improved employee morale resulted from their human resource Intranet capabilities. They used their Intranet to avoid a dreaded annual crunch by allowing employees to enter their own data during a limited time each year when employees were allowed to change health plans and deductions. Human resource employees were less stressed and other employees felt empowered by their control of their own information.

Knowledge management (KM) portals can be a very valuable component of a company's Intranet. They provide single point personalized access to multiple sources of geographically dispersed information. Users can get the information in one place using a KM. Previously, they would have had to go to multiple sources and locations for the information. Carl Frappaolo, executive vice president and cofounder of Delphi Group in Boston,

> *Why build a corporate Intranet? Developers will tell you because we can. A better answer is that it is an effective tool to combat the waste of time, effort, and materials within an organization at the same time generating new opportunities for collaboration and productivity. For the first time, an organization has the ability to put one, open-standards, thin client (the Web browser) as the interface to their corporate data and business processes.*
>
> —OPENCONSULT, INC.,
> "INTRANET ROAD MAP"

*Tip* Intranets are not expensive to implement but provide many benefits.

## Kimberly Clark: Using the Web for Interaction

In the late 1990s Kimberly Clark treated the Web like traditional advertising media for broadcasting information and purchasing banner advertising that directed traffic to product-related sites like Huggies. Their results were not impressive.

Mark Scott, marketing director for infant-care products in North America, and other executives complained that the company was missing an opportunity for interacting with customers. At his suggestion, they developed a parenting Web site, Parentstages.com, containing lots of information to help people be better parents. The site contains articles offering advice from a number of independent sources, the capability to search medical literature, a recipe finder, calculator to help parents make sure their children are growing at a normal rate, message boards, and links to a multitude of child-related Web sites. Throughout a visitor's use of the site and all related sites a banner ad at the top of all pages and links displays the logos of Kimberly Clark products.

They concentrate on informing customers rather than trying to sell to them. In the words of Britt Beemer, chairman of America's Research Group, a consumer-research firm in Charleston, South Carolina, "If you really want to impress the customer, spend zero time selling and all your time informing." Kimberly Clark designed their site to help parents keep their children and families healthier. It is designed to create loyal customers rather than to sell products.

—EMILY NELSON, "THE SOFT SELL," THE WALL STREET JOURNAL

*Tip* Posting information can save money and time. It can improve accuracy of information.

Massachusetts, calls KM portals "the first killer implementation of the knowledge management philosophy."

Frito-Lay used a KM to remedy the negative impacts of having information dispersed in disparate systems throughout the corporation. Not only was information hard to find and unavailable in a timely manner, corporate sales and marketing staff were having to repetitively conduct consuming research on trends and consumer behavior as requested by sales people. Also, there was a lot of valuable information on individual computers that was not available to all employees who would benefit from it.

They decided to develop a pilot KM portal that consolidated access to information from multiple sources into a single access point. Prior to implementing it throughout the company, they conducted a pilot with a test team and got very positive results. The test team doubled the growth rate of the customer's business in the salty snack category. According to Mike Marino, vice president of customer development of Frito-Lay, "The retailer is happy because they're doing more business in their market, and we're doing business at a faster growth

> *Certain statistics quote that 18 percent of corporate printed material becomes outdated after 30 days. Imagine that after 60 or 90 days. Now, imagine if that material were always online and current.*
>
> *—OPENCONSULT, INC., "INTRANET ROAD MAP"*

## Company Profile: Ketchum's Knowledge Portal

The Ketchum Global Network's employee portal features applications for storing and sharing information. It has an expertise locator that helps find capabilities within Ketchum, provides their employees with online phone directories, allows self-service human resource forms, and gives employees access to vacation information. In addition, they provide information on the company, relevant news and articles on brainstorming and creativity, and job openings. Ketchum reported that 70 percent of their employees looked at the site daily and 80 to 90 percent looked at it several times a week.

Ketchum hired the research firm, Meta Group, to study the costs and benefits of its impressive employee portal. For an investment of $13.79 million, the Meta Group estimates the firm will achieve benefits of $30 million dollars with an ROI of $15.5 million. Meta found the most significant benefit was being able to provide clients with faster, smarter service. It also has improved productivity, allowed new employees to get up to speed more quickly, and enabled employees to feel like a member of the Ketchum community.

*—MEL DUVALL, "CULTIVATING PROFIT," INTERACTIVE WEEK*

> *I*ntranets allow for a place where boundaries are lowered and information exchange is encouraged. This leads to more informed employees with the ability to make better, faster decisions. This in turn leads to better productivity and more time for revenue generation.
>
> —*OPENCONSULT, INC., "INTRANET ROAD MAP"*

**Tip** Immediate access to timely and accurate information is a major benefit of having an Intranet.

rate with this customer than with other customers." Timeliness of information acquisition was an important consideration for Equilon in developing their KM portal. The portal gives employees immediate access to data so that they can analyze, manipulate, and share information quickly and easily. Prior to the portal, the information was stored in a number of databases throughout the company. It was both difficult and time consuming to locate and distribute needed information. According to the business manager, Cynthia Flash reports in "Knowledge Management Meets a Portal" that according to the business manager, "It's not so much that the information hasn't been available, it's the timeliness the portal brings to us. We can get that information in real-time and make decisions quicker based on the information. It's getting the right information to the right people at the right time."

## Extranets

Extranets provide information to selected customers and suppliers. Companies may let customers check order information status, service information, new product listings, helpful hints, and specialized catalogs tailored to meet their needs. According to the Extranet Benchmarking Association (EBA), Extranets are presently being used for

- project management tools for companies and collaborating third parties.
- sharing proprietary ideas with a select group.
- online training for re-sellers.
- a way of dealing with high volumes of data using electronic data interchange (EDI).
- sharing product catalogs and inventory levels exclusively with partners.

- collaborating with other companies on joint development efforts.
- providing services offered by one company to a group of other companies, such as an online banking application managed by one company on behalf of affiliated banks.
- sharing news of common interest exclusively with partner companies.

Companies may allow suppliers to answer questions and receive updates about products, submit proposals, obtain bids, and collect payments. For example, the automobile industry has been providing their suppliers with password-protected access so they can obtain this information on their systems. Suppliers can obtain information about needed parts including design changes and anticipated needs. The system allows both automobile manufacturers and their suppliers to save money and reduce the time it takes for an automobile to be produced. Some companies are sharing information and joining forces to improve production and services through collaborative commerce. Other types of Extranets provide services to their subscribers. For example, Healthcare Technologies (www.healthxnet.com) provides access to view documentation, download meeting minutes, review current project plans, streamline the flow of information between companies, view demos of new products, and test new programs and software.

The farm equipment manufacturer, Deere & Co., uses its Extranet to post an electronic catalog. Dow Jones provides links with sources of information on securities transactions on its Extranet. Northern Trust Co., a Chicago bank, has launched an Extranet to help its commercial customers prevent bank fraud. Federal Express allows online status queries from customers, which saves

*Tip* Sharing information can be invaluable. The paradigm is changing from privacy to sharing.

*F*lexibility in time of delivery of knowledge is gained as information is always a click away.

—OPENCONSULT, INC., "INTRANET ROAD MAP"

couriers time and eliminates paper handling. According to Rob Carter, chief technologist at FDX Corporation, FedEx's parent company, "As Internet usage has exploded the online population, we have a natural means of reaching more and more customers this way."

The Extranet potential is limited only by the business strategies and methods employed. Extranets are a natural evolution, taking advantage of the Internet infrastructure and previous Internet investments to focus communications on the exchange of information and shared applications with business partners, suppliers, and customers.

Like Intranets, Extranets can save money, provide more accurate, up-to-date, and consistent information to users, lend to a sense of community, and be used any time from almost anywhere. To realize these savings businesses can use their Web site to post forms, newsletters, notices, announcements, and answers to frequently asked questions such as hours of operation, directions, repair information, and other commonly asked questions. Extranets can provide the same or different information as do Intranets.

> *Technically known as Extranets, business partner networks have proven to be much more effective than more traditional methods of communication such as phone or fax—and most corporations are catching on.*
>
> *—Extranet Strategist, "If You Build it Will they Come?"*

## Summary

Simply posting information can provide valuable benefits and increase both organizational effectiveness and efficiency. Companies can use the Internet and Extranets to improve customer service and at the same time saving money and personnel time. Companies can use Intranets to create a sense of community, improve company morale, save money, reduce paper transactions, and increase timeliness and accuracy of information.

Particularly useful are knowledge management (KM) portals that provide single point personalized access to

*Tip* There are many uses for Extranets depending on the needs of your business partners.

multiple sources of geographical information. Human resource applications, such as posting of benefits, insurance, and other forms can help both employers and employees.

Companies can use Extranets to improve efficiencies and effectiveness of their operations. They can improve value chain and information sharing with business partners and customers. They can use Extranets to engage in collaborative commerce applications.

> *Productivity increases as corporate knowledge is more accessible and the data is more accurate.*
>
> —OPENCONSULT, INC.,
> "INTRANET ROAD MAP"

## Chapter Key Points

- ✎ Intranets are private Internet-like networks for internal use by company employees.

- ✎ Extranets are private Internet-like networks for internal use by company employees and specified users.

- ✎ Companies can use Intranets to create a sense of community, improve company morale, save money, reduce paper transactions, and increase timeliness and accuracy of information.

- ✎ KM portals offer single point personalized access to multiple sources of geographically dispersed information.

- ✎ Human resource applications are particularly suited for Intranets.

- ✎ Intranets and Extranets can be used to improve customer service while preserving company resources.

- ✎ Companies can use Extranets to improve efficiencies and effectiveness of their operations. They can improve value chain and information sharing with business partners and customers. They can use Extranets to engage in collaborative commerce applications.

Companies can use the Internet, Intranets, and Extranets to improve relationships, increase effectiveness, and reduce inefficiencies.

## Web Sources for More Information

▶ **CIO Magazine's Intranet/Extranet Research Center** (www.cio.com/forums/intranet) contains information and an "ask the expert" service devoted to Intranet design and applications.

▶ **Extranet Benchmarking Association** (www.extranetbenchmarking.com) provides a newsletter, advice, and information to members.

▶ **Extranet News** (www.extranet.cc) is a portal site for Intranets and Extranets.

▶ **Extranet Reference Page** (www.viktoria.informatik.gu.se/~kerstinf/extranet.htm) provides information about the Internet and third wave Internet applications.

▶ **Extranet Resource Center** (www.netcom.com) offers applications and Extranet building tools.

▶ **Extranet Strategist** (www.extranet-strategist.com) is a quarterly news magazine focusing on Extranet management, security, and other Extranet issues.

▶ **Intrack.com** (www.intrack.com) is an excellent Intranet site with discussions, links to articles, links to vendors, and lots of information on a variety of Intranet-related topics.

▶ **Intranet Benchmarking Association** (www.intranetbenchmarking.com) offers a newsletter, advice, and information to members.

# RELATIONSHIPS MEAN REVENUES
## *Making and Keeping Customers Happy*

SUCCESS MAY BE DETERMINED BY THE QUALITY OF YOUR RELATIONSHIPS. ◀

*The widow had always known that developing relationships with her customers was a key to the success of the farm stand. She was proud that every summer many of the same families would visit the farm stand each week on their way to and from the shore. Even after the new highway was opened, many of these families drove several miles out of their way to visit the farm stand.*

*The widow had worked hard at getting to know her customers so that she could anticipate their needs. She tried to predict when repeat customers would visit and made sure she always had their favorite products in stock. She saved the best produce for repeat customers. She learned about customer tastes and family needs. She always provided refreshments specifically selected for particular customers. For adults she served drinks and snacks she knew they liked. For children she served cookies and milk or juice. She knew that traveling with children was difficult and made sure to always have inexpensive travel games on hand along with activities for different ages. She kept maps of the area and listings of activities and sites to give to new customers and others not familiar with the area. She would give these to families with children to make their trips easier. Not only were the adults grateful for the diversions she provided, the children were excited to visit the farm stand and would beg their parents to come back. The widow wondered how she could develop such strong customer relationships electronically.*

## Success Requires Strong Customer Relationships

In the cutthroat world of e-commerce, you can't afford the luxury of treating customers badly. On the Web, the cost of switching to another company may be minimal. Since it takes so much more money to acquire a new customer than to please your current ones, you must do everything you can to delight your customers and gain their loyalty. That means seeing everything from their perspective.

Relationships have always been key to doing business. Prior to the advent of the superstore, customers chose where to shop based primarily on location and convenience. Local merchants and their customers developed mutual trust through face-to-face interactions and honest exchanges of goods, services, and payments. Often merchants and their customers were willing to exchange goods, services, or payments for the other's word that they would make a payment, perform a service, or provide a good sometime in the future. Customers trusted their favorite merchants to sell goods and services at fair prices.

The advent of large department stores, warehouse stores, superstores, and discount chains changed all that. These stores compete on the basis of price and the convenience of having everything under one roof in a central location. Even the most loyal customers were usually persuaded that they should switch from the local merchants due to the lower-priced merchandise available from these large businesses, and the main streets of small town America began to fail.

Many of the most successful large stores attempted to create the personal "small town" feeling through advertising and customer service policies aimed at

> *C*onsidering that it is five to eight times more expensive to gain a new customer than it is to sell to an existing customer, the stakes are high indeed.
>
> —PETER FINGAR, HARSHNA KUMAR, AND TARUN SHIRMA, "21ST CENTURY MARKETS"

*Tip* Treat your customers well. Treat them as you would want to be treated.

## Focusing on Customer Wants: Foster and Smith

While many online retailers spend their money on advertising their Web site, Drs. Foster and Smith, vendors of pet care products, have spent nothing advertising their site. Yet their revenues have been growing at 15 percent a year and they continue to be profitable. Drs. Foster and Smith watched as dotcom failures, such as Pets.com, spent millions advertising their site only to go bankrupt after an expensive and memorable initial splash.

Rather than spending their money on advertising, Foster and Smith have been focusing on developing loyal and happy customers.

Drs. Foster and Smith began as a traditional catalog company and developed their Web site to provide customers with another channel for ordering products. Instead of advertising, Drs. Foster and Smith have spent money on Web site development. They have focused on providing customers with the site content they want. They spend money on shipping, making sure orders go out within 24 hours.

—LEE GOMES, "JUST SAY NO," THE WALL STREET JOURNAL

projecting personal caring and developing trust. They tried to create the same feel of the small town retailers but were able to offer lower prices due to their high sales volume. They located their stores to conveniently serve large numbers of people.

The Web is now making location less important. Whether they want to or not, all businesses are competing in a global marketplace. For many customers price has become the major, if not only, factor in many purchasing decisions. Unless you can be the low price leader, which is often difficult for small businesses, you will lose if you can't find other ways to gain and retain customers.

Forming relationships and loyal customers by providing excellent customer service is one way to win on the Web. Developing customer loyalty means developing

> *D*espite starry-eyed visions of hyperpersonalization and solemn vows of customer-centrism, many companies continue to thwart, frustrate, and punish their customers. I find this very upsetting. Why should I care? Apart from being a customer myself, I get most upset because the reputation of the entire Internet is damaged every time a customer goes away unhappy. We can't expect to attract more people and more money to the Internet if we continue to screw things up.
>
> —*JEFFREY GRAHAM,*
> *"E-CRM FOR DUMMIES"*

processes for the benefit of your customers. This chapter describes how you can develop these relationships throughout the entire life of your business. Although automated customer relationship management (CRM) systems help automate some CRM processes, to succeed you must understand customer relationships and what you can do to improve them before automating. That is where most businesses are lacking. With all the talk about improving customer service and personalization, many businesses still don't seem to care about their customers. You can gain a competitive advantage in the Internet marketplace by showing that you understand and care about your customers.

## Getting to Know Your Customers

To establish relationships with customers you must try to understand them and know what they want from your products and services. As in any human relationships, people want to be heard and understood. A local merchant had face-to-face conversations with customers. On the Web, there are a number of ways to encourage customers to communicate with you. Juniper Communications, a well-known consumer e-commerce market research firm, recommends a multichannel approach to customer service including:

- e-mail
- toll-free numbers
- chat rooms
- bulletin boards
- frequently asked questions

The idea is to give your customers ample opportunities to communicate with you. Next, you must listen to what they have to say.

## Measure Customer Reactions

To get an accurate idea of what your customers are saying, you need to measure their feedback. You should choose a way to measure customer feedback, make improvements, remeasure feedback, and keep improving and measuring indefinitely. In other words, implement a system for continuous improvement.

The experts at About.com recommend a formal but easy to administer quality assurance process for even very small Web-based businesses. They suggest first choosing an accurate but easy and inexpensive method for measuring quality (e.g., counting customer complaints or problems by area). Next, you would divide your customer processes into detailed small component processes, which would be assigned a code (the smaller the component processes the more accurate). For example, a B2C e-tailer might divide items into components in the areas of advertising, catalog, shopping cart, and ordering. Using customer complaints as a measure, as customer complaints occur these would be coded in the component area. At the end of a period (you can choose any period—a month, a quarter or whatever is convenient), you tally up the complaints and see which processes caused the most problems. It should be obvious at this point what processes are causing trouble. It is more difficult to decide why the process is causing difficulty and what you should do to improve it. For example, a slow Web site may indicate that you need a new ISP, should redesign your Web site, or have a problem that needs to be outsourced. In any event, continual measurement is necessary to ensure you are properly addressing the problems. Even after you are confident you have solved the underlying problem you should continue to improve your processes.

> *Relationships are critical in e-commerce to overcome the high cost of customer acquisition.... It means designing and operating the business from the customer perspective and recognizing that all aspects of your operation affect the customer including processes such as shipping that were traditionally viewed as being in the back office. E-commerce success rests on building relationships and repeat business.*
>
> —Martin V. Deise, Conrad Nowikow, Patrick King, and Amy Wright, Executive's Guide to E-Business

*Tip* ▷ Give your customers ways to give feedback.

## Google

Google (www.google.com) is proof that you can succeed on the Web by giving people what they want. In the very competitive arena of search engines, Google has become the 15th most visited Web site in the United States without spending anything on marketing. The business has been growing at more than 10 percent per quarter, largely from selling advertising and their search technology to other sites.

Google has built its following based on the capabilities of its search engine, which not only looks for keywords inside Web pages but also rates the importance of each search by the number and popularity of other sites linked to that page. Users have found the approach successful. This summer, a survey by market researcher NPD Group ranked Google the most effective search engine, with 97 percent of users saying they located what they were looking for "every time" or "most of the time." Google has recently added the capacity for users to search by groups and images or by using a subject directory to narrow their search. Google users get what they want and keep coming back for more.

—*Ben Elgin and Jim Kerstetter, "Why They're Agog over Google,"* BusinessWeek Online

## Guarantee Quality

In *Marketing Without Advertising: Inspire Customers to Rave about Your Business to Create Lasting Success* (Nolo Press, 1996) Michael R. Phillips and Salli Rasberry define the elements of an effective customer satisfaction policy as:

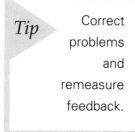

*Tip* ▷ Correct problems and remeasure feedback.

- customers should be encouraged to tell you about any problems.
- customers should know their rights and responsibilities from the beginning.
- customers should know the circumstances under which they are entitled to get their money back and how to take advantage of other rights.
- customers, not you, should feel in control. It's far better to provide a full refund if the customer is

dissatisfied than to demand that the customer come up with a "good reason" for the refund.

Whether you're selling products or services, go further than is legally required in anticipating and responding to the problems of your customers. How you do this depends in part on the nature of the products or services you offer. But for starters, consider the policy of Eddie Bauer, a highly successful national company that sells outdoor goods through its catalog and retail outlets: "OUR GUARANTEE: 'Every item we sell will give you complete satisfaction or you may return it for a full refund.'"

## Service

After the sale and delivery are complete, you have an opportunity to distinguish your business and build relationships during a number of processes.

- Customer follow-up
- Return process
- Customer service
- Complaint handling
- Ongoing relationship

### Customer Follow-Up

An effective way to catch potential problems before they become real is to send customers an e-mail about two or three days after anticipated delivery. If the product has not yet been delivered, you have the opportunity to correct the problem for the customer before they complain. If the product has been delivered the customer has an opportunity to express concerns or appreciation for good service.

*O*f course it doesn't stop there. Anything that can be monitored can be used to improve the quality of a business and this often involves setting your own goals. For example you may set an objective of delivering all orders within three days, or getting repeat orders from 30 percent of your customers within a month. Again you measure performance over a period, analyze which business process is causing the most problems, refine the process, and then repeat. Simple! The important point is that improving the quality of your processes should be a core part of your business. You need to be continually raising standards and finding better ways of doing things. Only the very best e-businesses succeed so make sure your business is one of them.

—GORDON WHYTE, "HOW TO MONITOR AND IMPROVE YOUR E-BUSINESS PROCESSES"

> *O*ne of the most over-looked aspects of any customer relationship management (CRM) strategy is the people on each end of the equation. Sure, we talk about being customer focused, but to what extent do we think that purchasing software to help manage relationships will make us so? And to what extent do we think we can rely on the existing skills that employees have to execute on a CRM strategy?
>
> —CHRIS MCTIERNAN,
> "PUTTING THE P INTO E-CRM"

*Tip* Great guarantees lead to great relationships.

### Returning Items

Not only should you guarantee items and allow returns without questions, customers must be able to easily return items. You need to have a simple, easy process for customers to turn in defective or unwanted items within reasonable guidelines. When customers have difficulty returning products and receiving refunds in a timely manner, they can easily become alienated.

Therefore, it is essential that you have a process in place for customers to return items easily and receive refunds quickly.

### Complaint Handling

You can approach customer complaints as either a huge burden or an opportunity to develop a relationship. While the other processes we have discussed in this chapter can be standardized and made routine, customer complaint processes are exceptions to the normal processes. These exceptions may fall into a number of categories and routine processes can be created for each type.

Exceptional processes offer an opportunity for your company to shine and develop solid customer relationships. By excelling at exceptional processes, you exceed expectations and can create strong customer relationships. According to Keen and McDonald, "How a company handles the exceptions may turn out to be a key to differentiating itself in a marketplace." A company can delight a customer by providing exceptional customer service, and hopefully, the company gains a loyal customer.

### Ongoing Relationships

The Internet provides many opportunities to establish an ongoing relationship with your customers. You can continue sending them e-mail notifications of specials,

## Outsourcing Returns

Janice Parker of Sincerely Yours, a home-décor business in Lewisville, Texas, out-sourced handling merchandise returns to a company, Newgistics Inc., which specializes in "reverse logistics." Parker reports that both the company and their customers are happy with the solution. It relieves them of the enormous logistical burdens of handling returned merchandise.

Dealing with returned merchandise is a thankless task for any business. It generates no profits while draining the company of both employee time and space. For small companies handling returned merchandise can be overwhelming. For many, such as Sincerely Yours, the solution may lie in outsourcing.

*—ELLEN NEUBORNE, "HAPPY RETURNS,"*
BUSINESSWEEK ONLINE

new products, and other information of interest to them. Ways that B2C and B2B businesses can establish these relationships are discussed in the chapters devoted to marketing.

### Automating CRM

There are a number of systems that help automate processes supporting CRM. For automating CRM to work you need to have a supportive attitude and processes that facilitate customer relations. There are CRM products that automate some sales functions, assist customer call center functions, support automated e-mail services, analyze and organize customer data, monitor traffic, and perform many other marketing and analysis functions. In *Executive's Guide to E-Business: From Tactics to Strategy* (John Wiley and Son, 2000) Martin V. Deise, Conrad Nowikow, Patrick King, and Amy Wright describe an ideal customer as supporting the following areas:

- General product information
- Product marketing information

*The scene is changing. Rather I would say, it has been already changed. Customers are king. Everybody is facing some kind of challenge. Not only sellers but the buyers too are facing challenges due to a changed environment.*

*—CHRIS MCTIERNAN,*
*"PUTTING THE P INTO e-CRM"*

> *Support, delivery, and maintenance activities should be viewed as cross-selling or up-selling opportunities for your existing customer base.*
>
> —PHILIP SAY, "SEVEN GREAT B2B MARKETING INITIATIVES"

- Ordering, placement, price quote, confirmation, and track status
- Customer care/service, including technical support, general inquiries, frequently asked questions (FAQs), and problem solvers
- Project/order administration, including invoicing and billing history, account summary, and unresolved issues
- Communications, including events, planned training, and promotions/incentives programs
- Collaborative demand planning workroom, including demand forecasts

There are numerous vendors of these products. Products, evaluations, and descriptions of products can be found at CRMguru.com.

## Summary

This chapter discussed the importance of customer relationships. Having good, loyal customers can make your business successful. Unfortunately, too many companies forget that. It does little good to automate if you do not have a customer-focused attitude.

## Chapter Key Points

🔑 Your customers are your greatest asset but too many companies forget that.

🔑 This chapter discussed the importance of customer relationships.

🔑 Having good, loyal customers can make your business successful.

🔑 It does little good to automate if you do not have a customer-focused attitude.

> *Bottom line: Treat your current customers as assets that must be protected diligently during these times. Do whatever it takes to keep your current franchise of customers productive and well served.*
>
> —PHILIP SAY, "SEVEN GREAT B2B MARKETING INITIATIVES"

## Web Sources for More Information

▶ **About.com** (www.about.com) provides articles, links, advice, and other information on B2B marketing and a host of other business topics.

▶ **ClickZ.com** (www.clickz.com) contains articles, links, advice, and other information on B2B marketing and many other e-commerce areas.

▶ **CRM Guru** (www.crmguru.com) is a great site that has links to a lot of information about CRM including vendor information and other help with buying CRM software.

▶ **Digitrends** (www.digitrends.net) offers articles and other information on the Internet and digital commerce.

▶ **ZDNet.com** (www.zdnet.com) has articles, links, advice, and other information on a number of e-commerce and businesses topics.

# BUILD IT AND WHO COMES?

*Getting Consumers to Come to You*

E-COMMERCE SUCCESS MEANS DEVELOPING
SOLID CUSTOMER RELATIONSHIPS. ◀

*The daughter put her floral wedding arrangement business on a portal but was still not generating the volume of business she needed. She was very disappointed and decided she should explore other ideas for marketing the business.*

*The daughter was getting to know other people who targeted wedding business. Several had Web sites. They decided to pool their resources. They formed reciprocal links with each other and approached other people in the wedding business about forming reciprocal links with them. The daughter and a few others decided to develop a newsletter offering tips and suggestions for having the wedding of your dreams. They would e-mail the newsletter to recipients and refer people to their sites. In addition, they pooled their customer databases and contact lists and bought an expensive e-mail list of potential customers.*

*The daughter decided to list her site and subscription information on the wedding newsletter on popular search engines. She knew that there were hundreds of people selling flowers on the Web and that she would have to make sure her site was listed early on the list when someone searched for wedding arrangements. She got listing information from each search engine and followed their instructions for obtaining a high listing. After finishing the instructed changes in her Web site she ran some tests on her favorite search engines. To her delight her site was near the top of all of the lists.*

*Within weeks of her new marketing efforts the daughter noted the increased visits to her Web site. She hoped that the traffic would continue and lead to increased sales.*

▲　▲　▲

> *Finding people of all sorts on the Internet is getting easier, because more and more people are coming online. And retail commerce is getting easier still, because more and more people are getting comfortable with the idea of using the Internet to do things.... Habits are changing, not in an Internet revolution, but at the normal slow, steady pace of human behavioral change.*
>
> —DAVID WALKER,
> "BEHIND THE GLOOM"

You have designed your site and found a great location. You can't just sit there and expect others to find you. You need to take steps to make sure that people come to your site. The many failures of B2C businesses and e-tailers demonstrate the importance of having an exceptional marketing plan. This chapter will discuss how you can use both Web-based and traditional marketing and sales options to maximize your success in the B2C marketplace, to bring traffic to your site, and to market to your customers after they have visited your site.

Smart marketing efforts and well thought out expenditures are more important to success than the dollar amount spent on advertising. In "Surviving in the Aftermath of the B2C Crash," authors Luis Arjona and Vikas Agrawal discuss how important it is to develop a marketing strategy. "Best practice players have built highly sophisticated marketing functions, instead of simply trying to outspend rivals with offbeat advertising campaigns and outlandish portal deals. They utilize multiple targeted offline and online media channels, track campaign effectiveness rigorously, and negotiate multi-layered traffic performance deals. As a result, the annual marketing dollars spent for the top quartile performers fell consistently in the $2m to $6m range, significantly below the $30 to $50m often quoted as being necessary for success."

Thus, smart small businesses can win even if they have less to spend on marketing. Knowing your customers and evaluating advertising costs and effectiveness

*Tip* How you spend marketing money is more important than how much you spend.

have been discussed. This chapter will explore the different avenues available for B2C advertising.

## The Power of Multichannel Marketing

Web marketing solutions range from online versions of business cards, advertisements, brochureware, and other promotional materials, to sophisticated online catalogs and e-mail campaigns. Unfortunately the B2C "road kill" that dots the Information Superhighway shows that using Web-based marketing alone is often inadequate. According to Ernst and Young, online retailers are realizing that multichannel marketing is a requirement for success: "The notion of a 'pure play' is turning out to be the wrong play…. To be successful, online retailers need to exploit other marketing channels simultaneously, such as in-store and catalog sales, as well as private labels. A number of apparel e-tailers are already doing this successfully. Our study shows that multichannel players can increase their share of the wallet, as many consumers are already browsing on the Web before buying in the store."

Companies succeed more often when they use multiple channels to get the message to their customers. It is a great idea to use as many channels as possible to publicize your Web site. List your Web address wherever possible. You can include the address in all traditional media: on your business card; in all advertisements whether in print, on the radio, or on TV; on all correspondence; on all brochures; in your catalog; and in press releases.

To be successful on the Web you must find ways to

- bring traffic to your site
- have customers make a purchase
- stimulate repeat customers

> *E*-Marketer's e-commerce B2C Report, which aggregates data from more than 100 research organizations, reveals that consumers spent $59.7 billion online last year, compared to $30.1 billion in 1999, a 98 percent increase.
>
> —E-MARKETER,
> "B2C E-COMMERCE REVENUES"

*Tip* Multichannel marketing works best in conjunction with both offline and online ads.

To be of maximum effectiveness in bringing traffic to your site you should use both traditional and online approaches for advertising. Studies have found that a combination of online and traditional marketing produces better results. In the words of Geoffrey Ramsey, a founder of eMarketer, a leading aggregator of Internet statistics and a recognized authority on business online, "In the mad race to build awareness, establish online brands, and drive site traffic, Web marketers will continue to divert the majority of their advertising and marketing budgets to offline media and their own corporate Web site development. The brand battle for Web marketers will be waged, not so much on banner ads, but on television sets, radios, and in magazines, as well as on company Web sites where real consumer interaction takes place."

In addition to listing your Web address everywhere possible, there are a number of online marketing techniques that can be used to bring traffic to your site.

- Registering on search engines
- Reciprocal links
- Banner ads
- Portal alliances
- Newsletters
- E-mail

> *E*-commerce is chugging along. It's a snowball that's grown and grown, and people that have bought online before will continue to buy online, and they're going to buy more.
>
> —JON WEISMAN, "THE E-BUSINESS AND TECHNOLOGY SUPERSITE REPORT"

*Tip* List your Web address and advertise the site everywhere you can.

## Registering on Search Engines

First, make sure that you list your site on search engines and use the Web design guidelines presented in Chapter 6 to ensure that your Web site is included toward the top of the list in searches. Not only do you want to register your site with popular search engines, you need to take the steps, as specified by each search engine, to make sure your site will be ranked highly. When people type in applicable key words, you want to make sure people see your site by having it appear near the top of the listings. Being listed and having a good position is so important that some companies have hired people to help them gain top positions on search engine lists. Using an inexpensive software package, like Web Position Gold (www.webpositiongold.com), to evaluate and manipulate your standing on search engines is a less costly alternative.

## Reciprocal Links

Reciprocal links are a great way to advertise your Web site. In "B2G Internet Marketing Strategies," author D. L. Bakuli explains how to use reciprocal links: "One of the most commonly used methods to advertise on the Internet is the use of free links. The system is simple yet quite powerful if you link with the right partners. You provide a link to your partners' Web sites and they in turn provide links to your Web site from theirs. For this program to be successful, you must provide compelling content, service, or give-aways that augment your product line." Companies like Amazon and Barnes and Noble demand a cut of profits for sales that result from clicks from their sites.

## Banner Advertisements and Pop-Up Ads

Banner advertisements are the rectangular advertising boxes containing promotions, offers, and Web address information that appear on Web sites. Pop-up advertisements are Web pages that open up to display advertisements, offers, and a Web address. Both include buttons that when clicked take the user to an advertiser's Web page.

> *E*-Marketer projects B2C global e-commerce revenues will reach $101 billion by year end, rising to $167 billion in 2002 and $250 billion by 2003.
>
> —E-MARKETER,
> "B2C E-COMMERCE REVENUES"

You should place banner and pop-up advertisements on sites that you feel will generate the type of traffic you are trying to attract. For example, you could place banner ads on popular sites, such as CNN, local or regional newspapers, or general Internet portals (Yahoo!, Lycos, or Netscape).

Alternatively, you can select specialized portals, trade associations, or other sites focusing on particular niches. You can choose to advertise on particular pages or to have the banner ads appear when certain actions are performed. One effective formula is having your banner ad appear on search engine listings when certain keywords are used for searches. For example, an online candy retailer could have a banner ad appear when someone includes the keyword, "chocolate," in a search. The cost of banner advertising can be expensive per sale. You usually pay each time your banner ad appears in this type of advertising. For example, at a cost of $20 (CPM) per thousand impressions, if 1 percent of the people who saw the ad clicked it, this would give you a cost of $2 per click (CPC).

The conversion rate, or number of people who click your ad and make a purchase, determines how much this form of advertising costs per sale. For example, if only 1 percent of the people who click purchase something, the cost to you would be $200 per sale.

## Portal Sites

You can develop an alliance with a portal site to market your products and services. The charge will be either a fee or percentage of sales. For example, gift retailers can list on AltaVista's Shopping Guide "gift" section, Go network's 911Gifts.com, AOL's listing of "Other Stores," or Yahoo!'s "Highlighted Merchant."

> *Deliver your message over and over again. There's no bigger waste of your marketing budget than an ad that runs only once. There is so much media clutter in our lives these days that it's unlikely that even a high-impact ad is going to make much of an impression without regular repetition.*
>
> —GEO PURDIE AND ANDY ROGERS, "MARKETING STRATEGIES"

*Tip* Reciprocal links can be a great way to get people to your site.

While these portals can be expensive, an added benefit of this approach is that store portals usually provide the software to automate retail stores. The Web site storefronts provided by these sites are usually standard so you may not be able to be creative with your site design. However, they do make it easy to get up and running and supply all items necessary to operate a retail store.

## Newsletters

You can use newsletters to market in three ways.

1. Advertising in a newsletter

2. Writing a column in a newsletter

3. Starting your own newsletter

Newsletters are great vehicles for advertising. First, they target people interested in the newsletter subject area. Second, people request them by subscribing. Finally, by writing in a newsletter you establish yourself as an expert in the area. If you choose to write for a newsletter or start your own you want to make sure to keep the reader in mind. Write short, two pages or less, articles on timely topics. Usually, the reader and newsletter owner, if not you, won't mind you doing some self-promotion. Make sure to include your company information along with information on who you are. Since the newsletter itself should be kept short, only a few articles should appear.

You can use either text or HTML e-mail messages. HTML e-mail messages include Web page features in the message itself. They can include special formatting, graphics, the ability to make secure purchases through the message, and other features. The downside is that some potential recipients may have e-mail programs

> *You must always be growing a tightly targeted list of prospects. It's the only way you can "capture" a percentage of the folks who visit your site and do not buy the first time (which is nearly all of them!). An opt-in strategy works best when you give something of value away in exchange for a visitor's name and e-mail address. Then you must stay in touch with these people on a regular basis, while providing value for them.*
>
> —JIM DANIELS, "OPINION: STEP-BY-STEP TO YOUR OWN PROFITABLE WEB BUSINESS"

*Tip* — Newsletters are a great tool for marketing your business.

## IBM: Customizing Recruiting

When IBM wanted to recruit prospective interview candidates in Boston two years ago, it used customized marketing to reach potential interviewees. Students were greeted with banner ads specifically geared to them. For example, Boston University students were greeted with "Boston University students, please click here."

The results of the campaign were impressive, with a "click-through" rate of 25 percent according to Double Click, Inc., a New York Web-advertising firm that developed the ads with IBM. In a typical campaign, banner ads produce a click-through rate of less than 1 percent. Thus, the campaign resulted in 25 times the number of students seeking more information than expected in a different type of campaign.

—*STEPHANIE MILES, "PEOPLE LIKE US,"*
*THE WALL STREET JOURNAL*

that do not support these features. Your browser and e-mail server will have directions on developing HTML messages.

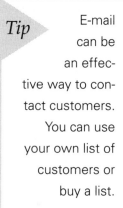

*Tip*  E-mail can be an effective way to contact customers. You can use your own list of customers or buy a list.

## Use E-Mail for Direct Mail

You can use e-mail to notify customers and Web visitors of new products, specials, and promotional items. You can use this in the same way that traditional retailers use direct mail approaches. Selected lists of e-mail addresses are sold just as they are in the traditional mail. You can find lists by searching using the keywords, "direct mail."

Your own lists are the best lists to send e-mail to. This can be especially effective if people have signed up to receive these notifications. Have customers choose to be notified of products and specials when they purchase something, subscribe to your newsletter, or join your Web site.

## Marketing from Your Site

Once you get people to your site you can use it for marketing. You can provide "freebies" to attract visitors and entice them to return. Once you post something it costs little to provide it to visitors. You can therefore use "freebies" to attract visitors and develop relationships.

You can post free information and links to information, and have search capabilities on your site to help individuals find information in your niche area. WebMD provides medical information and links on a wide range of medical topics. Search capabilities let visitors easily find the information they seek.

If your products and services can be used as gifts, you can set up a more sophisticated tool, the "Gift Search." The shopper enters relevant information such as occasion (e.g., anniversary), their relationship to recipient, price range, and other information. The search returns a listing of all items that meet the criteria. All that is needed to do this is a shopping cart system that is linked to a programmable relational database.

Providing customer reviews or listings of popular products bought by people with similar profiles can entice people to pick a particular gift since they will tend to feel more comfortable and attracted if an item is identified as popular. A gift registry is another method of getting your customers to get their friends to come to your site. Reminders of important events, such as a relative's birthday, and gift suggestions can also be used to increase traffic and repeat business. However, this requires a database, automatic e-mail generation, and customized messages.

There are a lot of things that you can give away. Software and tech companies may give away free software. Bluemountain.com, Amazon.com, and 1-800-Flowers have

> *If there is one aspect that kills Web site sales it is poor sales copy. You may think your site is fine, but tiny details in your sales copy can be costing you thousands of dollars a month.*
>
> —JIM DANIELS, "OPINION: STEP-BY-STEP TO YOUR OWN PROFITABLE WEB BUSINESS"

*Tip* ▸ Once they get to your site you can market to people more easily.

> **Tip** Customer feedback helps others feel comfortable buying from your site.

> *T*he dotcoms have begun to branch out by using "old economy" ways to create brand awareness, obtain credibility, attract a wider customer base, and maximize sales.
>
> —ERNST AND YOUNG,
> "GLOBAL ONLINE: RETAILING: 2001"

> **Tip** If your site is a store, people will feel more comfortable if it feels like a traditional store.

gained customers and gotten their customers to market their site for them by suggesting that they send "virtual cards" and "virtual bouquets." Similar postcard programs can be set up inexpensively. There are free postcard programs, given away as freebies on other sites, you can use to send virtual gifts. A Web search can be used to find free postcard software Web sites such as 1001.com, Freegraphics.com, and Win-shareware.com.

You can use your Web site to feature some things that may actually attract customers. Some of those things may be special sound and animation effects, freebies, or sweepstakes. You can also offer your customers incentives like free information (reports, newsletters), discounts, sweepstakes, and product samples.

## Enticing Customers to Make a Purchase

Once you get people to visit your site you must get them to buy. Design your Web store to provide visitors with a shopping experience as similar as possible to a real one. Peter Fingar et al. in "21st Century Markets" explains how to do this, "A well-designed consumer-oriented system will mimic the way people shop....People already know how to shop. A well-designed business-to-consumer application will capitalize on what they already know. Understanding and modeling the consumption process is key to designing a system that is not only simple to use, but can add significant value for the shopper. It is not enough to take a company's catalog and place it on a Web site with an order form. Consumer-oriented systems need to be designed from the customer's perspective, from the outside, in."

Merchandising through coupons, sales, and promotions can be used for business-to-consumer e-commerce. Consumer-oriented systems need to include the digital counterparts for coupons, promotions, and sales.

Shoppers like to browse and bargain shop. A retail Web site must have an attractive storefront that entices the potential buyer inside. Giving away useful information or digital coupons for entering your Web site are two such techniques.

## Summary

Competing on the Web requires B2C firms to effectively market their products and services. A Web site does not automatically attract customers. Survival may depend on the ability to effectively market. This chapter discussed both online and offline ways to bring traffic to your site. In addition to traditional advertising, there are several ways to get people to your site including registering on search engines, using reciprocal links, running banner and pop-up ads, forming portal alliances, using newsletters, and sending e-mail messages. Once you get people to your site, you can market to them by giving away freebies like free virtual bouquets and postcards, information, and newsletter subscriptions.

> *Adapt your message to the specific needs of your customers. It's likely your business has different types of customers who buy your product or services for different reasons. What's important to one audience may be secondary or completely irrelevant to another.*
>
> *—Geo Purdie and Andy Rogers, "Marketing Strategies"*

## Zagat.com

Zagat.com, a publisher of restaurant guides, used HTML-based messages for its most recent holiday promotion. It distributed a well-designed e-mail offering a discount for purchasing their packs of guides and maps for multiple cities. The message also encouraged recipients to forward the message to others.

Zagat.com was encouraged by the positive response to the promotion. The conversion rate for the program was five times the usual rate. As more potential buyers embrace these new technologies, the conversion rates may even be higher.

*—Fiona Ross, "Make the Most of Web Marketing," SmartBusinessMag.com*

> *irect response ads either drive traffic with a large "click here to go to this site" or they consummate the sale immediately. Click here and if you buy we'll give you a special deal which expires tomorrow.*
>
> —Geo Purdie and Andy Rogers, "Marketing Strategies"

## Chapter Key Points

- Due to the competitive nature of the Internet, you need to have very effective marketing to succeed on the Web.

- This chapter covers how to bring customers to your site and how to market to them from your site.

- You should use both online and offline methods of advertising. All advertising should mention your Web site and list your site address.

- Multichannel methods are associated with success.

- Online techniques for bringing people to your site include registering on search engines, using reciprocal links, running banner and pop-up ads, forming portal alliances, using newsletters, and sending e-mail messages.

- You can market once people are on your site by giving away freebies like free virtual bouquets and postcards, information, and newsletter subscriptions.

## Web Sources for More Information

▶ **Activmediaresearch.com** (www.activmediaresearch.com) has many articles and white pages on B2C commerce.

▶ **B2C Retail Commerce** (www.retailindustry.about.com/cs/b2cecommerce) has articles, forums, chats, and a newsletter.

▶ **ECommerce: B2C Report** (www.emarketer.com/ereports/ecommerce_b2c) reports on the state of B2C commerce.

▶ **E-Marketer.com** (www.emarketer.com) provides statistics and information about commerce on the Internet.

▶ **Internetweek.com** (www.internetweek.com) is a periodical that contains articles on B2C and other types of e-commerce.

▶ **ZDNet.com** (www.zdnet.com) offers articles, links, and information on B2C and related topics.

# MARKETING MEANS MONEY
## *Succeeding in B2B*

MARKETING TO OTHER BUSINESSES REQUIRES SPECIAL CARE. ◀

*The younger daughter was surprised at the amount of competition to sell seeds in the B2B arena. She knew that she would have to find ways to distinguish her seeds from others. She wanted to create a brand image for them. She was sure that her seeds were better but how could she communicate that?*

*She decided that she first needed to present herself as an expert at developing seeds and crops. She began writing newsletter articles for the B2B site on which she sold her produce and seeds. Writing articles was an inexpensive way to publicize her expertise to people who opted to receive the newsletter.*

*She also looked into other forms of Web advertising but was not convinced that any were worth the expense. Banner and pop-up ads were expensive, and she did not think they were likely to provide the branding she wanted.*

*She decided to take the time to develop a more personal approach. She purchased an e-mail list of farmers. The list contained address information and a list of recent purchases. She could tell where the farmers lived and what they grew. From this information she developed several e-mail messages to send. Each was designed for specific crops and regions of the country. She personalized her messages based on the information so she could more accurately address the needs of farmers. She took general information on where the farmers lived and what they grew. She combined those facts with data on weather conditions, crop demand, and other relevant items to provide more personalized messages.*

With only a fraction of the B2Bs expected to survive, developing an effective marketing campaign is critical to success in the B2B marketplace. Like B2C marketing, a multichannel approach, also called "integrated marketing," is also appropriate for B2B. Businesses can benefit by using traditional tools, such as participating in trade shows, advertising in print media, public relations, and direct mail. These should be augmented by online marketing methods. Philip Mowris, Director of Interactive and Media Services for FolioZ (www.folioz.com), the Southeast's first technology marketing firm, has made "a huge point of the importance of integrated offline/online campaigns." He says that "the more often we can engage [prospects] through direct mail, sales calls, banners, e-mail, when they are actively looking for solutions, the better the chance of success. The approach we take is to look at it from end to end.... So we couple the Internet with offline activities. We package a campaign together so it works in several tiers."

While advertising in multiple channels is most effective, so is an industry-focused campaign. Philip Say explores this topic in "Seven Great B2B Marketing Initiatives." He says, "Industry specialization or domain expertise is a mandate under tight market conditions. Over the last two years, the growth of competition in every space required companies to develop specific capabilities for discrete industry segments. Developing deep expertise within a target market is more effective than attempting to do everything for every market."

Experts agree that building your brand is essential to B2B success. The "nobody-ever-got-fired-for-buying-IBM" adage plays a role in purchase decisions.

Try to project a quality image in all your advertising and dealings with customers. In "B2B Advertising,"

> *What is it that distinguishes your company from your competition? It may be your industry experience, customer service, or distribution system. Whatever it is that sets you apart, you need to be sure your potential customers — and current customers — hear about it.*
>
> GEO PURDIE AND ANDY ROGERS, "MARKETING STRATEGIES"

*Tip* Repeat your message over and over in many online and offline ads.

Elaine Morris Palmer writes, "Alvin Toffler has said that exchange is a social dynamic, not a technological one. Brand builds aura around an institution. It's like your social life...who do you want to hang out with? (WebMD only took on partners with established brands.) Until now, it's been mostly about availability and pricing but with the advent of the Internet, brands have become more transparent. No more saying one thing and doing another."

## Branding and Business Buyers

Brand is particularly important to business buyers. While some of the advertising venues are similar, there are several differences between business buyers and consumers. Business customers want and often need to buy your product. Your job is to convince them to buy from you rather than someone else. Business buyers tend to be more knowledgeable. They either know about the products or services they are buying or at least have an idea what problem they are trying to solve. Consumers can buy something in just one step. Business buying involves multiple steps, levels of approval, and people for all but inexpensive products. Since different members of a buying team have different concerns, you have to successfully sell to several people. Therefore, many business marketing efforts are attempting to establish brand recognition and generate leads rather than immediate sales.

This chapter will discuss how you can use both Web-based and traditional marketing and sales options to maximize your success in the B2C marketplace. It will help you to

- bring traffic to your site
- market from your site

> *T*he rule of thumb for media allocation in B2B is still deployment of the old-fashioned sales and promotion tools in order: trade show, print, direct mail.
>
> —*Elaine Morris Palmer*, *"B2B Advertising"*

*Tip* ▶ Branding is critical for B2B. Business buyers care about brand.

- entice the customer to purchase

The recommendations in this chapter are supported by data gathered by B2BMarketingBiz.com during interviews with 100 B2B marketers from large firms (IBM , VerticalNet, UPS), small firms (SilverStream, WantedTechnologies), and marketing firms (FolioZ and Passaic Parc). The interviews focused on finding out which techniques worked for B2B marketing. Interviewees reported that the best techniques for B2B marketing were:

- banner and pop-up advertisements
- newsletter sponsorships
- e-mail campaigns
- online directories and buying guides

## Banner and Pop-Up Advertisements

In spite of reports that banner advertising is slipping in popularity, Network Solutions and other companies that gather information and test media have reported responses from banner results ranging from 0.5 percent to 2.0 percent and higher. Much of the business from banner advertising does not come immediately when people first click a banner. As much as 33 percent of the business comes from "View-Thru Trackers" or people who remember the banner and later visit the Web site. Because they remember and come back to your site, they may be better prospects than the people who clicked the banner on impulse when they saw the ad.

Banner ads can have several purposes. Some are aimed at educating people on a company's product line and what they are doing. Some are aimed at showing how a company fits into its marketplace. Others show the features and benefits of company products and services.

> *The proliferation of online market exchanges…has encouraged the commoditization of products and services so now, brand is more important than ever.*
>
> —ELAINE MORRIS PALMER, "B2B ADVERTISING"

*Tip*  Business buying involves more steps, approvals, and people than consumer buying.

You can run test programs to determine the success of banner advertising for your firm. Research firms, like Third Level Data.com (www.thirdleveldata.com) can help you to run test campaigns for a reasonable cost. Those interviewed said banner advertising works best when select sites were chosen based on the type of traffic they generated.

Just because a site gets a lot of traffic does not mean that it is the best site for you to use for advertising. Also, be careful about ad placement. Place banner ads only in specific locations on specific pages, those that generate the right kind of traffic for your business and let you specify placement of the ad on the site. The marketers reported that specifying the ad location on the site produced much better results, well worth any added cost. B2B online marketers who participated in the B2BMarketingBiz.com study were asked what they thought was the biggest mistake other marketers were making. Over and over again they said, "Banner ad and e-mail campaign links that just go to a regular home page."

Ads placed on search engines also work well. The marketers reported that general ads on search engines such as Yahoo didn't work, but ads linked to specific search terms worked very well. They also reported that text ads such as those that appear on Google (www.google.com) or Northern Light (www.northern light.com) worked better than graphical banner ads as the searcher is most likely looking for text to learn more about the search topic.

## E-Mail Campaigns

You can get excellent results from e-mail. The marketers in the study reported that e-mail campaigns to targeted lists of potential customers were 50 to 100 percent more

> *Remind them (your customers) on a regular basis why they should be doing business with you or why they've made a good choice if they are already a customer.*
>
> —GEO PURDIE AND ANDY ROGERS, "MARKETING STRATEGIES"

*Tip* The right traffic on a site is more important than the most traffic.

effective than average banner click-throughs. E-mail to registered visitors and customers also has excellent results. You need to be careful to obtain permission before sending e-mail, and not bombarding those who gave permission with unwanted e-mail.

The marketers surveyed by B2BMarketingBiz.com reported that, "As with banner media buys, broad, general e-mail lists usually are not worth the investment. You must hand-select every list and list segment you e-mail for good results." The major challenge in creating an effective e-mail marketing campaign is getting the best directed e-mail lists for your business. Developing your own "in-house" list works best.

Once you develop a list what should you say in the e-mail? The marketers in the B2BMarketingBiz.com study recommended sending a half to three-quarters of a page letter offering a pitch. Personalized and specifically targeted messages produce the best results. For example,

## Co-Branding at LatPro.com

LatPro.com, a 12-person online career center for Spanish and Portuguese professionals, found an affordable way to advertise its business by "co-branding" with related Web businesses. LatPro.com found that some high traffic Web sites were interested in including its career listings and embedded its content on those sites. It now relies on co-branding with related Web businesses for its marketing.

Dan Canning, LatPro.com's marketing director, credits co-branding with generating 30 percent of the site's recent traffic and the resulting 8,500 new registered users. He thinks that it would have cost the company between $7,000 and $10,000 to gain that much traffic using either traditional advertising or affiliate programs. The co-branding program has only cost $1,000 a month, mostly in salary for the program's manager.

—FIONA ROSS, "MAKE THE MOST OF WEB MARKETING,"
SMARTBUSINESSMAG.COM

IBM has been very successful with specifically targeted e-mail messages and newsletters to customers who have opted-in. The marketers from IBM reported that "the most critical factor was in personalizing each newsletter to its recipient." This doesn't just mean sticking the customer's name at the top of the message. It means making sure the news inside the message is specifically of interest to that individual. Their advice is that "if you have more than one product, service, or target demographic, make sure your house list is set up to gather and identify those separately." Nobody, even regular customers, cares enough to want to read regular news about your company. Everyone cares about news they need.

You can choose to use either text or HTML e-mail messages. HTML messages can provide more features and options for recipients. However, some recipients may not be able to receive these messages. In the United States HTML works well when marketing to business customers. Due to bandwidth concerns, text might work better in some other countries.

## Newsletter Sponsorships

Advertising in a newsletter was the "winner tactic" for B2B marketers. Newsletters produced results somewhere between the banner advertisements and e-mail campaigns. Their main benefit was that they acted as a branding vehicle and allowed a company to repeatedly send to the same subscribers without potentially alienating customers. Repeat e-mails can be annoying. On the other hand, customers will usually not be annoyed by receiving a newsletter because they opted to receive it. The cost of newsletter advertising is approximately the same as banner advertising depending on relative position on the page.

> *More and more, all elements of the advertising have specific roles and should support the buyer through the decision-making process. Each part builds on the others to reach the right customer with the right message at the right time in the buying cycle and can add value or detract from the brand image and ultimate results. Inclusion of the Internet in the mix only enforces that the right combination of price and supplier wins the customer.*
>
> —ELAINE MORRIS PALMER, *"B2B ADVERTISING"*

*Y*our Web site should be about your market, not about you. Gamse and many other B2B experts recommend basing your site's navigational flow on the needs that your most common visitor demographics have when they enter a site. For example, if you serve IT technicians and CIOs you might have a site section labeled "IT Techs" and another labeled "For CIOs."

—*B2BMarketingBiz.com, "Special Report: Top 10 B2B Internet Marketing Tactics"*

You can also purchase a newsletter subscriber list. These list customers who have opted to receive a newsletter on a specific subject. Therefore, they include people interested in the newsletter subject area. There are more than 25,000 opt-in B2B e-mail newsletters while only perhaps 1,500 total opt-in e-mail lists available.

B2B Works and other online ad networks can help you place your ads. Ads should be four to eight lines long and 60 to 65 characters wide. These ads can be tricky to write. According to Christopher Knight, CEO of newsletter ad network Opt-Influence (www.opt-influence), "50 percent of success lies in your headline." You should therefore give particular attention to it.

## Search Engine Listings

Not surprisingly, registering with search engines and getting a good position is necessary here also. Many businesses use a software package, like the inexpensive software Web Position Gold (www.webposition gold.com), to evaluate their Web site positioning or outsource search engine optimization tasks to an expert consultant, such as a professional listed in a Web search for Web developers.

## List on Online Directories

B2B firms should make sure they are listed on online directories and in buying guides. According to the Thomas Register, an online and offline industrial buying guide (www.thomasregister.com), approximately 54 percent of business buyers find new suppliers through online buying guides.

## Less Conventional Marketing Techniques

Sometimes you can reach the top decision makers in a company by doing what Hemmings refers to as B2B showmanship; that is, performing a direct marketing effort so out of the ordinary it opens previously closed doors. In "B2B Largest Growth Area in Direct Marketing," Michael Ogden illustrates: "Nextel, for example, used B2B Showmanship to reach 1,500 key executives of Fortune 500 companies in the Chicago area. The executives were sent a box that when opened played 'Take Me Out to the Ball Game' and contained a free T-shirt with the theme line 'I Do My Best Business from Wrigley Field,' plus a great offer. Those who agreed to a Nextel demonstration received two tickets to a Cubs game and a chance to win a Wrigley Field Upper Deck Party."

To succeed with this kind of campaign requires knowing about the customer's interests so that you can tie a theme-oriented campaign to the recipient's personal interests.

## Online Chat

Holding an online chat with an expert that people will want to interact with can bring people to your site and provide you with leads. B2BMarketingBiz.com recommends that, "To gain attendance you may want to give away some 'freebie," a white paper or something more concrete. Require registration via e-mail, create an e-mail ticket, and a few days before the chat send a reminder. Ask people to send their ticket to someone else if they can't attend." Online chats can also improve your brand image, especially if you are able to get highly esteemed experts. You can follow up online chats with an e-mail,

> *Narrow your target. Macro marketing is fine if you're Coke, Microsoft, or some other mega-corporation with an advertising budget the size of Mount Rainier. But most companies can't afford—and don't need—billboards, blimps, or Super Bowl ads. They need to reach a highly targeted audience of potential customers. Which is exactly what business-to-business marketing should do.*
>
> *—Geo Purdie and Andy Rogers, "Marketing Strategies"*

*B*2B sites, he (a prominent Chicago marketer) says, will thrive only by developing a strong corporate brand to attract a cohesive community of buyers and sellers, the critical "liquidity" every business exchange site is looking for. That type of traffic will be generated not by the site's technology, but by brand marketing which highlights the site's fairness and price transparency.

—*David M. Katz,*
*"Branding the B2B"*

*Tip*   It can take something unusual and innovative to reach the higher level executives.

and then use e-mail to notify them of other events and promotions as appropriate.

## Stimulating Repeat Customers

There are a number of other things you can do to effectively market to customers. Make sure you create value for your customers. With difficult economic times, business customers are particularly concerned with adding value for their employers. Convince them that being your customer adds to their profitability. Now it's time to take the next step.

Test integrated campaigns in different media with overlapping lists. For example, try a campaign using an e-mail list, direct mail list, and banners from the same trade magazine. Although precisely integrating specific online and offline media is still hard to do, many sites are now offering package discounts for banner advertisers who also run spots in their newsletters.

## Summary

As with B2C commerce, you should use both online and traditional marketing venues to market. However, the B2B and B2C buying processes differ. While consumer buying may be spur of the moment, business buying, for all but inexpensive items, is a multistep, multiple approval, and many person process. Branding is very important for B2B commerce.

Many of the venues reported by marketers to be effective for B2B advertising are the same as used for B2C. These include banner and pop-up advertising, newsletters, and e-mail messages. Online directories and buying guides are also effective in B2B marketing. The chapter presented advice on how to advertise in each venue. You should be careful about banner placement when using banner ads. E-mail messages should be personalized. Newsletters can be effective and inexpensive relative to other forms.

*Tip*  Current customers are more valuable than potential, so don't ignore them.

## Chapter Key Points

- Use as many channels as possible to advertise. Repeating your message is key to success.

- Branding is very important in B2B commerce. Business buyers want safe decisions.

- Be selective about where to advertise. Being industry focused is usually a good idea.

- According to marketers, effective B2B advertising includes: banner and pop-up advertising, e-mail messages, newsletters, online directories, and buying guides.

- The chapter presented advice on how to advertise in each venue.

- You should be careful about banner placement when using banner ads.

- Newsletters can be effective and inexpensive relative to other forms.

- E-mail messages should be personalized.

*Because online exposure has the potential to brand and direct market at the same time, it's essential that your marketing team bring to light what it's like to be the customer you're trying to reach—not just how he perceives the information but how he buys the product and uses it. Often talking openly with the customer in a brand-free exchange about what's working and what isn't in each medium can be useful.*

*—ELAINE MORRIS PALMER,*
*"B2B ADVERTISING"*

## Web Sources for More Information

▶ **About.com** (www.about.com) provides articles, links, advice, and other information on B2B marketing and a host of other business topics.

▶ **B2BMarketingBiz.com** (www.b2bmarketingbiz.com) includes articles, information, and numerous links to B2B marketing sites.

▶ **ClickZ.com** (www.clickz.com) contains articles, links, advice, and other information on B2B marketing and many other e-commerce areas.

▶ **Digitrends** (www.digitrends.net) offers articles and other information on the Internet and digital commerce.

▶ **ZDNet.com** (www.zdnet.com) includes articles, links, advice, and other information on a number of e-commerce and businesses topics.

*B*e the solution, not just a sale. Most people don't want to buy a drill; they need holes. Far too many companies overemphasize the features of their product, rather than the real benefits to their customer. Don't just tell your audience what your product can do; explain what it can do for them.

—MARTIN V. DEISE, CONRAD NOWIKOW, PATRICK KING, AND AMY WRIGHT, EXECUTIVE'S GUIDE TO E-BUSINESS

# CUSTOMER CONVENIENCE
## *Creating Easy Buying Processes*

BUYING PROCESSES MUST BE DESIGNED FOR THE CUSTOMER. ◄

*T*he grandson's online delivery business was going well. He was making a profit on the youth facility groceries and had numerous customers subscribing to his farm stand delivery program. Area merchants were delighted by the extra business his delivery service generated and had given him a generous discount on their products and services. He had been able to purchase necessary equipment by charging an annual fee of $50 for the service. He had originally gotten 78 people to pay the annual membership fee. With the $3,900 he had been able to purchase a freezer and a large refrigerator, and repair the family truck.

The only problem the grandson was having was processing the orders. He had sent an e-mail order form but few people were using it. Taking orders from e-mail, phone, and the fax machine was very time consuming. It was not always easy to figure out what people were ordering. The phone and fax orders came in a variety of formats. He had to enter the orders on his form again, and then calculate individual item prices, totals, and taxes. He then had to return to the farm stand to collect order information. It was a difficult process.

The grandson wanted to keep the ordering process easy for the customer but he wanted orders to be in a consistent electronic format. He wanted to stop entering the information again and to have individual item prices, order totals, and sales taxes calculated automatically. He wanted to be able to receive order information without returning to the farm stand.

> *R*esearch shows that only delighted customers are truly loyal customers. Customer delight provides a level of customer satisfaction that keeps them coming back. Providing a relationship that is merely satisfying as opposed to delightful leaves a company vulnerable to others seeking to take customers away because they are easier for the customer to do business with.
>
> —*MARTIN V. DEISE, CONRAD NOWIKOW, PATRICK KING, AND AMY WRIGHT, EXECUTIVE'S GUIDE TO E-BUSINESS*

*Tip* The buying process must be kept as easy and quick as possible.

Once you have customers on your site ready to buy, what comes next? You want to have them complete their order, receive the merchandise or service as promised, and become loyal customers. How can this be accomplished? Customer relationships are developed throughout the entire Internet service value chain including:

- *Customer acquisition*. Selecting, contacting, and acquiring customers.
- *Purchase support*. Facilitating ordering and sales transactions.
- *Fulfillment support*. Delivering on time.
- *Customer retention*. Keeping customers happy.

This chapter will explore how you can expedite the buying process, making it easier for you and your customers.

## Ordering Process

The ordering process should be as simple as possible. Customers should be able to get to the order Web page quickly, with only a few clicks. E-mail marketing expert, Tecbrand, offers this advice: "If a company is executing a campaign with a special offer, people clicking through expect to be presented with information pertaining to that offer, not a home page they have to surf through looking for where to go next. Normally companies only have two to three clicks to hold a prospect's attention. If they have to click more than that to reach an end objective, they will have been lost to the company."

Once on the right page, ordering should be easy. Customers are impatient and likely to abandon a lengthy or unyielding ordering process. Customer ordering should take as few keystrokes as possible. Asking customers to provide unnecessary information or to retype information you already possess can create aggravation and may result in not getting the order. If a customer has already registered at your site use the information you have to fill in the order form for them.

Amazon.com does an excellent job expediting the ordering process by using previously obtained customer information to fill in the order form rather than requiring the customer to enter the information again. After a customer logs in, Amazon.com uses their information already on file to complete the order form for them. They fill in the customer name, shipping address, billing address, and even payment information. The customer can either confirm the information or edit it as needed to complete the current order.

One of the most frustrating things for a business owner is to have customers ready to purchase and then to lose them. Once you have gotten the customer to add goods to their shopping cart you certainly don't want them to abandon their shopping cart without purchasing the goods. Yet 75 percent of online shoppers report they have abandoned at least one shopping cart during the last 90 days. A survey by Bizrate.com, rated the number one Web mall by Media Metrix, found that shoppers had abandoned an average of between one and two shopping carts, average value of $175, during the past summer. The survey of over 9,500 online abandoners found that 55 percent left their carts prior to checkout, and an additional 32 percent abandoned purchases at the point of sale, when entering billing and shipping information, or after the final calculation of the sale. Expensive shipping and handling charges were the reason cited for abandonment by more than 40 percent of shoppers. Thirty-one percent stated that they had changed their minds, and another 21 percent cited slow-loading pages as their reason for terminating the sale.

> *F*irms such as Dell.com and Amazon.com have created huge markets for selling their products directly to the consumer, by bypassing the traditional intermediaries.
>
> —MERRILL WARKENTIN, RAVI BAPNA, AND VIJAYAN SUGUMARAN, "THE ROLE OF MASS CUSTOMIZATION IN ENHANCING SUPPLY CHAIN RELATIONSHIPS IN B2C E-COMMERCE MARKETS"

*Tip* Minimize the number of steps and keystrokes it takes to make a purchase.

> *Not all things should be delivered via the Web, and not all interactions should occur on the Web. All too often, features are built because it is possible to build them—not because there is a need or demand for them. Make sure that those responsible for your CRM efforts understand the difference and can demonstrate the impact of certain features on customer relationships.*
>
> —Chris McTiernan,
> "Putting the P Into e-CRM"

Some of the abandoned sales were later completed. More than half of abandoned shopping carts on consumer sites are purchased at a later date, according to BizRate.com respondents. Unfortunately, 44 percent of the items are later purchased from a merchant's competitor, either another site or an offline store.

While abandoned shopping carts can be frustrating, failing to meet customer expectations later can be even worse for long-term customer relationships. To prevent this, many customer-focused e-tailers take steps to set realistic expectations. For example, Amazon.com is very careful to make sure that the customer gets a realistic idea of when delivery will occur. When information on an item is displayed, it includes a statement about when it can be delivered. Customers are told whether or not each item displayed is in stock. If there is no stock the customer is given an approximate waiting time and is updated by e-mail if it changes. During the order process, the customer is given choices on shipping options with estimated delivery dates for each. Amazon.com repeats approximate delivery date information more than once to help customers set realistic expectations about when they will receive their order.

## Payment

In B2C commerce, almost all purchases are made using a credit card. In fact it is often impossible for consumers to order on the Web without one. In B2B commerce, things are not so clear.

### B2C Payments

An online merchant has a number of choices for how to conduct credit card processing on the Web. Storefront services such as Yahoo! Store, MerchandiZer, iCat Web

Store, or Bigstep often have credit card processing functions built in so that the merchant has to do little to implement credit card use on their Web site. For those who choose to do it themselves there are a few steps that need to be taken before credit cards can be accepted.

First, to accept online payments you need to get an Internet merchant account from a bank. This account is different from a regular merchant credit card account. A merchant account provider (MAP) processes the transaction and deposits the funds in your account. They will charge you either a percent of the orders, usually 2.5 percent, or a transaction fee, a standard cost per transaction. Fees are higher than those charged by traditional credit card merchant accounts due to the increased risk resulting from the absence of the physical card.

MAPs can be found easily by searching the Web or through Web site listings. A listing of MAPs along with rate and fee comparisons can be found at MerchantWorkz. Some MAPs will not accept high risk accounts, such as adult entertainment sites, gambling sites, start-ups, and firms with bad credit. Some will charge higher fees for such accounts. MAPs may have a screening process and operating policies.

MAPs can either be banks or independent service organizations (ISOs). Banks are more secure and covered by federal regulations, but may charge higher fees than the ISOs and are not as likely to accept high risk clients. You also need to have an online transaction processing service to connect your Web site and the credit card company in order to enable immediate credit card authorization for online transactions.

Online credit card losses are higher for online merchants than for traditional merchants, and you will want to protect yourself against fraud. Since fraud can be an

*Tip* Shipping costs are a major concern for buyers and a cause of shopping cart abandonment.

*C*orrectly delivering products and services to customers requires correlating customer needs with the products and services available. Whether you are selling chemicals or infrastructure services, make sure those who are managing CRM efforts are well versed in both marketing and products.

—CHRIS MCTIERNAN,
"PUTTING THE P INTO E-CRM"

*M* ore recently, a host of credit card companies have jumped in to offer their own payment options tailored to e-commerce, from one-use credit cards to e-wallets. In fact, a recent report from Ovum consulting predicted that online payments made without credit cards will grow to $126 billion by 2005.

—KEITH REGAN, "ONLINE PAYMENT FIRM TARGETS B2B MARKET"

*Tip* Express appreciation by sending a message after order completion.

enormous expense for an online retailer, you will want to take steps to decrease your risks. First, always verify the address submitted online and the one the bank has on file. Unfortunately, in so doing you risk throwing out legitimate orders, like gift orders and orders by customers with post offices boxes. According to ActivMedia, one sale in ten will be rejected this way. Thus, it can be very expensive but may be necessary to throw out orders or at least confirm them to avoid the higher expenses associated with fraud.

Next, ask for the card verification value (CVV), a three-digit number on the back of the credit card. People without the physical card cannot provide this. You want to make sure that you store payment information only on secure servers and delete it as soon as possible. You will want to pay close attention to large orders and those requiring high shipping charges. You can also use transaction risk scoring software to identify potentially shaky transactions. Such software is available from Clear Commerce, CrediView, CyberSource, Digital Courier Technologies, HNC Software, and Mindwave Software.

Be sure to limit employee access to data and be particularly aware of former employees who may be angry with your company. Make sure you secure credit card transactions across the Internet by using a secure transmission protocol such Secure Electronic Transaction (SET) or Secure Sockets Layer (SSL) and have your site certified. Most merchants use SSL encryption technology, which protects information in transit as a basic e-commerce safety measure. You can have your site certified if it meets certain criteria. Certifying organizations include VeriSign, TRUSTe, and Better Business Bureau OnLine. These organizations can also help you to make sure you do all the things necessary to properly implement and secure credit card transactions.

### B2B Payments

Things are less certain for B2B as there are several different payment alternatives, but procurement cards, also known as purchase cards, are the favorite. Purchase cards allow approved companies to buy electronically without going through the traditional purchase order or billing process. Clare Saliba, in her article "E-Gift Market Hinges on Reliability" cites Avivah Litan, research director of Gartner Payment Systems, as saying, "Gartner's new survey of over 85 Web-enabled merchants shows that purchase cards are currently the dominant payment vehicle for B2B epayments. Purchase cards are practical for low dollar value B2B payments, and merchants are seeking solutions to enable the acceptance of them. With

> *I*t should also be easy for visitors to navigate between pages. If you see that a large proportion of people take a long route to search for products, fill out a form, or update an account, find ways to reduce the number of steps involved.
>
> —CADE METZ , "DESIGN PRIMER"

# Dell Computer: Efficiency not Innovation

Michael Dell has conquered the cutthroat personal computer market, by giving the customer what they want—custom-built quality products at the lowest possible prices. Since beginning his computer business in a college dorm room in 1984, Dell has been taking direct orders from customers. By doing so, he avoids the excess inventory that can result from inexact sales forecasts, is able to build products to fit individual customer specifications, and eliminates any distribution or fees from intermediaries. The benefits of bypassing the intermediaries alone are many, including reduced costs, quicker delivery, and the ability to create a purchasing experience that suits the customer and customize the product to meet individual customer needs.

Dell has been able to continually lower prices by focusing on efficiency rather than research and development. Dell has used the Web to shorten computer delivery times, take advantage of the latest component prices, and shorten cycle times through supply chain management. In the words of *BusinessWeek Online*, "Dell never fancied himself a product innovator. Rather, his brilliance is in identifying innovative business models and then executing them to perfection."

> *M*ost small Web-based businesses have discovered the importance of customer care. It's obvious that complaints should be dealt with quickly and efficiently and that there should be user-friendly support options to help solve problems using the Web site. A whole mini-industry has evolved producing Web-based CRM systems to add that personal touch to Web sites. However, it could be argued that this focus on customer care tends to overshadow the question of why the customer has problems or complaints in the first place.
>
> —*Gordon Whyte, "How to Monitor and Improve Your E-Business Processes"*

new emerging XML-based standards for processing invoice details on p-card payments, they are becoming an even more attractive payment vehicle for both buyers and sellers."

Businesses are developing systems for B2B commerce. Other methods include direct electronic transfers between businesses, purchase orders, credit cards, and charge accounts. Participants in B2B commerce will need to decide the method of payment prior to completing the order.

## Order Confirmation and Appreciation

The order acknowledgment process is an opportunity for you to develop a relationship with the customer. After an order is placed it is helpful to send an e-mail confirming the order and thanking the customer for their business. Confirming the order both reassures the customer that the order was placed correctly and provides an opportunity to correct mistakes early in the process. Expressing appreciation for the order lets the customer know that you value them and appreciate their business.

## Order Tracking

You should provide customers with a way to track their orders prior to receipt. Traditionally, this has been accomplished by phone. Customers call in and a company representative accesses the computer records to check their order. E-commerce enables you to empower your customer so that they can check the order on the Internet. FedEx and UPS have been allowing customers to track packages for years. Similarly, airlines let customers use the Web to check on lost baggage, register complaints, check on flight status, and make reservations. Not only are customers empowered, but you can save money through decreased phone and personnel costs.

## Customer Fulfillment

Failing to meet customer expectations for delivery can destroy customer confidence and trust in your business. During Christmas 1999, many Internet retailers learned this the hard way. Due to the large, unanticipated volume of orders, many retailers either did not fill orders as promised or were unable to deliver goods on time.

Trying to get customers to give them a second chance, some retailers allowed clients to keep canceled orders without paying. Some spent a lot of money delivering products on time by paying for unconventional delivery methods. Others simply did nothing and alienated customers.

To avoid these problems, you need to set realistic expectations for delivery dates, then keep them. This is why Amazon.com is so careful to set realistic expectations during the initial product information stage and throughout the ordering process. Keeping promises means anticipating spikes in ordering and planning for them by staying informed of probable demand for products. To ensure you can meet spikes, make sure that shipping options can be scaled to accommodate spikes, and that workers are available. Also, make sure that Web sites are finished at least two or three months before anticipated spikes.

The following steps are recommended for improving your fulfillment process.

- Learn about the potential obstacles to fulfillment

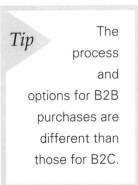

*Tip*

The process and options for B2B purchases are different than those for B2C.

*Remember that you are dealing with a more powerful customer since the advent of the Internet. During the industrial revolution, companies were in the "driver's seat." People were satisfied with mass-produced goods. Today, during the customer age, with easy and inexpensive access to a computer and the Internet, businesses must accept that customers are in the driver's seat. Today's customers are savvy. They know that there are thousands of businesses vying for their attention and money via the Internet and traditional means.*

—SHASHI TRIPATHI, "CHALLENGES AND MAIN COMPONENTS IN CRMS"

## Empowering Customers through Access to Data

Federal Express has improved its customer service and saved an enormous amount of time and paperwork by giving their customers online access through the Internet. They provide access to their tracking information so that the customer can track their own shipments through the Web.

Federal Express also provides customers with software to automate their shipping process. Customers are able to simplify their shipping process when they use Federal Express. The system fosters loyalty while saving labor for Federal Express employees.

- Know customer expectations
- Know your shipping options
- Tackle other fulfillment options
- Utilize information technology that enables high speed fulfillment

Customers submit information and purchase goods or services via the Web only when they are confident that their personal information, such as credit card numbers and financial data, is secure.

—CO-CREATIVE.NET, "BUILDING AN E-COMMERCE TRUST INFRASTRUCTURE"

## Summary

It is essential to keep the order and buying process as simple and quick as possible for people. Otherwise you risk losing customers. Customer abandonment, prior to the final purchase, has become a major problem for retailers.

This chapter looks at how you can improve your order and payment processes to ensure that it is easy and safe for customers to order from you. One of the most important components of keeping customers is developing trust. The next chapter discusses how you can establish trust by addressing the Web site issues of confidence, privacy, and security.

## Chapter Key Points

🔑 It is essential to keep the order and buying process as simple and quick as possible for people.

🔑 Customer abandonment, or aborting purchases after filling their shopping cart, is a major problem for online businesses.

🔑 You must keep online shopping as easy and safe as possible.

🔑 B2C processes need to ensure credit card safety.

🔑 B2B uses other payment schemes that are still being developed.

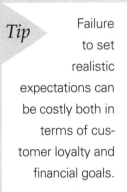

*Tip* Failure to set realistic expectations can be costly both in terms of customer loyalty and financial goals.

## Web Sources for More Information

▶ **About.com** (www.about.com) contains articles, links, advice, and information on B2B marketing and a host of other business topics.

▶ **ClickZ.com** (www.clickz.com) includes articles, links, advice, and other information on B2B marketing and many other e-commerce areas.

▶ **CRM Guru** (www.crmguru.com) is a great site that has links to a lot of information about CRM including vendor information and other help with buying CRM software.

▶ **Digitrends** (www.digitrends.net) offers articles and other information on the Internet and digital commerce.

▶ **ZDNet.com** (www.zdnet.com) provides articles, links, advice, and other information on a number of e-commerce and businesses topics.

# TRUST IS EVERYTHING
## *Ensuring Confidence, Privacy, and Security*

BUILDING TRUST IS CRITICAL TO BUILDING A SUCCESSFUL WEB BUSINESS. ◀

*The family was so proud of the relationships they had built with their loyal customers. They were concerned about how to develop customer trust as they changed their focus from a face-to-face business to one dependent on electronic forms of communication. The family had based its business on personal contact, meeting and talking with their customers. Customers were able to meet the family and see the flowers and produce they sold. Trust had never been an issue.*

*The family was unsure about how they could establish trust with their online customers, because they would not have the personal interaction with their online patrons. The family wanted to find ways to develop trusting customer relationships in the absence of personal contacts.*

*Each member of the family had been reviewing everything they could find on establishing online trust and had been studying successful businesses. Based on their findings they decided that the most important thing was to always do what they said they were going to do and set customer expectations to be realistic and then either meet or exceed those expectations. Also, they decided to develop, post, and follow a plan for protecting customer privacy and security.*

In face-to-face interactions, people use visual and verbal cues such as body language, tone of voice, and facial expressions to evaluate whether a person is worthy of their trust. When customers can see and touch merchandise and form judgments about the trustworthiness of the store, they are more willing to accept the risks of using a credit card than they would on the Internet. Your business must come up with other ways to build trusting relationships in absence of physical cues.

The absence of trust can be a barrier to business. A study by the Better Business Bureau Online (BBBOnline) reported that over 80 percent of online shoppers cited security as their primary worry when conducting business over the Internet. BBBOnline also reported that nearly 75 percent of online shoppers have abandoned an online transaction when asked for a credit card number due to their concern about inadequate online safety precautions and security technology.

Similar results were reported in an American Express survey in which nearly 80 percent of respondents voiced serious concern about privacy and security issues. In a study by VeriSign Inc., 85 percent of the surveyed Web users reported that concerns over a lack of security made them uncomfortable sending credit card numbers over the Internet. While establishing security on the Internet can be tricky, it is possible. There are enormous opportunities for those businesses able to overcome the obstacles and gain customer loyalty.

There are three important aspects of building customer trust.

1. Privacy
2. Security
3. Confidence

> *There is only one thing that can slow down the Internet and e-commerce growth surge: a loss of confidence among customers about the protection of their privacy and the security of systems. To date, there have been surprisingly few safety problems with online business.*
>
> —PETER KEEN, "ENSURING E-TRUST"

*Tip* Building trust in an electronic environment is hard but can be critical to your business success.

## Privacy

On the Internet, information is seen as a valuable asset. People are asked to share information about themselves, often in exchange for subscriptions to newsletters, access to more information, or other benefits. Businesses can use the information gathered to develop customer profiles, develop better marketing campaigns, better target advertising and marketing efforts, create products that meet customer needs, and personalize products and services.

While most businesses use information internally, others sell the information to the highest bidder. On the Web, some business models are even explicitly based on capitalizing on the value of information. For example, Bounty Brokers sell information about people: their addresses, past records, and current location. Search agents provide information about where to find products and consumer reviews about products. Infomediaries sell information about people's habits on the Web.

It is not surprising that people are a little wary about providing information on the Web. In "Companies Must Draft Privacy Plans for Web Sites," Deborah L. Stone says "As Internet use expands, there is a growing tension between the desirability for Internet businesses to gather and use information obtained from visitors to their sites and the rights of Internet users to individual privacy." Businesses with Web sites want to get the most they can out of their customer data but need to minimize potential liability for invading the privacy of their users.

### *Addressing Customer Fears and Concerns*

The answer to addressing customer fears and concerns may be to develop and follow privacy plans and policies.

> *To succeed in the fiercely competitive e-commerce marketplace, businesses must become fully aware of Internet security threats, take advantage of the technology that overcomes them, and win customers' trust.*
>
> —CO-CREATIVE.NET, "BUILDING AN E-COMMERCE TRUST INFRASTRUCTURE"

> *By defining and clearly posting your policies, procedures, and company values, you go a long way toward securing immediate trust and founding a long-term relationship with customers. Moreover, you avoid future confusion and conflict, as well as unnecessary burdens on your customer care department. Last, publicizing the way in which you secure transactions and protect credit card data is also intelligent strategy.*
>
> —*INTERNET LABS,*
> *"GETTING TRANSPARENT"*

*Tip*  Set policies for security and privacy, publicize them, and follow them.

Setting, publicizing, and following privacy policies can make customers more comfortable with your site and also work as a marketing approach. You should include in the policy how you will protect customer data from unauthorized use by others. Publicizing your security measures on your Web site will help secure customer trust and loyalty.

If you are going to use the customer information for anything other than completion of the transaction tell them. For example, if you are going to give or sell the information to another company you might tell them and give them the ability to fill in or check off a box if they do not want the information shared.

### Following Set Policies

Of course, once you set and post your privacy policies you must follow them. Using customer data in ways that would violate the policy could be deadly for your company. Certainly, your customers would never trust you again.

## Security

You need to make sure that your customers know all transactions are processed by a secure server, which encrypts the data taken during the ordering process. The current recognized way to ensure that information like credit card number and passwords is kept private is to use Secure Sockets Layer (SSL). Visa, MasterCard, and a number of major banks are developing an alternative system, Secure Electronic Transaction (SET).

Make sure that all financial transactions are conducted on a secure server and that customers know the site is secure. For SSL servers, a closed padlock on the status bars of major browsers and an "s" following the URL "http:" lets users know that the site is secure. A security certificate issued by a third party certificate authority will let customers know that your site is secure.

According to Internet Labs, "SSL server certificates and payment management services are the two essential tools you need to secure and e-commerce-enable your site for the most trustworthy Web experience possible." There are numerous companies that offer SSL services and certificates. Subscribing to one of them not only simplifies your security concerns but assures your customers that your site is safe.

Make sure that your security efforts are visible to users by posting your policies and procedures on your site. Internet Labs adds that "by boldly advertising your privacy and security policies (and posting more general information about the advantages of shopping online) you provide a means to convert customer anxiety into a sustainable one-to-one relationship based on trust."

Make sure that customers are always aware of all the privacy measures you are taking to ensure their security. You must make sure you address the concerns of customers in the following areas:

- *Authentication.* Customers need to know that they are doing business with a legitimate bank, store, or other business.

- *Confidentiality.* Customers must be sure that sensitive Internet communications and transactions, such as the transmission of credit card information, will be kept private.

- *Data integrity.* Data must be protected from undetectable alteration by third parties during transmission.

*T*o take advantage of the opportunities of e-commerce and avoid the risks of communicating and transacting business online, every business must address practical problems and questions involving privacy, security, and overall confidence.

—CO-CREATIVE.NET, "BUILDING AN E-COMMERCE TRUST INFRASTRUCTURE"

*Tip* Tell your customer how you will use their information.

- *Nonrepudiation.* The sender must not be able to reasonably claim that they did not send a secured communication or did not make an online purchase.

## Confidence

Customer confidence is critical to building customer trust and loyalty. One of the major builders of confidence is making sure that you do what you say you are going to do. Make sure that you set customer expectations to be realistic. Never promise more than you can do. Of course, there are instances that for reasons totally out of your control, you are unable to meet expectations. Try your best to make that an extremely rare occasion. When it does happen, be honest with the customer and make every effort to deliver the goods quickly.

Always try to make it right in the customer's eyes even if you lose money on the transaction. If you fail to fulfill a promise, but are honest with a customer and genuinely make every attempt to make it right, you may end up with a loyal customer and some positive word-of-mouth advertising. This can be worth much more than what you lost on the transaction. As discussed earlier, you can use the exceptions, the deviations from the norm to develop loyal customers by showing them you are willing to go to every length to ensure that they remain not only satisfied but delighted.

Other ways to build confidence are to use what *The Wall Street Journal* calls "reputation managers" that include posting customer feedback, ratings, and comments about your products and service on your site. For each book, Amazon.com solicits customer reviews and posts these reviews and ratings on the Web pages describing the book. eBay posts ratings based on prior customer feedback for all buyers and sellers for whom it

*M*arket share will go to those companies which differentiate themselves from the competition in terms of customer knowledge, customer service, respect for customer privacy, and the establishment of customer trust.

—*Thomas M. Siebel, Tom Siebel, and Charles R. Schwab,* "Cyber Rules"

*Tip*

Misusing customer data can cost you business.

has sufficient information. Finally, educating customers on your site and company can help compensate for the lack of personal human contact on the Internet.

You can gain your visitors' trust by helping them with their security concerns. Assure customers that buying products on the Web is probably safer than reading your credit card number on the phone. Remind them to only do business with secure sites and reputable businesses. Also, remind them that credit card companies will usually cover fraudulent transactions. You might post the Web site addresses of large credit card companies so the consumer can check their credit card company's policy.

Since the media tends to dramatize risks, you can endear customers by providing accurate and reasonable advice on legitimate online concerns such as how to avoid hackers. It can help to educate your visitors about the real risks. For example, you can include in your policy statements what security measures you have taken and let the customer know what to look for before doing business with other Web based businesses.

## Summary

To reach their full revenue potential, e-commerce firms must find ways to inspire trust in the absence of the physical cues we relied on in traditional marketplaces. You can develop customer trust by making sure that your company keeps all promises, protects customer privacy, and maintains a secure site. Equally important is publicizing the plans, policies, and procedures you have developed for gaining customer trust. Developing customer trust enables you to form strong relationships with your customers so they will keep doing business with you. The next chapter discusses the benefits of forming relationships with other businesses.

> *B*usinesses that can manage and process e-commerce transactions can gain a competitive edge by reaching a worldwide audience, at a very low cost. But the Web poses a unique set of trust issues, which businesses must address at the outset to minimize risk.
>
> —CO-CREATIVE.NET, "BUILDING AN E-COMMERCE TRUST INFRASTRUCTURE"

> *B*ut reliability is more crucial than flashiness. [Trust is] a highly qualitative factor...developed over time, painstakingly, and it could be lost in a single transaction if the site's technology is not up to speed. Trust in the technology is a much bigger factor than [a] killer application.
>
> —MICHAEL WEISER IN DAVID M. KATZ'S, "BRANDING THE B2B"

## Chapter Key Points

🗝 Web businesses must operate without the physical, visual, and verbal cues that build trust between people.

🗝 E-commerce success requires that you find ways to build trust online.

🗝 Three areas in which you need to build trust are: privacy, security, and confidentiality.

🗝 Information is becoming more of a commodity on the Web. You should always post your privacy policies and you must follow them exactly. Never do anything with a customer's information without their permission and knowledge.

🗝 Security certificates and other security measures are necessary to perform safe e-commerce on the Web.

🗝 You need to find ways to build confidence. Helping people solve problems and avoid security problems can build confidence and relationships.

## Web Sources for More Information

▶ **Building an E-Commerce Trust Infrastructure** (www.co-creative.net/ecommerce/BuildingAnE-CommerceTrustInfrastructure.htm) discusses building an e-commerce trust infrastructure including SSL server, certificates, and online payment services.

▶ **E-commerce Times** (www.ecommercetimes.com) has printed several articles on e-commerce trust including "Ernst and Young Debuts E-commerce Trust Community" (www.ecommerce times.com/perl/story/1653.html) and "E-Commerce News: In E-Commerce We Trust ... Not" by Paul A. Greenberg (www.ecommercetimes.com/perl/story/7194.html).

▶ **E-Commerce Trust Metrics and Models** (www.computer.org/internet/ic2000/w2036abs.htm) has Daniel W. Manchala's article about the e-commerce trust metrics and traditional models of trust.

## Web Sources for More Information, continued

▶ **Internet.com** (www.internet.com) is a Web-based publication with e-commerce news and articles on trust. One offering is "Trust: Initiative to Offer Cross-Border Dispute Resolution" by Beth Cox (ecommerce.internet.com/news/news/article/0,,5061_).

▶ **The Standard** (www.thestandard.com) contains articles on e-commerce and trust including "In E-Commerce We Trust" by Eric Young (www.thestandard.com/article/0,1902,26711,00.html).

▶ **ZDNet.com** (www.zdnet.com) has articles about e-commerce trust and other aspects of both B2B and B2C commerce. For example, "Business & Tech E-Commerce: Give us your trust" (www.zdnet.com/ecommerce/stories/main/0,10475,2699024-2,00.html).

*P*roviding information can "humanize" your online presence. Outside of familiar e-communities, the Internet can be a pretty shadowy place. The solution? Personalize your online presence by honestly disclosing information and details about who you are, your mission statement, your corporate culture, your business values, and any work you do in your community. By showing a human face, you make your e-storefront a more trustworthy place to conduct business.

—*CRMGURU.COM,
"THE CRM PRIMER"*

*Tip*

# DOLLARS FOR DATA
## *Mining the Store*

*In spite of their fears about the highway, the farm stand had earned their highest revenues. Unfortunately, their profits had been a little disappointing. Costs had been very high. Some of that was expected with the Web site and other expenses related to the changes in their business. However, they noticed that ongoing costs were higher than they anticipated. Since some sales resulted in higher costs than other sales, they wanted to know which were their most profitable sales and customers. With all of their data this seemed a daunting task and they were not sure how to accomplish it.*

*One of their highest ongoing costs was for the large amount of unsold produce they had each month. They also regularly ran out of other produce and were unable to complete some orders. Even after integrating their value chain and linking closely with their top customers, they were still running short of some things and left with the excess of others. It seemed to be different every week with no obvious pattern.*

*The family knew that they had the answers in their massive computer files. They had compiled a huge database with all customer and sales information; however, they did not know how to make heads or tails of it.*

> *Guesstimating customer preferences is no way to maintain an edge in today's frenetic and fiercely competitive e-commerce landscape. With Web logs essentially providing a detailed roadmap of how visitors move through a site, companies are sitting on a wealth of information that can be mined to answer basic questions like what customers are buying and what promotions are generating the most traffic.*
>
> —BETH STACKPOLE, "TARGETING ONE BUYER—OR A MILLION"

*Tip* — Your data is a valuable resource. Use it for competitive advantage.

The data collected by businesses is very valuable. Businesses can use customer data to better serve their clients, identify new customers to solicit to, or sell the information to other organizations. As price competition becomes fiercer due to electronic information and the Web, businesses must find ways to better reach, retain, and service their customers. Analysis of customer behavior, measurement, and data mining can help businesses to accomplish these goals.

Businesses have performed metrics and analyzed data for many years. Data mining is a very powerful tool that has recently been added to the data analysis tool kit. Data mining is the discovery of valuable information through analysis of enormous amounts of information, usually through pattern recognition. The practice of data mining had its start in 1987 when Usama Fayyad, a Tunisian-born computer scientist and University of Michigan graduate student, took a summer job at General Motors. While compiling a huge database, he developed a pattern recognition algorithm to help find answers to questions from data based on such factors as car model and engine capacity. Fayyad later applied his algorithms to helping Nasa find patterns in astronomical data, helping military intelligence, and working with the medical community. In 1996 he went to work for Microsoft and applied his findings to corporate "data warehouses."

This chapter will look at how data collection, data analysis, and data mining can help you to establish and maintain a successful e-commerce business. In the competitive landscape in which e-commerce businesses operate, you need to increase your ability to acquire and retain customers. The data analysis techniques outlined in this chapter can help you survive in this environment.

The business world has utilized data mining for a number of purposes. Data mining can help determine the interests of specific groups and individual databases by discerning patterns, correlations, and other useful relationships. The benefits of this type of information can be invaluable. In the business world, data collection, analysis, and mining can help you to:

- acquire customers
- know your customers and forecast behaviors
- identify the most profitable customers
- deliver a more personalized buying experience
- design products to better meet customer needs

## Acquiring Customers

Acquiring and retaining customers is critical for any e-commerce business. In the cutthroat world of e-commerce, you cannot afford to waste money on ineffective advertising, spending excessively on customer acquisition, or replacing customers rather than retaining them. To compete you need to optimize your customer acquisition process.

Knowing your cost of customer acquisition (CCA), or how much it costs you to acquire each customer, can help you assess your competitive position in your industry and the effectiveness of your advertising channels. To calculate your CCA you first need to know how much you spend on each customer and where each customer came from. One way to find out where your customers came from is to ask them. You can supply a place on a Web form to collect this information. While some people may answer this question, others will be hesitant. Having customers answer questions can be burdensome for the customer and may make some feel intruded

> *The cost of acquiring new customers in these choppy waters is very expensive. Sales cycles have increased, new buyers are apathetic, and marketing messages have diminishing impact. Initiatives focused on mining current relationships will prove to be very effective in these lean times.*
>
> —PHILIP SAY, "SEVEN GREAT B2B MARKETING INITIATIVES"

> *T*he current economy dictates that companies divest their underperforming assets. For marketing managers, this means carefully evaluating the performance of your sales channels and partnerships.
>
> —PHILIP SAY, "SEVEN GREAT B2B MARKETING INITIATIVES"

*Tip* CCA can tell you about your competitiveness in your industry and help you evaluate the relative value of advertising venues.

upon. Automated data collection and analysis programs like those from Datamine Limited or Datamining.com can help you determine where your customers came from without you needing to ask them.

You also need to keep careful records of where your advertising dollars are going. Knowing where customers came from and what you paid for advertising allows you to calculate an important measure of e-business success.

To calculate the cost of customer acquisition (CCA), you simply take the number of customers obtained from a particular marketing channel divided by the amount spent on that source. Looking at the CCA can help you weigh the comparative value of your advertising channels. When Cyberian Outpost (now Outpost.com) switched from TV ads to print and Internet advertising, it lowered its CCA from about $90 to $40. You should make sure that your CCA is lower than your competitors. The failed dotcom, Petstore.com, had a very high CCA of about $200 for ads at Yahoo!'s portal site when the industry norm was closer to $20, says John Berry in "Eye on ROI: Acquiring Customers." A CCA ten times the industry norm might be an indication that a business is not competing effectively and needs to change. Early detection of problems can help save a business that would fail if needed changes are not made. You are likely to find industry CCA through trade associations and marketing publications.

## Know Your Customers and Predict Their Behavior

Understanding the trends, relationships, and other patterns in customer data can also help you forecast customer behavior so that you are better able to plan advertising, promotions, and manufacturing. Knowing your current customers better can help you to acquire more customers and successfully market to current ones. You can use data mining to analyze your customer data and identify the most profitable customers, find ways to retain customers, sell more to current customers, and develop profiles of people most likely to become customers. From the results you can better direct your customer acquisition activities. Also, you can use your findings to direct promotions to the current customers most likely to buy additional items.

Understanding your customers is invaluable. Through in-depth data analysis, you are able to construct more customer profiles. These profiles help you to put together marketing campaigns more likely to be accepted by their recipients. Recognition of patterns in customer data can help you better target promotions and advertising to the people most likely to become customers.

You can use the information to design different Web pages so customers "land" on the right page. You can use customer knowledge to design pages targeted to specific groups. You may want to have specific Web pages, landing pages, appear in different advertisements or after clicking on different sites. For example, you might have teens land on a Web page with a more youthful site address and feel, and more mature customers land on a more conservative page. This way you can specifically market to those customers.

Prior to initiating an expensive campaign, you can test advertisements and promotions. You can use the data obtained by the test to improve campaigns before full implementation. For example, a free service from Market Tools lets you create surveys so you can perform

> *A* relatively high CCA is not in and of itself a sign of trouble. Again the measure is contextual. A CCA of $400 for new brokerage customers is certainly not as unreasonable as the same amount needed to get someone to visit 800.com to buy a VCR. The nature of brokerages as a business suggests a much deeper and potentially longer-lasting relationship financially than that with a consumer goods retailer.
>
> —JOHN BERRY, "EYE ON ROI"

*Tip* Having a high cost of customer acquisition can be an indicator of problems.

these tests. For $199 annually they will let you use detailed reporting and analysis of your data and give you the ability to customize surveys. ZTelligence, their high-end service, is designed for large corporations and market research firms.

In addition, you may want to supplement your information. There are other sources of statistics that can be valuable to you. For example, for a base subscription rate of about $3,500, Net Value collects and sells information on consumer behavior on the Web. Free U.S. Census data and other fee sites like DemographicsNow.com allow you to look at your customer demographics and perform analysis on geographic data, determine likely future trends, and analyze how people spend their money.

## Identifying Your Most Profitable Customers

Not all customers are equal. Some are more profitable than others. Data mining can be used to discover your most profitable customers so that you can develop ways to maximize your sales to those customers. For example, Della.com has used data mining to determine which advertising vehicles have brought them the most profitable customers and have created different Web pages for people coming from different advertising vehicles.

By data mining, More.com has been able to identify profitable customers and then reach out to them with custom marketing and cross-selling programs. According to Andy Felong, CEO of More.com, "We're looking for that competitive edge, and we believe by obtaining the information and mining it, we can get it."

Similarly, you can determine customer profiles and identify trends. Through data mining their wedding

*S*mart marketers often supplement their customer database (usually containing information such as buying or service history) with information gathered through surveys, Web clickstream data, and marketing data from outside sources to create a single view of the customer.

—KAREN HOWARD, "BEYOND PERSONALIZATION 101"

*Tip*  Create different Web landing pages for different groups of customers.

registry site, E.piphany discovered that its high-end business was seasonal. The summer and fall/winter holiday season were the busy times. To achieve year-round business, the company decided to transform itself into a lucrative general gift registry, broadening their customer focus.

## Deliver a Personalized Buying Experience

Since price is such a dominant factor in purchasing on the Internet, many more products are becoming commodity items. At the same time some Internet companies are raising the bar for customer interactions by using those interactions, as well as Web browsing habits, prior purchases, and other data to determine and meet customer wants and needs. These companies anticipate customer needs and meet them during every interaction. Competing in this market means you need to use all the tools at your disposal. In "Beyond Personalization 101" Karen Howard says, "with the competition often just a click away, and price no longer a deciding factor, it has come down to the customer experience. Delivering a consistent and positive experience is what attracts and keeps the customers coming back."

Building customer profiles and personalizing the buying experience is essential. Amazon.com is an expert at this. They use their data to personalize visitors' experiences. They use information gleaned from customer purchases to provide visitors with suggestions about what other books they may be interested in.

Gift selection systems that recommend gifts are also an example. These systems use personal and demographic data and purchases made by similar groups to make the right recommendations based on prior shopping habits.

*Tip* Personalization is the face of future marketing.

> *To gain this razor-sharp understanding, retailers must have a personalization engine that is built upon a sophisticated analytic or data mining technology. These superior technologies use advanced algorithms to glean trends, often invisible to even the most sophisticated marketing mind, from reams of data.*
>
> —KAREN HOWARD, "BEYOND PERSONALIZATION 101"

Personalization has been found to have the following benefits:

- It allows retailers to present a consistent face, and offer consistent treatment, across all the channels a customer may choose.
- It is a key contributor to customer satisfaction and loyalty.
- It enables retailers to increase order size.
- It helps retailers close sales and reduce shopping cart abandonment.
- It encourages repeat orders.

In order to personalize interactions, companies need to understand buying habits, likes and dislikes, browsing habits, buying channels used (online, catalog, physical store), importance of price, what type promotions are effective, and profitability of a customer. There are statistical tools that companies can use for personalization. These tools help companies adapt promotional offers to best fit an individual. Personalization uses predictive technologies to help companies meet the needs of an individual including:

- *Collaborative filtering*. Making predictions based on past purchases by people with similar characteristics. For example, aiming a promotion for skateboards for an 11-year-old boy based on the purchases of other 11-year-old boys. Recommending books based on educational level and age is another.
- *Rating the probability*. Knowing the odds of offer acceptance when a person clicked through from a particular advertisement. By looking at probabilities based on past response behavior, you can better predict and market to that individual.

> *If you know precisely who your customers are, you can do whatever it takes to keep them coming back. Luckily there are lots of ways to slice demographic data on household makeup, buying trends, and more. Doing some coordinated geographic research can keep you one step ahead of the other guys.*
>
> —KAREN HOWARD, "BEYOND PERSONALIZATION 101"

*Tip* Make sure you don't irritate people by sending offers for things they are unlikely to want. Target solicitations.

- *Stopping inappropriate offers*. This can be extremely important to retaining customers and not alienating potential ones. So many people get annoyed by legitimate offers. You do not want to send inappropriate ones, like an offer for a new car to a single female who just purchased a new vehicle after having her last car for ten years, or a lawn mower to someone who lives in an apartment.

## Customizing for the Masses

Using data to customize product design is increasingly used as a competitive strategy by smart companies. Companies are fully using data along with data analysis and mining techniques to personalize interactions. Gift recommendation systems are an indication of where the industry is going. These systems use personal and demographic data and purchases made by similar groups to make the right recommendations based on prior shopping habits. For manufacturers, the Internet enables all companies to gather the data needed to better anticipate and meet consumer demands through increasing levels of product and service customization. Ralph Szygenda, CIO of General Motors Corporation, describes the situation:

> From the consumer's point of view, we're moving from the age of mass consumerism to the age of individual consumerism. Customers' needs are being filled by custom-tailored services or by product designs that reflect their individual desires more closely than ever before....The manufacturers that can anticipate their customers' needs and suggest solutions tailored to their buying patterns, and socioeconomic, and lifestyle backgrounds will be

*R*etailers will be assured that real-time personalization is the best method to acquire, retain, and advance customer relationships and convert visitors to buyers.

—KAREN HOWARD, "BEYOND PERSONALIZATION 101"

*Tip* Collaborative filtering allows you to make recommendations to customers with similar characteristics.

*T*he cost of gaining incremental sales from a current relationship can often be less than that from a new customer.

—WEBTOMORROW.COM, "DEFINITIONS"

## Nike: Creating Customized Shoes

Nike.com allows customers to create customized shoes, bats, and gloves. A customer logs on to Nike.com and builds their products with custom colors and a personal moniker. The site displays a rendering of the product built with the customer choices.

If the product is approved the customer completes the order and payment. The site then orders the product automatically and puts it into production. The moniker is programmed into the stitching machine automatically based on customer input. Finally, the completed product is shipped to the customer.

—LAURA LOREK, "HAVE-IT-YOUR-WAY WEB SITES START TO CATCH ON," INTERACTIVE WEEK

the clear winners in the brutally competitive global business environment.

## Protecting Privacy

As more companies use customer data to perform data analysis, data mining, personalization, and customization, privacy becomes a concern. You must take steps to protect customer data and make sure that customers are informed about how their data is being used. Again, you need to assure them that their data is not being used against them, sold to another marketer, or shared without their permission. Karen Howard explains in "Beyond Personalization 101" that "consumers want to protect their privacy and need assurance that personal information will remain secure. Assure them that you request this information only to provide better customer service. Once customers realize the benefits of these personalized interactions, they'll readily offer relevant personal details. You must uphold your part of the bargain and develop truly personalized service."

*Today's customers have seen the bleak side of e-commerce (spam, mishandled orders, and poor customer service) but true real-time personalization that uses real-time knowledge and insight to tailor offers, information, and discounts to each individual is the sunnier alternative that can help fulfill the promise of e-commerce.*

*—KAREN HOWARD, "BEYOND PERSONALIZATION 101"*

On the other hand, you may be planning to sell their data. That is all right as long as you have their permission. The important thing is to inform people of your policies, then stick to them.

## Summary

Customer data is very valuable. Companies can sell data or use it to market to potential and current customers. This chapter explored how you can use data analysis and data mining to generate revenues.

Data mining is analysis of massive databases to find valuable information, usually by finding patterns in the data. For companies, these analyses help identify customer profiles, better target marketing campaigns, and make more appropriate offers to the right customers. Companies can access advertising markets and their position relative to their industry. They can test market campaigns before spending enormous amounts of money on them.

> *With the movement toward one-to-one customer marketing, the idea of catalogs that are custom-produced for each customer is moving closer to reality.*
>
> —ALEX BERSON, STEPHEN SMITH, AND KURT THEARLING, BUILDING DATA MINING APPLICATIONS FOR CRM

### Chapter Key Points

- In the cutthroat environment of the Web, businesses need to use all the available tools to compete.

- Knowing your customers is essential to compete in this environment.

- Data analysis and data mining allow companies to identify potential customers, target new customers, direct promotional offers and marketing campaigns, test advertising and promotional campaigns, access advertising methods, and personalize marketing.

*Tip* Always make sure you inform customers of how you use their data.

🔑 Data mining is finding relationships and trends in data, usually by finding patterns in the data.

🔑 Personalization is becoming more important in the competitive Web environment.

## Web Sources for More Information

▶ **Data Mining and Knowledge Discovery Journal** (www.digimine.com/usama/datamine) is a journal devoted to the understanding and application of data mining.

▶ **The Data Mining Group Web Site** (www.dmg.org) is a consortium of industry and academics formed to facilitate the creation of useful standards for the data mining community.

▶ **Data Mining Tutorial** (www3.shore.net/~kht/dmintro/dmintro.htm) provides an introduction to data mining.

▶ **KDNuggets.com** (www.kdnuggets.com) provides a newsletter, information, links, news, consulting, software, and other resources for data mining.

▶ **Kurt Thearling's Web Site** (www3.shore.net/~kht/index.shtml) Dr. Thearling is a senior director for Development of the Wheelhouse Corporation. He has created a data mining information site with recommendations, links, and other information.

# WIN-WIN STRATEGIES
## *Creating Profitable Alliances*

E-BUSINESS MAY REQUIRE WIN-WIN RELATIONSHIPS
WITH OTHER COMPANIES.

*The younger daughter convinced the family to pursue her plan for selling floral wedding arrangements on the Web. After consulting with the Web designer, she was ready to develop the site. To save money, one of her nieces did the work. They decided to create a simple Web site with a main page listing the types of arrangements available with small pictures of each. When each of the small pictures was clicked, it took the user to a page with an enlarged picture, a description of the arrangement, and prices for different packages featuring that type of arrangement. People were then given the phone number to get information and order a package. The daughter chose to not provide Web-based ordering capacity as she felt the personal contact was needed due to the intimate nature of weddings.*

*The Web site was posted on an ISP and listed with several search engines. However, the site generated few calls. The daughter began to question her plan.*

*Then, the niece had an idea. A friend's sister had recently gotten married and told her about the great wedding sites she had found on the Web. There were several portals and sites that linked future brides and grooms to a variety of wedding-related sites and services. The niece suggested they list the site with these portals. The daughter took the niece's advice, and formed relationships with related sites. Almost immediately, their business increased.*

*I*n the B2C world, alliances are often necessary for survival. There are several types including:

- Product and/or service alliances, where one company licenses another to make its product, or two companies jointly market their complementary products or a new product.

- Promotions, where one company agrees to carry a promotion for another company's product or service, such as Sears and AOL.

- Logistics, which offer warehousing and/or distribution services.

- Pricing collaborations, where companies offer mutual price discounts like rental cars and hotels or airlines.

—ERNST AND YOUNG, "GLOBAL ONLINE: RETAILING: 2001"

The Internet has resulted in some unexpected partnerships. Many businesses have realized that in the online world it is often beneficial to join together. In fact, business survival may depend on the ability to form alliances with other businesses. These businesses are switching from the "win-loss" paradigm that often characterizes business relationships in the traditional world to a "win-win" paradigm according to Covey (1990) that characterizes many online business relationships. Increasingly businesses are learning that there is often a synergy that results from joining forces. Two or more businesses are stronger together than they are standing alone. This is particularly true for small businesses where joining with complementary companies can give each the power to effectively compete with the "big guys."

Historically, hierarchical companies developed because transaction costs were lower for internal operations and more expensive externally. To bring down their costs, companies brought multiple functions in-house, building large hierarchical organizations. Electronic communications are changing that by reducing the costs of conducting external transactions between organizations according to Malone, Yates, and Benjamin in "Electronic Markets and Electronic Hierarchies."

These reductions in external transaction costs present a real opportunity for small businesses. Due to the availability of electronic communications, you can expect to see more and more businesses form interorganizational systems and alliances. Small businesses can use these reduced transaction costs to their own benefit.

## Links and Portals

Having links to your site from other Web sites and portals featuring related products and services can be an excellent way to get new customers and add value to your Web site. Since you are trying to bring as many customers to your site as possible, it makes sense to have links at the sites and portals you think customers are likely to frequent, usually sites on related topics. People visiting the related sites and portals can simply click a button to arrive at your site. Therefore, you want to make sure to have as many relevant links as possible.

It takes only a few lines of HTML code to put a "Link to Us" button on your site and this may result in some new links and increased traffic. One of the easiest ways to get links to your site is to form agreements for reciprocal links with other sites. Other companies are usually more likely to feature a link to your Web site on their site if you are willing to feature a link to their site on yours. Forming reciprocal links to other sites can provide you with more visitors in two ways. First, a link on their site is likely to result in more visits to your site. Second, posting their link on your Web site increases the information on your site and adds value for users.

*Tip*  Think win-win. On the Web, it's cooperation, not just competition.

It may be to your advantage to participate in a *vortex*, or large varied portal such as Yahoo!, Amazon.com, or Excite.com. On the other hand, as the story at the beginning of the chapter illustrates, it can be very valuable for a company to join a *niche portal* or a specialized portal. Fruit of the Loom realized the value of owning "the" niche portals when it developed a portal for Activewear. To attract as many potential customers as possible and establish the dominant niche portal in that market, it allowed even distributors to carry competitive brands.

It is often expensive to participate in a portal. However, the costs may be justified by the benefits. The portal traffic, sales resulting from the portal's marketing and advertising programs, and other services may produce revenues far exceeding the cost of participating.

## Business-to-Business Hubs

Participating in a B2B exchange or trading hub can be very beneficial. B2B trading hubs are marketplaces in which buyers and sellers can buy, sell, or participate in auctions for products, services, or capacity. These trading hubs are often referred to in different ways including independent trading exchanges (ITEs), vortexes, vortals (vertical portals), virtual marketplaces, butterfly markets, fat butterflies, electronic markets, e-markets, internet markets, i-markets, vertical hubs, digital exchanges, metamediaries, intermediaries, and online exchanges.

There are two basic types of markets—vertical markets and horizontal markets. Vertical markets, like vortals, target specific industries and segments offering specialized goods and services. Horizontal markets sell a specific type or category of product or service to a wide range of industries and companies. (Chapter 7 provides a detailed discussion of B2B exchanges.) In her article, "E-Business and E-Commerce," Kristina Eriksson summarizes how small businesses can often benefit from participating in a B2B hub, "These so-called *e-markets* are trading exchanges that facilitate and promote buying, selling, and business community among trading partners within certain industries. The e-markets are typically sponsored and driven by a market maker who brings suppliers and vendors together by using the Web. Buyers benefit by being able to get product specific information and by taking advantage of lower prices from competing suppliers. Sellers get a new, efficient distribution channel to new

> *J*oint ventures, partnerships, and outsourcing agreements allow you to adapt quickly to the changing demands of the e-customer, and to provide relevant products, services, consulting, and resources.
>
> —GEOFFREY RAMSWEY IN PETER FINGAR, HARSHNA KUMAR, AND TARUN SHIRMA'S, "21ST CENTURY MARKETS"

*Tip* Reciprocal links can bring business to both of you.

markets and the opportunity to compete with other vendors. In short, one could say that e-markets bring product availability, reduce transaction costs, increase price leverage, and improve service levels because of the competition."

As described in the farm stand story in the beginning of this chapter, online programs help smaller businesses join together to offer services that were previously available only to larger businesses. In "Business Models on the Web," Michael Rappa describes how "business trading communities, such as VerticalNet and Buzzsaw.com, assist in B2B exchanges by aggregating information on products, suppliers, industry news, job listings, and classified advertisements for their users. Buyer aggregators, such as Mobshop, Volumebuy, and Etrana, gather small purchasers so they can unite and get volume discounts." These sites aggregate buyers so they can benefit from quantity discounts and service packages as larger firms

> *"If you're a small dot-com, you have to build alliances with bigger companies. You have no choice,"* says Philip Anderson, an associate professor at the Tuck School of Business at Dartmouth College in Hanover, New Hampshire.
>
> —ROBERT MCGARVEY, *"FIND YOUR PARTNER"*

## eBay and AOL

Co-opting a much larger rival can mean success for a new and smaller company. Web auction leader eBay.com's CEO, Meg Whitman, anticipated that AOL would want to enter the auction market. In 1998 excitement about the potential of auction markets was high and Whitman knew that AOL would want a role in the marketplace. Rather than face the prospect of competition from AOL, Whitman turned AOL into a partner.

Whitman made a deal to create links from key AOL Web pages to the eBay site. Eventually, she agreed to make ebay the exclusive provider for all AOL properties. Thus, she was able to take a potential rival and form a successful and profitable partnership.

—STEVE KAMM, *"TURNING YOUR COMPETITORS' STRENGTH TO YOUR ADVANTAGE,"* BUSINESSWEEK ONLINE

do. In addition, they get product information, customer feedback, and other information that may help them to select products and services.

By using auction sites, very small businesses are able to keep costs to a minimum and still run a profitable business. Without the Internet and these brokerage sites, many of these small businesses could not exist. In "The Mighty Mini-Dots," Arlene Weintraub explains, "Of course, size matters, even in the New Economy. But in some crucial ways, the Net helps level the playing field for small outfits. For one thing, the cost savings of selling online and dispensing with store rents or direct-mail costs makes some businesses viable that otherwise wouldn't be." By linking with other businesses and selling through auction and other brokerage sites, companies are able have the business while sharing the costs.

> *Increasingly businesses are learning that there is often a synergy that results from joining forces. Two or more businesses are stronger together than they are standing alone.*
>
> —ARLENE WEINTRAUB,
> "THE MIGHTY MINI-DOTS"

## Affiliate Programs and Advertising

Sites can make money from either selling products and services or advertising revenue. For example, you can join an "affiliate" network, or an intermediary. For this, you can get paid in a number of different ways.

*Tip* Don't ever forget that the most important thing is the conversion rate: how many site visitors make a purchase.

- *Pay per hit.* Under this plan you get paid every time the banner is displayed, usually each time your site is hit. You get paid cost per thousand (CPM) hits so the rate per hit is very low.
- *Pay per click.* You can also get paid per click; that is, when people actually click your banner rather than it just being displayed. Although the rate per click is higher than the rate per display, you are paid only when the banner is clicked.
- *Pay per lead of sale.* There are higher payment rates for actual sales or leads. They are not necessarily

more expensive. Only a fraction of the people visiting your site will click on the banner, then make a purchase.

You can find a listing of affiliate sites along with reviews of each at: www.thefreecountry.com/eccentricity/affiliate.shtml. The affiliate networks pay different amounts and provide different links. It is probably most beneficial to pick the network with the most relevant links. For example, if you want to attract technical people, links to software and computer sites would be better than links to children's clothing.

## Interorganizational Information Systems

Interorganizational systems are the result of two or more information systems joining with each other and using information technology to reduce costs and more effectively compete. Businesses entering into these systems realize they can benefit more through cooperation than competition.

People are now used to using bank cards at the grocery store, the gas station, and the ATM machines of competing banks. Fifteen years ago these interorganizational systems were nonexistent. Now, there are links to payment systems, such as bank ATMs, in most stores and gas stations. Such systems are convenient for customers and provide the companies with more business and expedited transactions.

Interorganizational systems benefit both the customer and organizations involved. They are becoming easier and cheaper to develop. You can expect to see more and more businesses form interorganizational systems and alliances.

> *Jim Datovech, 45, president of ComVersant, an e-commerce consulting firm in Gaithersburg, Maryland, adds, "Speed to market is critical today, and that's why alliances make so much sense. An alliance brings more strengths together."*
>
> —ROBERT MCGARVEY, *"FIND YOUR PARTNER"*

## Summary

Partnerships are becoming more and more a part of the e-commerce landscape. On the Internet, these partnerships take several forms. Small businesses can join with each other to create reciprocal links and portals. Businesses can form alliances through B2B exchanges. They can make money through affiliate programs and advertising. Finally, businesses can form interorganizational information systems to cut costs and create greater convenience for the consumer.

**Tip**  Small businesses gain power by joining together.

### Chapter Key Points

🔑 E-commerce firms are increasingly forming alliances to do business on the Web.

🔑 On the Internet, these partnerships take several forms. Businesses can

- develop reciprocal links and join portals.
- use B2 exchanges.
- make money through affiliate programs and advertising.
- use auctions and other sites.
- form interorganizational information systems.

## Web Sources for More Information

▶ **Association of Strategic Alliance Professionals** (www.strategic-alliances.org) lets you talk with a pro before saying yes (or no) to a marriage proposal. And don't miss the white paper on putting together an alliance that achieves big returns at www.logosnet.com/main/alliance_law.htm.*

▶ **"Dispelling the Myths of Alliances"** (www.ac.com/overview/Outlook/special99/over_specialed.html) is a thoughtful article written by a couple of Andersen Consulting partners, who say that 30 percent of alliances are outright failures (compared to 39 percent that are deemed unequivocal successes). They offer tips for getting your alliances in with the 39 percent.*

▶ **"Eat or Be Eaten! Strategic Alliances in Business"** (www.ocri.ca/presentations/Zone5ive/ Freeman/ppframe.htm) is a fast-moving slide show optimized for display on the Web. This site walks viewers through the how-tos of minimizing risk and maximizing gains.*

▶ **Entrepreneur.com** (www.entrepreneur.com) provides a wide array of resources and information for entrepreneurs and small businesses.

▶ **"Mergers and Corporate Consolidation in the New Economy"** (www.ftc.gov/os/1998/9806/ merger98.tes.htm), is a statement from the Federal Trade Commission (FTC) supported by rich statistical analysis, gives you the goods on alliances and the economy.*

▶ **SmartAlliances.com** (www.smartalliances.com), put up by consulting giant Booz-Allen & Hamilton, offers the firm's advice to clients considering alliances. Don't miss the "Chart of the Week," which offers at-a-glance visuals on how to do an alliance right (and how most have been done wrong).*

▶ **"Strategic Alliances"** (www.larrainesegil.com/strategicalliances.htm) is an overview of alliances from Larraine Segil, an international consultant specializing in alliances. The site is packed with plenty of stats and facts.*

▶ **"There's Strength in Numbers"** (http://onlinewbc.org/docs/expanding/alliances.html), sponsored by the SBA, is a one-page site offering tips on the benefits of alliances.*

▶ **The Free Country** (www.thefreecountry.com/eccentricity/affiliate.shtml) has a listing of affiliate programs with ratings for each.

▶ **The Site Wizard** (thesitewizard.com) offers a lot of information and tips for starting an affiliate program.

*from the *Entrepreneur* magazine article, "Find Your Partner: When Industry Giants and Dotcoms Come Together, It's Profits That Fly Round and Round."

# WORLDWIDE IS NOT FOR WIMPS

## *Competing in the Global Market*

GO GLOBAL IF YOU WANT TO GROW. ◀

*T*he older brother was a little concerned. He had been selling his produce to several grocery stores. He had just gotten a message late Friday afternoon from one of his largest customers telling him to reduce his prices for some produce or risk losing the grocer's account. The brother knew that no other farms in the area could provide produce for less and did not think that anyone from the states producing similar produce would be able to undercut his price after paying for shipping.

Over what seemed to be a very long weekend, the brother called all of his contacts locally and out-of-state trying to solve the mystery. He knew his produce sold well and was excellent quality. What was going on?

Monday morning finally arrived and the brother was able to reach the grocer. The grocer directed him to a Web site, a B2B portal for purchasing wholesale groceries. The brother was horrified to see produce from below the U.S. border being sold for unbelievably low prices. The non-U.S. farmers were able to pay lower wages and had long been a threat to many U.S. farmers who competed in metropolitan markets. However, local produce had been immune to this competition due to their remote location and the resulting, expensive shipping costs. Now the brother could see that the portal was allowing the growers and grocers to coordinate shipping and reduce these costs.

The brother was caught off guard by this new unexpected source of competition. He saw that he was in danger of losing more and more business to non-

*U.S. growers unless he could come up with ways to effectively compete.*

▲   ▲   ▲

> *I*nternet commerce will accelerate to $5 trillion in 2005, fueled by nearly one billion global Internet users, or 15 percent of the world's population. That's a 70 percent compound annual growth rate from the $354 billion in Internet spending in 2000.
>
> —MARY MOSQUERA,
> "GLOBAL E-COMMERCE"

*Tip* ▸ E-commerce is expanding more quickly outside the U.S. than inside.

## Global E-Commerce

Going global on the Web can be an excellent way to expand your business as described in "Going Global: Study Your Markets, Develop a Strategic Plan" by AdvancingWomen.com, "Not only will you expand your market, but you will access a diverse revenue stream which is more stable since you will no longer be as vulnerable to periodic downturns in any one economy. Global companies outperform domestics, growing twice as fast with significantly higher returns."

Global e-commerce revenues are enormous and growing rapidly. Global revenues for retail e-commerce sales were $286 billion in 2000 and a report by eMarketer says they will be more than $3.2 trillion in 2004. Similarly, IDC predicts that total Internet commerce will increase $354 billion in 2000, to $5 trillion in 2005 with one billion global Internet users, or 15 percent of the world's population. According to John Gantz, IDC's chief research officer, "More than 100 million new users come onto the Web every year, and corporate volume purchasing over the Web is just getting cranked up. Add to that the proliferation of mobile phones and other Internet access devices that will allow people to access the Internet anytime, anywhere, and you have a scenario for explosive growth."

Growth rates in other parts of the world are expected to be higher than in the United States. While in 2000 the United States accounted for 46 percent of e-commerce revenues, by 2005 the share accounted for by the United

States is expected to decrease to 36 percent. While all regions are expected to have healthy e-commerce growth, Asia/Pacific and Western Europe are expected to have the fastest growth between 2000 and 2005 according to Mary Mosquera in "Global E-Commerce."

Internet use will also increase in other regions more than in the United States. In 2000, the United States was home to 34 percent of all Internet users. Europe had 29 percent, Asia/Pacific (excluding Japan) 16 percent, Japan 10 percent, and the remaining countries 11 percent according to Mosquera. Even if you are not convinced by the potential of the international market, the Internet forces you to compete in a global marketplace so you should consider marketing worldwide. Experts predict dire consequences for businesses that don't go global.

Meg Whitman, eBay CEO, regrets that eBay did not move into global markets more quickly so they could have avoided the formidable competition they faced when they entered each new market internationally. In "Global E-Commerce," Mary Mosquera conveys Meg Whitman's warning: "Today, emerging start-ups must get global fast. If not, they will find themselves in a situation like eBay, and lose dominance quickly since the U.S. market will shortly comprise only one third of the total world market."

Currently, American technologies dominate globally, both on the Web and on land. However, if American firms do not act more quickly to establish international businesses we risk that global dominance. In "Go Global," Sawhney warns, "If American firms do not move faster, or know how to play a global strategic game with other giants being formed in Europe, Asia, Israel, etc. then they stand to lose significant financial status, possibly losing the entire game within the next five

*M*ore than 100 million new users come onto the Web every year, and corporate volume purchasing over the Web is just getting cranked up. Add to that the proliferation of mobile phones and other Internet access devices that will allow people to access the Internet anytime, anywhere, and you have a scenario for explosive growth.

—*MARY MOSQUERA,*
*"GLOBAL E-COMMERCE"*

*Tip* You are global whether you care to be or not.

years—where will they be positioned when the 2005 numbers show U.S. share of the world Internet market is less than 30 percent of total world Internet commerce?"

## Challenges of Going Global

Unfortunately, going global is not without dangers. It can be dangerous to go into the global arena without an understanding of the issues and challenges. In Ernst and Young's "Global Online: Retailing 2001," Deirdre Mendez, Ph.D., President of Foreign Business Management Consultants in Austin, Texas, reflects on the problems companies have had: "Small companies enter international markets without a clear strategy, and without adequate preparation. They don't research foreign markets, perform due diligence on foreign partners, protect their intellectual property, or understand the customer culture of their overseas operations. They create partnerships that don't work and must be renegotiated or terminated. All of these mistakes take time to rectify and cost money. Some of them cannot be undone. But all of them can be avoided by strategic planning."

### Understanding the Culture

Your success may depend on your ability to understand local issues. It can be very tricky to understand and respect all social and cultural conventions. Having a trusted, local representative to help in these areas can be a great help. In addition, customer expectations vary by country. A representative can help you to understand the differences so that you can develop satisfied and loyal customers.

To accommodate local customs and tastes, you are likely to need to customize your product. You usually need to do some type of "product localization," even if it is only changing the product packaging. Be especially

> *M*any companies are looking to duplicate the success of the e-business efforts in the United States in other countries, but they're finding that it isn't as easy as it might seem. Companies can't create a single Web site and expect to reach customers and distributors around the world, according to industry analysts. "Global e-commerce doesn't exist," says Martha Bennett, VP of research for Giga Information Group. "The moment you have to deliver physical goods, you're up against every piece of legislation that exists in the real world." Not to mention every cultural and language barrier.
>
> —NATALIE ENGLER, "GLOBAL E-COMMERCE"

careful in this area as your success may largely depend on your ability to understand, respect, and cater to the norms, customs, and tastes of the local population.

### Planning for Order Fulfillment

Prior to opening up an online global retailer, you need to have a plan for payment, shipping, and other logistical issues. You need to have an infrastructure for receiving payments and shipping merchandise. While the United States depends on credit cards for payments, other countries may have different conventions. In "Go Global," Mohanbir Sawhney describes "Credit cards are not widely used for e-commerce in Japan. Less than 10 percent of transactions are conducted using credit cards. 7-Eleven in Japan has a payment acceptance service for products and services purchased from Web merchants. 7-Eleven charges a fee for collecting payment and transferring it to the merchant. Consumers can select 'payment at a 7-Eleven Store' as one of the payment options for small purchases, and print out a payment slip that they present at their nearest 7-Eleven store."

Many customers find online shipping costs already too high. Internationally, these costs are even higher. In some markets even exorbitant shipping rates may be acceptable as the product is otherwise unavailable. Prior to beginning a global online business, you will want to find strategies to minimize these costs and make sure that even after adding shipping costs, your prices are competitive. Plus, you need to plan how merchandise can be returned and money refunded.

### Laws and Regulations

Tax laws and other regulations must be understood in order to maximize profits. Prior to entering a new

*Tip* U.S. firms risk losing global dominance if they do not act soon.

*C*ompanies looking for potential new e-commerce growth markets after the dotcom crash should consider countries such as Estonia, Brazil, Chile, and South Korea, according to e-readiness ratings released today by a consulting firm based here. But they should also be prepared for some challenges.

—MITCH BETTS, "GLOBAL E-COMMERCE STILL FACES BIG CHALLENGES"

> *Companies that attempt to reach other markets via the Web run into a host of issues. Chief among them are organizational problems, according to a survey by Forrester Research of 50 companies creating a global Web presence. These include dealing with different marketing strategies in different markets, securing adequate resources, and managing channel conflicts. Other difficulties include managing content, technical obstacles, and cultural and legal barriers. The manner in which companies handle these is critical.*
>
> —*MICHAEL PUTNAM,*
> *AN ANALYST AT FORRESTER*

country, it is important that you understand the tax laws, contract formation practices and requirements, consumption laws, consumer protection laws, and protection of electronic resources such as your Web site and databases.

You can improve your profitability by developing an expertise in the local tax laws or by hiring someone to advise you. While duty charges are usually unavoidable, you can sometimes be creative with taxes by doing things in low-tax jurisdictions rather than high-tax ones. By setting up a subsidiary in a low-tax district, multi-channel retailers may be able to take advantage of lower tax expenses. In addition, several strategies can be used to reduce your taxes including "tariff reengineering," or having local customs agencies reclassify products to a lower duty category, reducing product valuations, importing from companies with preferential treatment under a treaty, using foreign trade zones, or using customs-bonded warehouses.

Thorough research and expert guidance into local laws will save headaches and increase profitability of global operations. Global online retailers may also be forced to adhere to specific guidelines wherever consumption occurs. These can be both expensive and difficult. You need to know what these are and how they impact your business prior to entering a global marketplace.

To avoid fines and financial losses, you will want to understand the consumer protection laws. Different countries have different regulations for protecting consumer privacy. You want to be careful not to violate them or any language requirements that might exist.

You will also want to understand your ownership rights regarding your Web site and databases prior to entering a country's market.

### Web Site Design

Design your Web site to meet the needs of your specific audience. You need to make sure that people in the international markets you want to target can read your Web page. If the local population does not speak English, translation will be necessary. There are translation services that can help you to achieve this.

Make sure that your Web site does not inadvertently offend anyone by violating local customs and culture. If you have the Web site translated make sure that it translates properly so it does not unnecessarily alienate or mislead the local population. Misuse of words can severely reduce your sales volume.

When you have online and land-based businesses in more than one country, it can be tricky to maintain a consistent pricing strategy. However, that can be essential to customer satisfaction and developing loyal customers. Make sure that you list international shipments in your shipping table.

Keep in mind that internationally, telecommunications infrastructures and technologies vary. In some countries, telecommunications infrastructures can be very unreliable and poor quality. Also, computers and browsers may be different than those used in the United States. You need to be careful that your site loads quickly on all browsers. Due to transmission times across long distances, using a mirror site (a duplicate of the original) in the country can help minimize load times.

> *T*o "act locally" is no different online than on land. Companies must understand consumer preferences, values, and shopping habits, as well as cultural conventions and regulations. Respecting the language of each target market is as critical to success as understanding what motivates consumers to buy online in their particular countries.
>
> —*ERNST AND YOUNG,* "*GLOBAL ONLINE: RETAILING: 2001*"

*Tip* — Use tax laws to your advantage when possible.

*T*ranslation is a key part of tailoring an e-business site for a particular market. A number of software translation products are available, but they're limited because they don't handle idioms or technical material well. So General Electric Information Services and others are turning to tools that simplify the workflow involved in using human-translation services to localize content for different markets.

—NATALIE ENGLER, "GLOBAL E-COMMERCE"

*Tip* — Make sure your Web site does not inadvertently offend anyone.

## How to Get Started

Finding a partner is an excellent strategy for going global. Large international firms have established infrastructures, brands, and reputations. They have already worked out the issues and are often willing to partner with a small firm.

A great way to get started may be finding an appropriate B2B marketplace that would fit with your business objectives. Make sure the marketplace has the needed infrastructure, can meet your logistical needs, allows you to deal directly with local and global counterparts, and only charges a small transaction fee.

Is going global worth it? Yes. It is a lot of work, however. In "Going Global: Study Your Markets, Develop a Strategic Plan," AdvancingWomen.com advises, "If you do your homework, get some help from locals and professionals, going global could be one of the smartest and most profitable moves you'll ever make."

## Summary

The new global economy requires us all to compete globally whether we want to or not. The United States has been dominant in e-commerce but will lose that position if more firms do not aggressively enter the global marketplace.

This chapter has discussed how you can take your business global. To succeed requires knowing as much about local laws, customs, language, and norms as possible. Make sure your Web site and all other communications are properly translated, respectful, and in line with local traditions. There are many challenges to global e-commerce. Local laws, shipping, authentication, and payments can be difficult.

While going global can be challenging, the potential revenues are enormous.

## Chapter Key Points

- Going global is no longer a choice. We are all competing in a global economy.

- The potential for revenues from global e-commerce is enormous as non-U.S. Internet growth is faster than U.S. growth.

- U.S. companies need to aggressively move into markets to be dominant. Firms such as eBay.com have lost market dominance due to late moves into an area.

- Shipping, payment, and authentication can be areas of challenge. Local laws, customs, language, and norms must be respected and followed to succeed.

> *The necessary mechanisms are still missing to establish trust in business transactions with new and constantly changing worldwide business partners.*
>
> —RICK DRUMMOND, "IS SECURITY INHIBITING GLOBAL E-COMMERCE?"

## Web Sources for More Information

▶ **E-commerce Times** (www.ecommercetimes.com) has printed several articles on global e-commerce including "Global E-commerce Standard, Ready to Roll" (5/13/2001), "U.S. Calls for Global E-Commerce Rules," "China's E-Commerce Shell Game" (10/04/00), "One World, One Internet?" (09/18/00), and "FTC Seeks Global E-Commerce Laws" (09/07/00).

▶ **Global E-commerce**: Revenue and Marketing Trends (www.budde.com.au/TOC/TOC1640.html) provides data and links to information on global e-commerce marketing and revenue.

## Web Sources for More Information, continued

▶ **ITworld.com** (www.itworld.com) includes reports on global commerce. For example, "Global e-Commerce," *Computerworld* 5/3/01 by Mitch Betts (www.itworld.com/Tech/2418/CWD010503 STO60164).

▶ **The Global e-Commerce Monitor** (www.rpifs.com/ecommerce) is a monthly nontechnical e-mail guide to the financial opportunities and pitfalls of global e-commerce. Includes a monthly e-mail survey of significant news about international e-commerce.

▶ **ZDNet.com** (www.zdnet.com) has articles about e-commerce trust and other aspects of global e-commerce.

*The lure of expanding a customer base with easy access and communication via the Internet is too great an opportunity for any serious company to ignore. Global expansion on the Internet promises expanded customer reach and greater revenues and profits for retailers.*

*—ERNST AND YOUNG, "GLOBAL ONLINE: RETAILING: 2001"*

### CHAPTER 23

# TRAVEL THE WEB, NOT THE WORLD
## *Web-Based Training, Conferencing, and Education*

NEW OFFERINGS CAN LET YOU USE THE WEB TO REDUCE TRAVEL. ◄

*After graduating from high school, the grandson devoted himself fully to expanding his grocery delivery business. He had applied to and was accepted by the state university, located approximately 100 miles away. He had planned to study business administration and come home on weekends to work on his growing delivery business. His uncle offered to oversee the business, and he had hired a friend to take orders and do the actual deliveries.*

*As the summer progressed, the grandson became reluctant to leave the business. Although he thought his uncle and friend could be relied upon to keep things running, he did not want to be so far away. On the other hand, he did not think the local colleges in commuting distance offered the quality programs offered by the state university.*

*The grandson decided to look into distance education programs and was thrilled to learn that he could take courses through the state university without leaving his home. Most of the courses he needed were available on the Web. He could graduate with a degree in business with very little time on the university campus. He enrolled in the business school. He kept his uncle as an overseer of the business, and his friend as a helper taking orders and making deliveries.*

> *I*t's not unusual for people in the technology business, especially consultants and sales types, to log 100,000 or more miles a year on airplanes. But given the recent disasters in New York, Pennsylvania, and Washington, D.C., a number of IT vendors and consultancies report that some of their people are unwilling to fly. Meanwhile, a number of companies are restricting air travel or are not allowing employees to fly at all, at least for the present.
>
> —*Laton McCartney,*
> *"Fear of Flying"*

**Tip** ▷ Web training, conferencing, and education can reduce travel.

$T$he World Wide Web provides a number of ways for you to save money and time by allowing you to participate in meetings, training, and classes without traveling to get to them. In addition, it reduces employee anxiety resulting from the September 11, 2001 attacks and allows them to avoid the increasing delays and other frustrations. Using the Web to replace travel for meetings, conventions, education, and training can result in enormous savings. These savings result from eliminating expenses for travel, lodging and other accommodations, facilities, equipment, support, and employee time.

Businesses have seen the benefits and are spending huge sums on distance education and training. International Data Corporation estimates that corporate distance education and training expenditure ranges between $7 to $60 billion depending on the factors analyzed and reported. As technology improves, Web conferencing is also seeing a rapid increase, particularly with companies and organizations wanting to decrease their travel for both economic and personal reasons. In response, Web conferencing vendors are responding with more powerful and affordable conferencing options that allow businesses to decrease corporate travel.

## Online Training

In addition to reducing travel-related expenses, online training can provide substantial benefits for your company. Online instruction is interactive and allows each student to progress at his or her pace. To enhance the learning experience, it integrates audio, video, animation, and text. You can also monitor and track your employee's progress through the training program.

## E-Learning at Cisco Systems

Cisco has developed an end-to-end e-learning system aimed at providing customers with the content distribution capabilities for use in a number of e-learning applications. They are streaming the tutorial to 2,000 people around the world rather than having 300 salespeople travel to learn about the product.

Cisco is saving a lot of money by their application of an e-learning system for the product launch. For each salesperson traveling to an off-site for training, the trip cost averages $2,000 for lodging, airline tickets, and other expenses. For each setup the remote training costs $35 per person. While the off-site training would cost $600,000 for 300 people, they are able to train 2,000 people for just $70,000. Their total savings from this application was a whopping $530,000.

—MAX SMETANNIKOV, "CONTENT DISTRIBUTION MEETS E-LEARNING," INTERACTIVE WEEK

There are numerous ways for your company to participate in e-training. In "How to Build an Online Training Program," Jason Compton lists several methods for a variety of budgets. At the low end, SmartPlanet.com offers hundreds of canned courses starting at $9.95 per student. For companies that need standard training programs their options work well. For companies requiring customized training packages, DigitalThink offers customized training but the costs tend to be many thousands of dollars. For a few thousand, Click2learn.com offers an e-learning course-creation system, expert help, and hosting of the course.

Online training is particularly popular with law firms, insurance companies, and corporate legal departments due to its potential for reducing workplace lawsuits. One of the major uses of online training is for compliance training to ensure that employees understand the legal workplace regulations, according to Anitha Reddy

*Tip* ▷ Online training can be cost effective and better than face-to-face in some cases.

*E*xpert training delivered exactly when you need it. Students and business partners who are always in touch. Less time and money spent on travel. These are the advantages promised by online learning, which lets companies train employees and contact business partners in a live conference setting via standard PCs.

—SMART COMPUTING, "TAKE THE TRAVEL OUT OF TRAINING"

*Tip*   Web conferencing can be achieved cheaply and easily.

in "A Training Solution That Clicks." She enumerates how online training has been used successfully for helping employees understand legal workplace regulations for safety, discrimination, sexual harassment, bribery, and corruption. Reddy describes the rising need for compliance training resulting from the 1999 Supreme Court ruling that allows companies to avoid paying punitive damages if they attempted to comply with federal antidiscrimination laws by taking actions such as instituting mandatory training. As evidence of the rise of online learning Reddy cites two business executives with expertise in e-learning. First, he quotes John Ivancevich, vice president of content development for the e-learning company Aegis, who says there are about 300 firms nationwide offering online harassment prevention training. He also cites Matt Feldman, chief executive of the e-learning business Learning Insights, who predicts that online legal compliance training will soon be a $100 million to $200 million market.

## Videoconferencing

As the technology improves and businesses reduce travel, we can expect increasing use of Web videoconferencing. In "Video-to-Desktop Set to Emerge as Killer App" Tom Kontzer relays the prediction by Joe Gegan, an analyst with Yankee Group, that there will be increasing demand for videoconferencing over the Internet and more offerings as the technological problems are eliminated. According to Kontzer, as online training technologies mature and the alternatives increase, these systems will become cheaper and more advantageous financially. Cathleen Moore in"Videoconferencing Takes Control," cites Christine Perey, a consultant and founder of Perey

Research and Consulting, as saying that businesses can get fast returns on their investments in videoconferencing systems, paying for systems within three months. Thus, videoconferencing systems are becoming a very wise option for many businesses.

## Distance Education

Distance education is not new. Its earliest forms can be traced back to the 1700s. During the 20th century, distance education has been conducted using mail for correspondence courses, radio, television, and computers. The growth of distance education has exploded since the National Science Foundation gave universities and other educational institutions access to the Internet in the mid-1980s.

Now, hundreds of accredited colleges and universities, including numerous state universities and other prestigious academic institutions, offer Web-based education. Degree programs and courses are offered in thousands of areas, with close to 500 business degree programs listed on the Web site of the nonprofit Global Network Academy (gnacademy.org). Hundreds of certificate programs are also available on the Web.

Distance education programs offer a viable alternative for obtaining a degree, certificate, or additional courses in an area. The offerings by so many respected academic institutions make Web-based education a flexible, cost-effective option for businesses and their employees. Information on specific offerings can be found through a number of organizations, particularly good sources are the GNA Academy (gnacademy.org) and University of Wisconsin's Extension University Clearinghouse (www.uwex.edu/disted/catalogs.html).

*O*nce a high ticket novelty for only the healthiest of large enterprise budgets, videoconferencing price points are dropping, opening the door to a variety of industries to use it as a communication tool to cut costs and ramp up employee productivity.

—*Cathleen Moore, "Videoconferencing Takes Control"*

*Tip*   Many quality colleges and universities offer distance courses.

*A*nd Internet videoconferencing isn't as complicated as you might think. Anyone with a Net connection and a speedy computer hooked to an inexpensive camera can do it, especially when it costs less in time and money than an airline flight or even a cab ride across town.

—DANIEL LEVINE,
"SEEING EYE TO EYE"

*Tip* The Web provides many alternatives for saving money in training, education, and conferencing.

## Summary

The World Wide Web increases the possibilities for remote training, videoconferencing, and education. As businesses face budget constraints and other reasons to limit travel, these systems provide a viable alternative. Offerings in online travel, videoconferencing, and education are becoming increasingly sophisticated and affordable.

### Chapter Key Points

- Web training, videoconferencing, and distance education offer new alternatives for companies.

- By replacing travel for training, education, and meetings, organizations save money in accommodations, support, facilities, equipment, and other expenses.

- There are both inexpensive and expensive options for online training, allowing you to buy canned packages or develop customized programs.

- Online training for legal regulation compliance is very popular.

- Web videoconferencing is becoming more technically and financially feasible.

- Web-based distance education programs are being offered by thousands of colleges and universities.

## Web Sources for More Information

▶ **Nerd Wide Web** (www.nerdworld.com/nw1934.html) provides information and links on communications and videoconferencing.

▶ **PC World** (www.pcworld.com) contains articles, information, and links to videoconferencing resources.

▶ **Smart Computing** (www.smartcomputing.com) has articles and information on videoconferencing options.

▶ **Search Networking.com** (http://searchnetworking.techtarget.com) has information, articles, and links on videoconferencing.

▶ **Videoconference Resource Center** (www.videoconference.com) is an independent site providing links to videoconferencing related sites.

*If business airline traffic suffers a lengthy slowdown, companies are likely to turn to electronic means of communications such as telephone and videoconferencing, and there are already clear signs of such an increase. This in turn could hasten the spread of broadband Internet access in the office, the home, and to mobile devices, analysts say.*

—ALMAR LATOUR AND KEVIN J. DELANEY PARIS, "RELUCTANCE TO FLY MAY BOOST TELECONFERENCING COST"

# MILEAGE FROM MOBILE
## *Doing Business from Anywhere*

THE NEXT WAVE OF BUSINESS WILL BE WIRELESS AND MOBILE.

*a*s international businesses entered the produce market, the brother realized he needed to find a way to add value to his products and services. He could not compete on price. While quality was important, it did not seem important enough to convince some of the grocers to buy produce from him. He would have to find other ways to distinguish his service.

Watching his nephew, he had an idea. His nephew had built a successful delivery business. While he was still getting some of the bugs worked out, it was turning out that delivering groceries along with other items could be profitable. As high profile online grocers had discovered, it is difficult to have a profitable business delivering groceries unless you charge a fee. However, the nephew had built a profitable business by charging a low fee and delivering higher margin items along with the groceries.

The brother thought he could work with his nephew and improve both his own and the nephew's business. The first step would be to combine their deliveries. He knew the nephew usually left the farm stand with less than a full truck load of produce. The brother believed the nephew could take additional produce and get it to the grocery stores at a lower cost than the brother incurred for a separate delivery. Second, he thought he could help the nephew to simplify his ordering process while adding value for his own customers. The brother proposed that he would buy Personal Digital Assistants (PDAs), one for the nephew and one for each grocer.

*The grocers could use the PDAs to order produce, check delivery times, and get needed information. The nephew could use the PDA to receive order information and better coordinate deliveries with his uncle.*

▲ ▲ ▲

## Mobile Commerce: The Future of E-Business

Many predict that mobile commerce (m-commerce) will be the future of electronic business. In "Go Mobile Now," Peter Keen predicts that "the next major shift in the use of IT will obviously be toward wireless and mobile commerce. It will happen in fits and starts, with the usual hype, chaos and clutter, disappointments, and brilliant innovations, just like with e-commerce."

M-commerce is doing business using mobile devices such as handheld personal digital assistants (PDAs), wireless laptops, and Web-enabled digital phones. Due to the potential of the mobile market, companies are spending billions to build the market for mobile technologies in the United States.

In Europe and Japan, mobile devices equipped with Web-ready microbrowsers are much more common than in the United States, where only 34 percent of the population had cellular phones in 2000. In Western Europe, the penetration of cell phones was above 50 percent according to Fiona Harvey in "The Internet in Your Hands."

The upward potential of this market is enormous. A number of manufacturers including Nokia, Ericsson, Motorola, and Qualcomm have joined with carriers such as AT&T Wireless and Sprint to help develop the mobile

> *As with the Web, the early wireless buzz has been about the consumer market. But, as with the Web, it became apparent that the payoffs are in the B2B arena.*
>
> —PETER KEEN,
> "WIRELESS PRODUCTIVITY"

market. Manufacturers are developing smart phones, which offer fax, e-mail, and phone capabilities all in one, paving the way for m-commerce to be accepted by an increasingly mobile workforce. Handheld computers, such as the most recent Palm Pilots models, can access the Web through either built-in antennas or by attaching to a mobile phone or a modem with an antenna. New cell phones have built-in microbrowsers that allow their customers to send e-mail and current events.

Other things are happening also. Companies are using the industry standard, Bluetooth, as the basis for providing short-range transmissions in products. Companies are also using short-range, last-mile broadband wireless (possibly a secure form of Bluetooth and/or 802.11b) for transmissions. At the high end, Motorola, Ericsson, and Nokia are working on 3G "super phones" that will look nothing like current phones. These will have sophisticated features such as color screens capable of presenting high-resolution graphics and video and data input devices like a keyboard, mouse, touch-sensitive screen, and stylus. For most people, cell phones with larger screens and better input devices will be sufficient to fill their needs for sending and receiving e-mail, accessing the Internet, and maybe, playing music. IBM and others are working on voice communications. Wearable devices worn on the wrist will provide another way to access the Web. For example, Hewlett Packard and Swatch are jointly developing an Internet watch that will look like a fashionable timepiece but contain a tiny radio transmitter allowing the wearer to access sports scores, news, e-mail, and music on the Web. Bluetooth devices will allow users to conduct transactions without cash, checks, or credit cards.

*Wireless data services may be the next big thing. WAP, the wireless application protocol, put together by a huge group of companies, permits Web surfing over mobile phones. It's going to come into its own when third-generation, high-speed mobile telephones roll out. Simultaneously, Bluetooth, a standard developed by a different set of companies, is expected to enable all kinds of personal networking (e.g., writing with a pen that later transmits the data to your PC). Neither company has taken over the world; in fact, there's a chance that neither will, considering the rise of 802.11b, which transmits data at up to 11 megabits per second. It is wireless broadband, and operates in a part of the spectrum (near microwaves) that requires no license.*

*—WENDY M. GROSSMAN, "WIRELESS WONDER"*

## Wireless E-Mail for Attorneys

Houghton Mifflin, a textbook and curriculum publisher, allows their legal staff easy access to corporate e-mail from any location via a wireless connection or telephone. In the past, attorneys had to carry a laptop on the road to have access to corporate e-mail. By using a wireless e-mail messaging system, the firm was able to provide easier e-mail access for their attorneys. For the cost of a laptop, roughly $1,000, and a monthly fee of $8 to $20 per person, Houghton Mifflin is able to provide their attorneys with convenient access to e-mail.

This year fans with Internet-enabled mobile phones or wirelessly connected handheld computers voted at Major League Baseball's new wireless site Mobile.mlb.com. They could also use mobile devices to get scores from recent and in-progress games. Even game manufacturers Nintendo and Sony, along with the manufacturers of portable music players, are planning to include wireless Internet access in future products.

*Tip* The United States is behind Japan and Western Europe in mobile phone use.

## M-Commerce and Your Business

The long-term potential for m-commerce is enormous. It provides your business with the opportunity to sell to consumers anywhere at any time. Consumers will be able to buy products and services, do immediate price comparisons on items they see in stores, get business addresses and maps , and conduct business on the go.

Some of the earliest benefits of m-commerce are being seen in the B2B arena. Current applications include use by field employees such as service technicians, delivery people, traveling sales personal, inspectors, and other mobile employees who need to communicate with each other and a central location. According to Ernst and Young, there will be many business applications when m-commerce becomes more "dependable, secure, and scalable." A number of industries will be affected by the rise of m-commerce such as:

- *Financial services*. These include mobile banking (when customers use their handheld devices to access their accounts and pay their bills) as well as brokerage services, in which stock quotes can be displayed and trading conducted from the same handheld device.

- *Information services*. Includes the delivery of financial news, sports scores, and traffic updates to a single mobile device.

- *Telecommunications*. Service changes, bill payment, and account reviews can all be conducted from the same handheld device.

- *Service/retail*. Consumers will be given the ability to place and pay for orders on-the-fly.

## Following the Lead of Western Europe and Japan

To get ready for m-commerce you need to look beyond the United States. Mobile devices are much more popular in Europe and Japan than they are in the United States. Due to problems with the technology, customers have been reluctant to purchase mobile Web phones. Part of this reluctance is due to dissatisfaction with the dismal state of the current cellular phone service in the United States. In a recent *Consumer Reports* study, consumers reported very low levels of satisfaction with mobile phones. This is not surprising due to the present state of U.S. cell phone service. It is costly in spite of its

> *S*imple Messaging System (SMS) is the foundation of the first generation of consumer m-commerce applications. It's almost nonexistent in the U.S., but in Europe, it's everywhere.
>
> —PETER KEEN, "WIRELESS PRODUCTIVITY"

*Tip* The United States wireless network still has a lot of problems.

unreliability, incompatible standards, clumsy user interfaces, low quality transmissions, and fragmented broadband services (such as Digital Subscriber Line, or DSL). Given the nature of cellular service, why would customers buy slow, awkward WAP phones and PDAs with add-ons that enable Web access?

Thus, while the United States has been a leader in e-commerce, it has been slow to catch on to m-commerce. Finland is the most advanced in m-commerce, having numerous, profitable, and highly demanded applications, and excellent mobile phone coverage according to Peter Keen in "Go Mobile Now." In Finland, people use the phone to perform applications including sending textual messages, paying bills, and conducting business.

In "The Future Is Here or Is It?," David Wilson recommends that we look at the experiences of Europeans and the Japanese to predict some of the uses of m-commerce in the United States: "If you want to see the future, watch a teenager in Japan. For young Japanese, the cell phone call—that phenomenon of modern living—is already going the way of 45-RPM vinyl. Phones aren't just for calling; they're for sending e-mail. Since its introduction in February 1999 the Internet-ready iMode phone has been taken up by some ten million Japanese."

The mobile Web market in the United States has been hampered by a number of problems. First, competing wireless networks use different technologies for transmitting their signals resulting in many of the current problems. Another problem hampering mobile Web adoption has been the slow speeds of wireless data transmissions, with only about one-fifth of the speed of a typical PC modem using a phone line. While that speed suffices for sending text messages, it is inadequate

> *M*-commerce is international, and the more that IT professionals look beyond the United States, the more they'll be able to accelerate their companies' moves into the next innovation space of online business.
>
> —PETER KEEN, "GO MOBILE NOW"

for other Web-based activities such as surfing and downloading large files like video, audio, and other data-intensive files. Along with slow speeds, the screens on mobile devices are too small to properly display most Web pages. To accommodate these problems, some sites have developed special additional sites to be used with mobile devices. A few like Google.com have developed the technology to convert a regular Web page into a page appropriate for a mobile device. Unfortunately, only a small fraction of the millions of Web pages can be displayed on a mobile device, and most of those are in Japan and Europe. Also, wireless data networks have been limited to major cities.

Developing wireless technologies will alleviate some of the problems. Current cellular phones are either first generation analog devices that use radio wave modulation and can only transmit voice, or second generation digital cell phones that transform voice messages into bits of data that are then transmitted by modulated radio or microwaves. Third-generation (3G) wireless networks are being developed that could increase data transmission speeds, with companies predicting as high as 2.4 megabits per second. At the higher speeds, it becomes more feasible to raise transmission speeds. According to Fiona Harvey in "The Internet in Your Hands," 3G is expected in Europe in 2002 and the United States in 2003. Unfortunately, Forrester Research predicts that 3G services will not be available outside of metropolitan areas until 2010. In the meantime, several U.S. companies are developing the General Packet Radio Service (GPRS) or 2.5G bit/sec. broadband wireless capability that fills the gap between first-generation digital phones and the massive, planned, and much-delayed, third generation wireless services. For example, Sprint PCS is using packet

> *While the hardware manufacturers battle it out, a similar competition will focus on the software that will control all these devices. One popular contender is the operating system developed by Palm for its handheld computers and also used in Handspring's Visor machines. Another is the EPOC operating system created by Psion, the British manufacturer of handheld computers, and also used in Web-browsing cell phones made by Nokia and Ericsson. The third player is Microsoft.... Because of the diversity of devices, most industry watchers agree that there is unlikely to be a single winner in this software war, in contrast with Microsoft's domination of PC operating systems.*
>
> —*Fiona Harvey,* "*The Internet in Your Hands*"

> *P*hone companies are not the only ones eyeing the market. The makers of handheld computers, which have until now been used primarily for scheduling appointments and compiling address lists, are also introducing devices that can access the Internet. Some manufacturers are planning to add voice communications to the machines as well so that they can compete directly with the super phones.
>
> —*FIONA HARVEY,*
> *"THE INTERNET IN YOUR HANDS"*

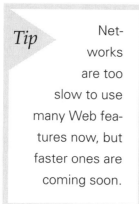

*Tip*     Networks are too slow to use many Web features now, but faster ones are coming soon.

switching to raise transmission speed according to Peter Keen in "Go Mobile Now."

An initial step towards a wireless Web is the Wireless Application Protocol (WAP), a set of technical specifications that essentially standardize transmissions of Web documents to cell phones, PDAs, pagers, and other handheld devices. Some U.S. and European wireless carriers are incorporating WAP standards into their networks. Currently, technical limitations such as the low bandwidth, slow transmission speeds, small screen sizes, and lack of processing power make it impossible for cellular phones and other handheld devices to properly handle the transmission of pages including graphics and pictures in HTML. Phone.com developed Handheld Device Markup Language (HDML), which allows the text portions of Web pages to be transmitted to cell phones and handheld devices. Many analysts believe that as high bandwidth and more sophisticated and powerful third generation technologies proliferate WAP will become obsolete.

Phone.com has joined with Motorola, Nokia, and Ericsson to develop a standardized language based on HDML called Wireless Markup Language (WML). They have also formed the WAP Forum. WML converts pages from HTML to WML, removing graphics and fancy formatting. Unfortunately, the resulting pages are sometimes unreadable so that companies are beginning to develop separate versions of their pages written in WML and expressly tailored for WAP devices.

U.S. companies are working diligently to solve the many current problems and keep up with Western Europe and Japan. In the future these problems will be alleviated enabling m-commerce to become a strong force in the future.

## Summary

Wireless technologies and mobile Web access are the future. A number of efforts are being made to make this a reality. Europe and Japan are much further ahead in the mobile arena. Mobile phone use is higher in Western Europe and Japan than in the United States.

The WAP is an attempt to bring the Web to mobile devices such as PDAs, mobile phones, and other handheld devices. Short-term communication platforms such as Bluetooth are being developed.

Some businesses are already using mobile commerce for mobile employees. We can expect mobile commerce to open many more arenas for business.

> *NTT DoCoMo is the world's most profitable and fastest-growing mobile Web and messaging service. It also shows the proven demand for wireless messaging everywhere.*
>
> —PETER KEEN,
> "WIRELESS PRODUCTIVITY"

### Chapter Key Points

- Mobile commerce is the way of the future. Wireless technologies are bringing the Web and commerce to mobile devices.

- The United States is behind Western Europe and Japan in use of mobile devices. Both have more mobile phones and smarter mobile phones than the United States does.

- The WAP is an attempt to bring the Web to mobile devices such as PDAs, mobile phones, and other handheld devices.

- Short-term communication platforms such as Bluetooth are being developed.

- Some businesses are already using mobile commerce for mobile employees.

- We can expect mobile commerce to open many more arenas for business.

## Web Sources for More Information

▶ **Ernst and Young** (www.ernstyoung.com) has research and information about m-commerce on their Web site.

▶ **Peter Keen's Computerworld Columns** (www.peterkeen.com) are frequently on mobile commerce and wireless technologies.

▶ **Scientific American** (www.sciam.com) has issues, articles, and series devoted to wireless technology and m-commerce.

*E*ven the makers of video-game consoles are joining the fray: Nintendo and Sony are expected to equip their GameBoy and Playstation consoles with Internet access in a year or two. As more and more consumers get their music from the Web rather than from tapes or CDs, the manufacturers of portable music players will start to build models that can wirelessly download the MP3 files on the Internet.

*—FIONA HARVEY,*
*"THE INTERNET IN YOUR HANDS"*

# INTO THE FUTURE
## *Combating Complacency*

ONLY EVER-EVOLVING COMPANIES WILL SURVIVE. ◀

*S*o many of the neighboring farms had gone out of business. With farming conglomerates and changing times, farmers had to be flexible and ingenious to survive. Some of the local farmers had simply refused to change. The family joked about some of their neighbors being in denial.

The farmer who had the largest and most profitable farm stand had insisted that the slump was temporary. He fully expected his farm to return to profitability. He had done so well for so many years and could not believe that his farm would go under. He refused to see the reality.

Another farmer had not believed the highway would really be built. He spent all of his time trying to figure out ways to stop the highway construction and trying to convince others to do the same. When the highway became a reality, he had no plans for adapting his business to accommodate the changing environment.

In a way, the widow was glad they had always had to struggle. Lately, things had gotten a bit worse but it had never been easy for the family. Their business had never achieved the level of prosperity of the largest farm stand. The widow and her family had always sought new ideas for making money. Her husband's death had forced all of them to work together. They had never had the opportunity to rest on their laurels and let complacency set in. They had and would always have to be adaptable, ever evolving, and searching for new opportunities.

> *IT and business developments are changing the business landscape at astronomical rates.*
>
> —*BILL GATES,*
> *BUSINESS AT THE SPEED OF THOUGHT*

$A$t this point you have probably already successfully developed your Web strategy and are doing business on the Web. However, now is not the time to relax and take it easy. In the new global, electronic world of business, staying the same means losing ground to other businesses that are continually evolving. Even after you have implemented a successful Web strategy, your business must continue to progress or risk becoming obsolete.

This chapter discusses how you can stay current and successful in this rapidly changing world. It talks about the danger of the complacency that can result from success and gives recommendations for keeping abreast of your situation. It includes a list of the trends that will be most important to business in the 21st century.

## Beware of Success

Success can breed complacency, and in today's rapidly changing world complacency can mean death to your business. In his book, *Business at the Speed of Thought: Using a Digital Nervous System*, Bill Gates discusses the dangers of being too confident due to past success. Ironically, as the profitable farmer demonstrated in the story at the beginning of the chapter, the most successful businesses may be the most resistant to change. It is easy for us to become enamored with strategies that have previously been successful. Change is always difficult for people. When we achieve success, we are likely to be even more tied to our previously successful ways and may be blind to the need to change. The *2,000 Percent Solution* describes this danger using IBM as an example. IBM's amazing turnaround was delayed due to the belief by employees that IBM was invincible. The authors say

> *Tip*
>
> In today's business world, evolve or risk becoming obsolete.

that "the most seductive source of stalls is the siren song of success."

An oft-cited episode, the 1980 decline of the American automobile industry, offers insights. For 40 years, from the 1930s through the early 1970s, U.S. automobile manufacturers dominated the world car market. During that time, gasoline prices were very low in the United States, and American consumers favored large, luxurious automobiles. However, in the early 1970s, gasoline prices began rising rapidly and gas supplies were insufficient to meet consumer demand. Gas shortages, rationing, and lengthy lines at gas stations resulted. Many Americans became disgusted with the amount of money they were spending to fuel their gas guzzling cars. The industry failed to see what was happening until it was too late to retain their previous market dominance.

While American automobile manufacturers kept making big, inefficient cars, Japanese manufacturers were exporting smaller, fuel efficient automobiles to the United States. American automobile manufacturers seemed surprised when Americans began to buy the Japanese automobiles in large numbers. Since Japanese automobiles better served the needs of the marketplace, the American automobile makers lost significant market share. Due to their inability to see changing consumer wants and needs, American automobile manufacturers took several years to produce cars that met the needs of their market. They lost dominance of the world market to other manufacturers that provided customers with more appropriate vehicles.

In a way the widow and her family were lucky to have never achieved the kind of success that breeds complacency. In the words of Bill Gates, "The best companies always worry and seek out bad news, as a way of staying

> *By 1990, sales of Britannica's multivolume sets had reached an all-time peak of about $650 million. Dominant market share, steady growth, generous margins, and a 200 year history all testified to an extraordinarily compelling and stable brand. Since 1990, however, sales of Britannica, and of all printed encyclopedias in the United States, have collapsed by over 80 percent. Britannica was blown away by a product of the late-20th century information revolution: the CD-ROM.*
>
> *Judging from their inaction, Britannica's executives at first seemed to have viewed the CD-ROM encyclopedia as a child's toy, one step above video games...hardly made for a serious rival to the Britannica—or so it seemed.*
>
> —THOMAS S. WURSTER,
> BLOWN TO BITS

on their toes. A competitive company must maintain an underdog attitude."

## Keeping on Your Toes

Keeping on your toes means being aware of both your internal and external environment. The earlier you become aware of potential problems and opportunities the more power you have to make the outcome successful.

### Communicate with Employees, Customers, Business Partners, and Suppliers

It takes a conscious effort for executives in Fortune 500 companies to not become far too removed from their customers, employees, and business partners. When they have lost touch as in the farming and automobile manufacturer examples, the results have been devastating. Hewlett Packard has used the technique of "Management by Walking Around" (MBWA) for years as a method of keeping managers and employees of all levels in touch with each other. They also have open office areas with few walls so that people are forced to interact with each other.

Never stop interacting with customers. Read their complaints as well as their compliments. Staying in touch with customers, employees, and business partners means that you hear about potential problems early.

### Measure, Measure, Measure

After initial strategic plans are developed, keep setting measurable objectives and make sure you are meeting them. Collect customer complaint information. Get customers and others to evaluate your services. Develop metrics for order processing, delivery, Web loading times, sales figures and all other measures which can

> *B*reak out the measuring stick. The emphasis on delivering tangible value requires marketing organizations to quantify results. Improving a relevant set of performance metrics for your customers should be the central objective of your business.
>
> —PHILIP SAY, "SEVEN GREAT B2B MARKETING INITIATIVES"

help to make sure that you are operating as you should. Make sure all of your internal processes are working properly.

If you sell products on the Web, count customer complaints, customer returns, and abandoned shopping carts. If you lose a regular customer or large account, follow up and ask why they no longer do business with you. You may want to collect data from current and past customers to make sure that they are satisfied with your service and ask them for suggestions for improving things. In sum, the more information you collect, and the more you measure how you are doing, the more you are able to improve the way you do things.

### Keep Abreast of External Happenings

Make sure that you have ways to keep informed about how things are going in the competitive environment. *The Wall Street Journal* and other national sources of business news are terrific for general business information. However, you need to make sure that you are current in your area. Join trade associations or business groups in your field, subscribe to specialized publications, and keep in contact with colleagues in your field. Never lose touch with your business environment.

### Take Advantage of Important Trends

Keeping you in touch with the external environment means knowing what trends are important. There are a number of e-commerce trends that we think will affect your business. You can choose to take advantage of these trends or risk being left behind.

*Trend 1: As more people use the Internet for commerce, customers are becoming more and more powerful.*

*Tip* — Know what is going on in your environment.

*Bottom line: Signing off on performance metric improvement may sound risky, but in these times, it's a risk that must be taken to survive today's downdraft.*

—PHILIP SAY, "SEVEN GREAT B2B MARKETING INITIATIVES"

> *Wireless Application Protocol (WAP) is a specification being developed in a European-led effort to bring the wireless Web to mobile phones and personal digital assistants. WAP has been a major disappointment so far, but the lessons for designers have been substantial. Trying to shrink HTML pages onto a phone display with deadly slow wireless transmission speeds doesn't work.*
>
> —PETER KEEN, "WIRELESS PRODUCTIVITY"

*Tip* Keep in touch with employees, customers, and other business partners.

As the Internet evolves competition is increasingly based on how well companies can anticipate and meet customer needs. Many of the traditional items to compete on are disappearing. A lower or equal price is only a click away. Location is irrelevant. The customer relationship is becoming more and more important. The use of technology to better meet customer needs is becoming a major factor in competition.

For e-commerce businesses this means increasing levels of personalization. The Internet allows organizations to maintain the customer preference information needed to provide individually customized products and services. Many predict that mass customization, tailoring products to individual customers, is the future of manufacturing.

*Trend 2: Alliances and collaborative commerce will become increasingly necessary to compete.*

E-commerce has evolved from consumers conducting basic transactions on the Web, to a complete retooling of the way partners, suppliers, and customers transact. The 21st century demands that businesses work together as partners in "win-win" relationships rather than the "win-lose" competitions that dominated much of 20th century business. For many businesses selling on the Web, alliances have become mandatory.

In their 2000 study of e-commerce in 12 countries, Ernst and Young found that, "Companies will look to leverage their strengths with complementary companies in all areas of the organization including marketing, supply chain operations, customer databases, and finance."

For manufacturers, alliances will support collaborative commerce. Manufacturers will increase their working relationships with suppliers, customers, and business partners. They will develop alliances and collaborative value chains. In "Ready for the New B2B," Peter Keen describes how we are already seeing this: "The year 2000 saw the focus of business-to-business (B2B) e-business shift from optimizing an individual enterprise to optimizing a network of businesses for competitive advantage. Indeed, during the year, more than 1000 public Collaborative Value Chains (e-markets) were established serving numerous industries and enterprises, and offering a vast array of choices for building closer relationships with customers and suppliers. By 2010, it is expected that 75 percent of online transactions will be through Collaborative Value Chains (e-markets)."

*Trend 3: People will conduct commerce "anywhere, anytime" using wireless, mobile, and global connections.*

A number of trends give rise to the trend towards people being able to conduct commerce from anywhere at anytime. Business will increasingly become global. As more of the worldwide population comes online, we can expect the Internet to become more of a global marketplace. According to J. Fonstad in "Start-ups Going Global; Global Strategy for Start-ups," "The European online population will exceed the U.S. online population by 2003. By 2005, U.S. users will represent only 30 percent of the world's online community."

*Trend 4: Smarter technology will be everywhere in our daily lives.*

An extension of the "anywhere, anytime" idea is the increasing "intelligence" of many of our everyday appliances. We are seeing this around us. For years, manufacturers have been adding microprocessors to automobiles, appliances, equipment, intelligent home

> *F*or multichannel retailers, the question is not, should we consider alliance; it is, how do we manage our alliances effectively, without jeopardizing the brand?
>
> —*ERNST AND YOUNG,*
> *"GLOBAL ONLINE: RETAILING: 2001"*

*Tip* You can add value by using information to personalize and customize products and services.

*L*arge corporations spend huge amounts of money on quality assurance, trying to make their products or services as error free as possible. Smaller businesses, in general, don't tend to worry about quality in the same way. They rely more on intuition, common sense, and comparisons with competitors to evaluate the quality of the business.

—*ABOUT.COM, "HOW TO MONITOR AND IMPROVE YOUR E-BUSINESS PROCESSES"*

*Tip* Wireless communications allow flexibility for conducting business.

monitoring systems, and other items we use daily. As the chips become cheaper, smarter, and smaller this will only increase. When "intelligence" is coupled with the ability to communicate, anything is possible. A global economy with wireless and mobile commerce communication using PDAs and other devices will be the future of business.

The "smart phone" is one example. On the Internet, "intelligent" agents already perform search tasks, combine information through syndication, and do many other tasks. We will see more and more applications of this "intelligence" combined with communications.

As these technologies become cheaper and more readily available, increasing numbers of businesses will use them to their competitive advantage. For example, even now, sites like Yahoo! are using intelligent agents to personalize information, help customers and site visitors search for material, and perform functions that make life on the Web a little easier. Soon, these opportunities will be more affordable for all businesses.

## Summary

Staying competitive means that businesses will have to evolve to be and stay successful. Staying the same in the 21st century business landscape means losing ground. Beware of success. It can bring complacency and that can mean death for your business.

Staying current means communicating with business partners, collecting data and measurements, and being aware of environmental changes. We expect personalization, mass customization, business alliances, collaborative commerce, and anywhere, anytime commerce.

## Chapter Key Points

🔑 The rapidly changing competitive business landscape of the 21st century makes it essential for businesses to continue to evolve.

🔑 Success can bring complacency, overconfidence, and resistance to change.

🔑 To stay current means communicating with customers, business partners, and employees; collecting data and measuring progress internally and externally; and keeping informed of the outside world.

🔑 In the future we expect firms to use data to personalize and customize products and services.

🔑 We expect more business alliances and collaborative commerce.

🔑 We expect anytime, anywhere commerce due to mobile communications and globalization.

🔑 To be successful, businesses need to change with future circumstances.

## Web Sources for More Information

▶ **Cnet.com** (www.cnet.com) has questions on e-commerce and e-commerce's future (http://builder.cnet.com/Webbuilding/pages/Business/Ecommerce20).

▶ **Cyberatlas** (www.cyberatlas.com) presents Internet and Web statistics. It includes the article, "Retailing: Future of E-Commerce May Rest on Customer Service" (cyberatlas.internet.com/markets/retailing/ article/0,1323,6061_274891,00.html).

## Web Sources for More Information, continued

▶ **E-commerce Times** (www.ecommercetimes.com) has printed several articles on the future of e-commerce including "Is There a Future for E-Commerce?" by Keith Regan (www.ecommerce times.com/perl/story/3914.html).

▶ **Overview of Present and Future e-Commerce** (www.jef.or.jp/en/jti/200011_007.html) includes Japanese Economic Foundation Article/Cover Story by Nakahara Tsuneo.

▶ **ZDNet.com** (www.zdnet.com) has articles about e-commerce future trends and other e-commerce areas. These include "Is Mobile E-Commerce the Future?" by Justin Pearse (www.zdnet.co.uk/news/1999/45/ns-11559.html).

# TERMS AND TECHNOLOGIES
## *Unraveling the Web*

*Java. Internet Protocol. SMTP, URL, TCP-IP...* These terms and acronyms are the language of the World Wide Web. What do they mean and how can we use them to make our businesses work better? And why does the Web seem so disorganized? It's frustrating.

When using the Web for business, you are using information sites and communication links that were designed for purposes very different from the ones for which you now use them. When you go on the Internet, you are actually using a graphical user interface, the World Wide Web, to help us navigate the Internet, a network of networks originally conceived by the military. Neither the Internet nor the Web were designed with commerce in mind. In fact, there was no commerce on the Internet until 1991.

To understand e-commerce you need to understand some basic technologies you will hear and read about when investigating e-commerce and the Web. A brief discussion of Internet history also helps you to understand the organization, or lack thereof, of the Web.

## What Is the Internet?

The Internet is a worldwide system of computer networks that allows users on one computer to get information from and send messages to another. The World Wide Web (WWW or Web) is a graphical user interface version of the Internet that uses hypertext (Hypertext Markup Language, HTML) to display and link Web sites and pages. HTML is the language that describes how text and pictures are to be displayed and how Web pages are linked so that clicking on the reference to the page takes the user to that page. HyperText Transport protocol is used to move information between computers.

Many of the limitations of the Internet and Web result from its history and the fact that it was not developed for commerce. The predecessor of the Internet began shortly after World War II as a way for military installations to exchange information. In 1969 the United States government formed ARPANET (Advanced Research Projects Agency Network) so that users at one research university could talk and exchange information with users at other universities. Later, the National Science Foundation took over the Internet and made it available for a much larger volume of traffic. Eventually the NSFNet evolved into the Internet. Due to government funding and related use restrictions, there was no commercial use of the Internet prior to 1991. At that time companies began to add links so they could transmit information. The transition from NSFnet, a government-funded research project, to the Internet, a largely commercial network of networks was completed in April 1995. Only being a commercial entity for a small portion of its history, it is not surprising that the Internet is not better organized for business use.

The Internet is distinguished by its use of Transmission Control Protocol/Internet Protocol (TCP/IP), a set of protocols, also used by Intranets and Extranets. In 1977, TCP/IP was invented. TCP/IP is the set of protocols that facilitate communication between computers linked to the Internet. Internet Protocol (IP) transmits data and Transmission Control Protocol (TCP) ensures that the data is delivered in the correct sequence.

Individual computers are identifiable by their IP addresses. (IP addresses are in binary code, which specifies a number to identify the computer, computer network, host, and host network. For example, 25.84.5.25 means computer named 25, on network 5, on host 84, of network 25.)

The Internet uses IP addresses to locate everything on the Web. IP addresses are translated from numbers to text before we see them. The Internet uses addresses in the form of Uniform Resource Locators (URLs) to identify locations. The format of a URL address is the "at" symbol, or "@," the name of the computer followed by a period, then the domain name followed by a period, and finally the type of organization.

To use the Web you must employ a Web browser, such as Netscape Navigator and Microsoft Internet Explorer. The browser is a computer program that provides the user's view of the Web. Browsers allow users to see formatted text, display pictures and motion videos, and hear audio. Different versions of Web browsers result in different Web page appearances. Later versions of Web browsers enable users to use more features on some Web pages such as animation, virtual reality, sound, and music.

The Web is based on client/server technology in which one computer program, the client, requests information from another program, the server, who fills the request. On the Web, your browser is the client program and the Web server containing the Web pages is the server. On the Web and other networks, computers can act as clients and servers depending on the situation. One example of this client/server application is the use of "cookies." A cookie is a message, a text file, which is given by the Web server to the browser for storage on a user's computer. Each time the browser requests a page from the server, a cookie is sent. Cookies are used to identify users and allow sites to prepare personalized sites for them. When you go to a site and are greeted by a message with your name or other personal information, that is due to the use of a cookie.

Most personal and corporate users gain access to the Web via the Internet Service Providers (ISPs). ISPs are companies that provide access to the Internet. The primary use of the Internet is for e-mail. For most people, the e-mail system is based on two servers, the Simple Mail Transfer Protocol (SMTP and Post Office Protocol (POP3). The SMTP server handles outgoing mail while incoming mail is handled by the POP3 server. Internet Message Access Protocol (IMAP) service is used for convenient, flexible e-mail access, especially if you send and receive e-mail from multiple locations. To write or read e-mail you use an e-mail client such as the stand-alone clients Microsoft Outlook, Outlook Express, or Eudora. There is also an e-mail client Web page for users of free services such as HotMail or Yahoo.

Many companies use Java™ technology when developing their Web sites. Java can be used to build extensive applications or to create miniature programs called "applets" that are used to expand the functions of Web pages and perform tasks such as creating animated cartoons and news tickers. Java allows users to manipulate data on networked systems, which reduces the need to write specialized software. The network then delivers only the applets required for a specific function.

The Java platform is based on the idea that the same software should run on many different kinds of machines including computers, phones, TVs, and handheld devices. Java allows you to use the same application on different types of computers, consumer gadgets, and other devices.

A new standard, eXtensible Markup Language (XML), is also gaining popularity on the Web. XML allows data with standardized names and semantics to be shared on the Web in the same way that HTML does with page formats. XML was developed by the World Wide Web Consortium (W3C) in 1998 to allow data sharing. It is a standard for defining and naming data that should increase the ability of companies to share data.

In summary, you can better understand the Web by understanding its history and some basic terms. This appendix provided a brief introduction. Additional information can be found on the following sites:

- *whatis.com* (www.whatis.com). This site defines things such as software applications, database, operating systems, Internet technology terms, Internet acronyms and lingo, Internet applications, and e-mail.

- *Webopedia* (www.zdwebopedia.com). An online dictionary and search engine for the computer and Internet technology. Definitions of many computer-related terms, from hardware to the Internet.

- *NetLingo Internet Dictionary* (www.netlingo.com). Dictionary and glossary of Internet jargon: definitions for terminology and words.

- *The Internet Glossary* (www.animatedsoftware.com/statglos/statglos.htm). A glossary of terms necessary for understanding the Internet and World Wide Web. Organized according to learning order for those unfamiliar with the subject.

- *CyberAtlas* (www.cyberatlas.com) The World's Online Populations CyberAtlas has compiled the latest surveys of the online populations of nations around the globe.

- *Square One Technology: Internet Glossary* (www.square onetech.com/glosaryf.html). A glossary of terms necessary for understanding the Internet and World Wide Web.

- *Marketing Manager Plain English Internet Glossary* (www.jaderiver.com/glossary.htm). A plain English, marketing oriented guide to understanding the Internet and terms.
- *CNET.com Glossary and Cite* (www.cnet.com). Provides downloads, a glossary, and a lot of information on the Internet and World Wide Web.

# Glossary of Terms

**Angel Investors** Individual investors who usually invest in the beginning stages of a business.

**Application Service Provider (ASP)** Companies that host, manage, and provide software over the Internet.

**Bandwidth** Pipeline to and from Web site through which data flows. Width determines how much information can be carried through communications lines at a given time and therefore, speed. Thus, bandwidth is usually used to refer to transmission speed. Speed measurements are given in terms of data transfer rates like kbs (kilobits, 1024 bits, per second), mbps (megabits or millions of bits per second) and gbps (gigabits or billions of bits per second).

**Banner Ads** These are the rectangular advertising boxes containing promotions, advertiser Web site addresses, and special offers that appear on Web pages.

**Bluetooth** A standard, for short range transmissions of data from device to device.

**Brochureware** Online versions of your brochures and other promotional materials. These materials are published on the Web so that visitors to the site can read or download them.

**Business-to-Business (B2B) Commerce** Transactions between businesses—businesses selling to other business customers.

**Business-to-Customer (B2C) Commerce** Transactions between businesses and individual customers—businesses selling to other nonbusiness consumers.

**Business-to-Employee Commerce (B2E)** Businesses using the Web for transactions with employees.

**Business-to-Government (B2G) Commerce** Transactions between businesses and government entities such as businesses selling to the government sites.

**Client** In client/server architectures, this is the computer that supplies the files, programs, and services to the client.

**Client/Server Architecture** A computing architecture in which one computer, a client, requests files, programs, and services from another computer, the server.

**Collaborative Commerce** Communications bring together employees, customers, and business partners who share information, develop trusting relationships, and design products and processes. Usually, companies sharing information to improve the production process.

**Collaborative Value Chains** Linking with business partners to automate and integrate your value chain.

**Cookie** A message, or a text file, which is given by the Web server to the browser for storage on a user's computer. Each time the browser requests a page from the server, the cookie is sent. Cookies are used to identify users and allow sites to prepare personalized sites for them. When you go to a site and are greeted by a message with your name or other personal information that is due to the use of a cookie.

**Customer Relationship Management (CRM)** A company's processes for communicating and dealing with its customers.

**Data Mining** Analyzing enormous databases to discover valuable and useful information.

**Data Units** In computing, BITs are the basic unit, Binary DigITs. Bytes are 8 bits.

**Disintermediation** The elimination of middlepeople as businesses link directly with their customers and suppliers.

**Domain** The address of each server on the Web. Each domain name stands for an Internet Protocol (IP) address.

**802.11b** An alternate standard, for short range transmissions of data from device to device.

**Electronic Data Interchange (EDI)** The exchange of data and processing of transactions using electronic networks rather than paper.

**E-tailers** Retailers who sell on the Web.

**Extensible Markup Language (XML)** A language that describes how data is formatted and exchanged. It allows organizations to share data.

**Extranet** A private, interactive Web-like network shared by organizational members and selected outsiders but not available to others on the Web, who are outside the firewall or barrier it allows access to only those authorized. Usually Extranets provide access to suppliers and customers.

**FTP** A method for transferring files on the Internet.

**Government-to-Business (G2B), Government-to-Consumer (G2C) Commerce** Government using the Web to provide services and sell to businesses and consumers.

**Government- to-Government (G2G) Commerce** Government agencies using the Web for transactions with each other.

**HyperText Markup Language (HTML)** The language that describes how text and pictures are displayed and how Web pages are linked. Web pages are written in HTML.

**HTML Messages** E-mail messages that allow customers to incorporate Web page features into an e-mail message.

**HTML Tags** Web page information that describes text style, placement of links and graphics, and formatting. http://computer. domain.organization/file (if no file is specified it will appear index.html).

**HyperText Transport Protocol (HTTP)** The language used to move information between computers.

**Internet Message Access Protocol (IMAP)** The language that provides convenient, flexible e-mail access.

**Infomediaries** Entities that link buyers and sellers. Infomediaries can provide information to buyers and sellers which allow them to compare options.

**Internet** A worldwide system of computer networks. With permission, the users on one computer can get information from other computers on the Internet and can send messages to one another.

**Internet Service Provider (ISP)** Companies that provide users with access to the Internet.

**Intranet** A private, interactive internal Web-like network shared by employees and other organizational members but not available to others on the World Wide Web who are outside the firewall or barrier it allows access to only those authorized.

**Knowledge Management (KM) Portals** Web sites that provide single point personalized access to geographically dispersed and multiple sources of information.

**Local Area Network (LAN)** A network over a local area, usually inside a company or building.

**Lines of Credit** Approval of a prespecified amount to be loaned by an institution for any purpose.

**Maintenance, Repair, and Operations (MRO)** The parts and other supplies used by a company for nonproduction maintenance, repair, and service.

**Mass Customization** Production of personalized goods and services in large numbers of customers.

**META Tags** Information accompanying Web pages that describes who created the page, update information, subject information, and which keywords represent the page's content. This information is often used by search engines.

**Mini-dots** Very small businesses doing commerce on the Web.

**Niche Portal** A portal specializing in an industry, product, or service niche.

**P2P Commerce (P2P)** Consumers interacting directly with each other on the Web. Usually, the sharing of hardware, programs, and files by individual personal computers and Internet connection devices directly with each other without first going through a centralized computer.

**Pop-Up Ads** These are Web pages that open up on top of the user's current Web page to display an advertiser's Web address, promotions, and special offers.

**Post Office Protocol (POP3)** This is the language or protocol that handles incoming mail. POP defines how e-mail is sent and received.

**Portal** A Web site that provides links to other Web sites and provides a good place to begin a Web search.

**Pure-Play** Businesses that exist only on the Internet and do not have physical stores to sell.

**Secure Sockets Layer (SSL)** A recognized security standard for Web sites. The protocol or language ensures that credit card information can be transmitted securely.

**Servers** In client/server architectures, this is the computer that supplies the files, programs, and services to the client.

**Shopping Cart** Software that allows customers to purchase products on the Web by adding them to a list of current items for purchase.

**Simple Mail Transfer Protocol (SMTP)** The language or protocol that handles outgoing mail.

**Streaming** The live flow of digital information that makes it possible to hear audio, see video, or view animation as a continuous stream when it arrives rather than having to wait for a file to be downloaded.

**Supply Chain Management** The series of activities that a business uses to maintain adequate inventories of their raw products to efficiently manufacture their products.

**Transmission Control Protocol/Internet Protocol (TCP/IP)** The set of protocols used to facilitate communication between computers linked to the Internet.

**Uniform Resource Locator (URL)** Internet addresses. The format of the address of each Web site.

**Value Chain** The series of activities that a business uses to turn raw materials into finished products or services.

**Venture Capitalist** Individuals or firms who are willing to provide funding for rapidly growing, profitable businesses.

**Vortal** A portal targeting a specific industry or segment.

**Vortex** A portal with a wide range of services and products.

**Web Host** The server (computer) on which you locate your Web site.

**Wireless Application Protocol (WAP)** An attempt to bring the wireless Web to mobile phones and personal digital assistants.

**World Wide Web** A graphical user interface version of the Internet.

# Chapter References

## Introduction

Advancing Women Network. Going Global...Study Your Markets, Develop a Strategic Plan or Take a Shortcut With Net B2B Marketplaces. *AdvancingWomen Network, 2000* October 20, 2001, www.advancingwomen.com/web/going_global.html.

Ghosh, Shikhar. Making Business Sense of the Internet. *Harvard Business Review* March-April 1998.

Hof, Robert D. Overview: The "Click Here" Economy. *Business Week*, June 22, 1998.

Moore, John. Does E-Commerce Hurt Small Business? *Smart Reseller*, November 4, 1998, www.zdnet.com/zdnn/stories/zdnn_rc_display/0,3443,2159790,00.html (September 30, 2001).

Say, Philip. Seven Great B2B Marketing Initiatives. *ClickZ.com* March 5, 2001, www.clickz.com/b2b_mkt/b2b_mkt/article.php/838111 (June 29, 2001).

SBA.org. The Facts about Small Business 1999. www.sba.gov/advo/stats/facts99.pdf (August 10, 2001).

Sculley, Arthur B. and W. William A Woods. Interview with the authors of *B2B Exchanges: The Killer Application in the Business-to-Business Internet Revolution.* March 2000 http://shop.barnesandnoble.com/booksearch/isbnInquiry.asp?isbn=9627762598&displayonly=authorInterview (August 10, 2001).

————. *B2B Exchanges: The Killer Application in the Business-to-Business Internet Revolution.* New York: ISI Publications, 1999.

Siebel, Thomas M., Tom Siebel, and Charles R. Schwab. *Cyber Rules: Strategies for Excelling at E-Business.* New York: DoubleDay, Inc., 1999.

Stewart, Trevor R. A Cause for Rational Exuberance: Cyberhype notwithstanding, the e-business revolution is taking the world to a whole new place. *Global Magazine* March 2000, Vol. 3, No. 1. www.deloitte.com/tidalwave/Exuberance.htm (July 29, 2001).

Walker, David. Behind the Gloom, Continuing Audience Growth. *Lighthouse on the Web* April 10, 2001, www.shorewalker.com/pages/audience_growing-1.html (July 29, 2001).

Yoffie, David in *The Wall Street Journal's* Millennium Forum broadcast on CNBC, October 22, 1999.

### Chapter 1

SBA.org. The Facts about Small Business 1999. www.sba.gov/advo/stats/facts99.pdf (August 10, 2001).

Weintraub, Arlene. The Mighty Mini-Dots: Small Frugal and Unflashy, They Are Making Money Where the Big Guys Couldn't. *BusinessWeek e.biz*, March 19, 2001.

### Chapter 2

Barker, Joel Arthur. *The Power of Vision.* Burnsville, MN: Chart House International, video.

Bizplus.com. Business Plans. www.bizplus.com/Zframes/info.html (June 23, 2001).

Carlton, Sean. Building a Successful Business in 2001. *ClickZ.com,* December 13, 2000 www.clickz.com/tech/lead_edge/article.php/834011 (March 5, 2001).

Covey, Stephen. *The 7 Habits of Highly Effective People: Powerful Lessons in Personal Change.* New York: Simon & Schuster Trade, 1990.

CPP Leadership Forum. The Power of Vision. *Forward Thinking, the newsletter of the National Labor Management Association,* December 2000 www.nlma.org/vision.htm (June 30, 2001).

Ebiz101.com. Business Plans. *ebiz101.com,* www.ebiz101.com/business_plans.htm (August 11, 2001).

Galleta, Dennis. Developing an Internet Business Plan. *Commerce on the Information Highway 2000 (BA MIS 2578),* University of Pittsburgh, Joseph M. Katz Graduate School of Business, www.pitt.edu/~galletta/iplan.html (May 30, 2001).

Henricks, Mark. Short and Sweet: Crafting an e-business plan. *Business Start-Ups magazine* May 2000, www.entrepreneur.com/magazines/MA_SegArticle/0,1539, 271149——1-,00.html (May, 30, 2001).

Hulme, George V. Sharing Lunch: Key to Keeping Business and IT Goals in Sync. *InfoWeek,* September 17, 2001, www.informationweek.com/story/IWK200109 16S0005 (October 18, 2001).

Levy, Mitchell quoted on *Ecnow.com.* http://ecnow.com/strategy.htmECnow.com (July 30, 2001).

Mason Rowe and Snyder Dickel. *Strategic Management: A Methodological Approach,* Reading MA: Addison-Wesley Publishing Company, 1986.

Nanus, Burt quoted in The University of North Carolina at Pembroke *Strategic Planning Model Explanations.* www.uncp.edu/ir/plan/explanations.htm (May 30, 2001).

Pitts, Michael W. "BIZStrat Strategic Management Lecture notes, Strategic Planning." Department of Management Business 434, Virginia Commonwealth University, Spring 1995, http://aiken.isy.vcu.edu/classes/bizstrat/lecture.htm (July 19, 2001).

Rutherford, Emelie. To E or not to E, a Retailer's Dilemma Part One: Defining an Online Strategy. *Darwin*, April 6, 2000, www.darwinmag.com/learn/ebusiness/crossing/column.html?ArticleID=11 (July 3, 2001).

Williams, Frank. Frank Williams' Quotes on Leadership. www.healylaw.com/williams.htm (August 11, 2001).

Young, Ken. Managers Fail Dot-com Firms. *IT Week*, October 30, 2000 www.zdnet.co.uk/itweek/analysis/2000/41/management/ (August 5, 2001).

### Chapter 3

Buzzmedia.com. Bozos Kill Small Business. *Xpress Press* April 16, 2001, www.xpress press.com/news/buzzmedia_041601.html (July 13, 2001).

Ideacafe.com. Financing Your Biz. *Ideacafe.com,* www.ideacafe.com/getmoney/financing.html (May 30, 2001).

Michael Visard. Venture Capitalist Is Cautious in Economic Slowdown. *Infoworld,* April 2, 2001 (Vol. 23, Issue 14) www.inquiry.com/pubs/infoworld/vol23/issue 14/010402tcvcview.asp (May 10, 2001).

### Chapter 4

About.com. *E-commerce Tips.* http://ecommerce.about.com/gi/dynamic/offsite. htm?site=http%3A%2F%2Fwww.ibguide.com%2Fectips.htm (July 12, 2001).

*Agentware Business Plan* 2000. www.agentware.net (November 20, 2000).

Daniels, Jim. 10 Key Components to Lasting Success on the Web. *BizWeb2000.com CyberMarketing Infoboard*, www.BizWeb2000.com (July 20, 2001).

Drier, Tony. Communicating. *PC Magazine*, February 20, 2001 p. 138, www.pc mag.com (June 30, 2001).

Graham, Jeffrey. E-CRM for Dummies. *ClickZ.com,* Wednesday, April 4, 2001, http://clickz.com/print.jsp?article=3698 (May 30, 2001).

Metz, Cade. Design Primer: It's Not Just the Visual. *PC Magazine,* February 20, 2001, www.ecommerce/filters/resources/0,10385,2181778,00.html (May 30, 2001).

Tweney, Dylan. Slim Down that Homepage. *Business2.com*, July 13, 2001, www.busi ness2.com/articles/web/0,1653,16483,FF.html (July 30, 2001).

Vickery, Lisa. Keeping the Cachet. *The Wall Street Journal*, page R28.

Wilson, Ralph F. Starting an E-Business on a Shoestring, Step 5: Obtain Professional Website Design. *Web Marketing Today*, March 1, 2001, www.wilsonweb.com/wmt6/start-design.htm (June 30, 2001).

WilsonWeb. Theme: Starting an E-Business on a Shoestring, Step 5. *Web Marketing Today,* Issue 97 March 1, 2001, www.wilsonweb.com/wmt6/issue97.ht (May 30, 2001).

### Chapter 5

About.com. Learn from Dot-com Failures: Hubris and "Greed." *Small Business Information,* http://sbinformation.about.com/library/weekly/aa011601a.htm (August 10, 2001).

———. What is Web Business? *About.com's Web 2000 Course,* http://ecommerce.about.com/gi/dynamic/offsite.htm?site=http://www.theproduct.com/education.htm (August 10, 2001).

Blankenhorn, Dana. This Week's Clue: Secrets. *A-Clue.Com,* November 27, 2000 v.4, No.48, www.a-clue.com/archive/00/cl001127.htm (July 30, 2001).

Carlton, Sean. Building a Successful Business in 2001. *ClickZ.com,* December 13, 2000, www.clickz.com/tech/lead_edge/article.php/834011 (March 5, 2001).

Cox, Beth. Is Pure Play the Wrong Play? Yes, Says New E-tail Study. *Start-up internet Marketing: Tip of the Week,* www.startupinternetmarketing.com/ezines/pureplay.html (August 20, 2001).

Deise, Martin V., Conrad Nowikow, Patrick King, and Amy Wright. *Executive's Guide to E-Business: From Tactics to Strategy.* New York: John Wiley and Sons, 2000.

Graham, Jeffrey. E-CRM for Dummies. *ClickZ.com,* Wednesday, April 4, 2001, http://clickz.com/print.jsp?article=3698 (May 30, 2001).

Kamm, Steve. The New Netrepreneurs: Dot-com veterans are creating smarter start-ups for a chastened world. *BusinessWeek* e.biz, October 1, 2001, www.businessweek.com/magazine/content/01_40/b3751601.htm (October 15, 2001).

Keen, Peter G. and Mark McDonald. *eProcess Edge: Creating Customer Value and Business Wealth in the Internet Era.* McGrawHill, New York, 2000.

Nickell, Joe Ashbrook. Radar: The Dot-Com Class of 2000 Grows Up. *Smart BusinessMag.com,* May 2001, page 32.

Pickering, Chris. E-Business Rule #2: Profits Matter. *Datamation* October 24, 2000, http://itmanagement.earthweb.com/article/0,,10454_622541,00.html (June 27, 2001).

———. E-Business Rule #4: Focus on Customers. *Datamation* December 19, 2000, http://itmanagement.earthweb.com/ecom/ecomstrat/article/0,,12169_622911_2,00.html (June 27, 2001).

Rayport, Jeffrey F. The Truth about Internet Business. *Strategy and Business,* Third Quarter, 1999, www.strategy-business.com/briefs/99301/page1.html (May 30, 2001).

Reinhardt, Andy. Tesco Bets Small—and Wins Big. Britain's top supermarket chain was slammed for its go-slow approach to selling goods over the Net. Now it's the world's largest online grocer. *BusinessWeek Online* October 1, 2001, www.businessweek.com/magazine/content/01_40/b3751622.htm (October 15, 2001).

Rowe, Alan J. *Strategic Management: A Methodological Approach.* Reading MA: Addison-Wesley Publishing Company, 1986).

Shook, David. The Davids of E-Commerce. *Business Week,* April 23, 2001, www.businessweek.com/bwdaily/dnflash/apr2001/nf20010423_511.htm (July 2, 2001).

Stewart, Trevor R., Succeeding in E-Business. *The E-Business Tidal Wave.* Deloitte Touche Tohmatsu, 1998, www.deloitte.com/tidalwave/default.htm (August 1, 2001).

Weintraub, Arlene. The Mighty Mini-Dots: Small Frugal and Unflashy, They Are Making Money Where the Big Guys Couldn't. *BusinessWeek e.biz,* March 19, 2001.

Whyte, Gordon. An E-Commerce Survival Guide: 10 ways to help your business through "interesting times." *About.com,* www.ecommerce.about.com/library/weekly/aa022801a.htm (June 4, 2001).

### Chapter 6

Afuah, Allan and Christopher L. Tucci. *Internet Business Models and Strategies: Text and Cases.* New York: McGraw-Hill, 2001, www.mhhe.com/business/management/afuahtucci/ (October 20, 2001).

Brea, Cesar. Many-2-Many: New Solutions in Collaborative Commerce. *ArsDigita* 2001, www.arsdigita.com/learning/whitepapers/many2many (July 12, 2001).

Buford, Tiger. Emerging Business Models on the Web. *Web Tomorrow,* www.webtomorrow.com/webonom.htm (June 20, 2001).

Fingar, Peter, Harshna Kumar, and Tarun Shirma. 21st Century Markets: From Places to Spaces. *First Monday* v. 12 no. 4, www.firstmonday.org/issues/issue4_12/fingar/index.html (July 5, 2001).

Fox, Chris. Business Models that have Succeeded and Business Models that have Failed—International Case Studies. www.chrisfoxinc.com/eCommerceBusinessModels.htm (June 30, 2001).

Karpinski, Richard. The Net Continues to Transform Business Models. *InternetWeek* March 31, 1999, http://content.techweb.com/wire/story/ TWB19990331S0019 (June 30, 2001).

Leebaert, Derek (editor). *The Future of the Electronic Marketplace.* Cambridge, MA: MIT Press, 1998.

University of South Carolina. E-commerce. *University of South Carolina Darla Moore School of Business,* http://dmsweb.badm.sc.edu/ibus737/g3/Ecommerce_Webpage.htm (August 4, 2001).

Webtomorrow.com. Emerging Business Models on the Web. www.webtomorrow.com/webonom.htm (June 1, 2001).

Wharton School. Creating Internet Strategies for Competitive Advantage. *Wharton School, University of Pennsylvania,* September 28, 2000, http://knowledge.wharton.upenn.edu/arti cles.cfm?catid=7&articleid=244&homep.age=yes (June 4, 2001).

### Chapter 7

Brea, Cesar. Many-2-Many: New Solutions in Collaborative Commerce. *ArsDigita* 2001, www.arsdigita.com/learning/whitepapers/many2many (July 12, 2001).

Buford, Tiger. Emerging Business Models on the Web. *Web Tomorrow,* www.webto morrow.com/webonom.htm (June 20, 2001).

Community B2B. B2B Fundamentals. *Community B2B,* www.communityb2b.com/library/b2bfundamentals.cfm (August 3, 2001).

Dembeck , Chet. U.S. B2B to Reach $6 Trillion by 2005. *Ecommerce Times,* June 27, 2000, www.ecommercetimes.com/perl/story/3653.html (August 20, 2001).

Enos, Lori. The Biggest Myths about B2B. *E-Commerce Times* June 22, 2001, www.ecommercetimes.com/perl/story/11327.html (August 5, 2001).

Fingar, Peter, Harshna Kumar, and Tarun Shirma. 21st Century Markets: From Places to Spaces. *First Monday* v. 12 no. 4, www.firstmonday.org/issues/issue4_12/fin gar/index.html (July 5, 2001).

Karpinski, Richard. The Net Continues to Transform Business Models. *InternetWeek* March 31, 1999, http://content.techweb.com/wire/story/TWB19990 331S0019 (June 30, 2001).

Katz, David M. Branding the B2B. *Brandera.com 2001,* www.brandera.com/b/B/fea tures/00/05/02/business.html (July 30, 2001).

Kovair, Inc. Strategically Speaking: SRM News and Facts. *Kovair Inc. Newsletter,* July 2001, www.kovair.com/news/Newsletters/july_2001.html (September 6, 2001).

Leebart, Derek (editor). *The Future of the Electronic Marketplace.* Cambridge, Massachusetts: MIT Press, 1998.

Trendlines. *CIO Magazine* September 15, 2000, www.cio.com/archive/091500_tl_num bers_content.html (June 30, 2001).

Turnolo, Marie. Business to Business Exchanges. *Information Systems Management* Spring 2001, www.brint.com/members/01040530/b2bexchanges (August 3, 2001).

## Chapter 8

Blankenhorn, Dana. This Week's Clue: Secrets. *A-Clue.Com ,* November 27, 2000 v.4, No.48, www.a-clue.com/archive/00/cl001127.htm (July 30, 2001).

Cox, Beth. Is Pure Play the Wrong Play? Yes, Says New E-tail Study. *Start-up internet Marketing: Tip of the Week,* www.startupinternetmarketing.com/ezines/pure play.html (August 20, 2001).

Dicksteen, Lisa Napell. Beauty site gets personal with Oracle, WebSphere Epiphany. *Techupdate,* October 1, 2000, techupdate.zdnet.com/techupdate/stories/main/0,14179,2814305,00.html (June 30, 2001).

Ernst and Young. Global Online: Retailing: 2001. www.ey.com/global/vault.nsf/Inter national/Globalization/$file/Globalization.pdf (January 12, 2002).

Fingar, Peter, Harshna Kumar, and Tarun Shirma. 21st Century Markets: From Places to Spaces. *First Monday* v. 12 no. 4, www.firstmonday.org/issues/issue4_12/fin gar/index.html (July 5, 2001).

Graduate School USDA. Why the World Wide Web? www.corpimages.net/USDA/ (March 1, 2002).

Rayasam, Renuka. Time Travel Expenses. *Smart Business Mag* March 1, 2001 www.smartbusinessmag.com/article/0,3658,s%253D1874%2526a%253D8309,00.asp - 67k (March 4, 2002).

Rutherford, Emelie. To E or not to E. *Darwin Online,* April 2000, www.darwinmag.com/learn/ebusiness/crossing/column.html?ArticleID=11 (August 7, 2001).

Vargas, Melody. The State of Online Retailing. http://retailindustry.about.com/library/weekly/01/aa010502a.htm (May 4, 2001).

### Chapter 9

Accenture. State Government Portals Create One-Stop Shops for Citizens. *Accenture.com,* www.accenture.com/xd/xd.asp?it=enWeb&xd=Industries%5CGovernment%5Cgove_portal.xml (August 21, 2001).

*CNET.* June 1, 2000, www.cnet.com (June 23, 2001).

Furth, John. Uncle Sam Wants B2G. *Line56,* February 21, 2001, www.line56.com/articles/default.asp?NewsID=2197 (April 5, 2001).

Hayes, Heather B. Dot-Coms pitch Public Service. *Federal Computer Week*, August 28, 2000, www.go.vic.gov.au/usportals.htm (August 1, 2001).

Konrad, Rachel. Will B2G Become the "Next Big Thing"? *CNET News.com*, June 1, 2000, http://news.cnet.com/news/0-1005-2001995229.html%3Ftag%3Drltdnws&e=42 (July 23, 2001).

Olsen, Marc. Technology and Nonprofit Management: Themes from the Conference of the Alliance for Nonprofit Management. *Non-profit Online News,* http://news.gilbert.org/features/featureReader$3842 (July 1, 2001).

Quintanilla, Francisco. B2G Commerce Will be Big Business. *Office.com,* July 18, 2000, www.office.com/global/0,2724,9-18748,FF.html (July 29, 2001).

Whatis.com. B2G. http://whatis.techtarget.com/definition/0,289893,sid9_gci503766,00.html (July 28, 2001).

Young, Eric. In E-Commerce U.S. Agencies Trust. *The Industry Standard,* May 29, 2001, www.computerworld.com/cwi/story/0,1199,NAV47_STO60911.00 (May 24, 2001).

### Chapter 10

Gomes, Lee. Is P2P Plunging off the Deep End? *The Wall Street Journal,* April 4, 2001, http://techupdate.zdnet.com/techupdate/stories/main/0,14179,2704598,00.html (March 4, 2002).

———. Peer-to-peer party comes to a halt. *The Wall Street Journal,* April 4, 2001, www.msnbc.com/news/554433.asp?cp1=1 (April 8, 2002).

Hachman, Mark. Peer-to-Peer Companies Discuss Napster Ruling. *TechWeb News,* February 13, 2001, www.techweb.com/wire/story/TWB20010213S0024 (December 19, 2001).

Peertopeercentral.com. What's Really Happening In Net User Land? Distributed comp players offer Web performance info. February 28, 2001, www.peertopeercentral.com/research.html (May 23, 2001).

Rapport, Marc. Microsoft, IBM Researchers Develop P2P Networking Technology Computing giants cooking up their own flavors of P2P. February 14, 2001, www.peertopeercentral.com/research.html (May 3, 2001).

Scannell, Ed. Ford to use peer-to-peer technology to boost fuel-efficient car designs. *Infoworld,* March 27, 2001, http://iwsun4.infoworld.com/articles/hn/xml/01/03/27/010327hnfordp2p.xml (June 30, 2001).

Solomon, Karen. Peering is your Future. *Web Building—CNET.com,* March 5, 2001, http://builder.cnet.com/webbuilding/0-7535-8-4950892-2.html (July 10, 2001).

Spooner, John. Intel likes what it hears in Napster. *ZDNet.com,* August 9 ,2000, www.zdnet.com/zdnn/stories/news/0,4586,2613163,00.html (June 30, 2001).

Whatis.com. Peer-to-peer. www.peer-to-peerwg.org/whatis/index.html (November 30, 2001).

### Chapter 11

Click Z.com. Five Important B2B Marketing Concepts for 2001. *ClickZ.com* November 27, www.clickz.com/article/cz.2893.html (June 25, 2001).

Community B2B. B2B Fundamentals. *Community B2B,* www.communityb2b.com/library/b2bfundamentals.cfm (August 3, 2001).

Drickhamer, Dick. Peak Performance. *SCMDigest* n.91 27 May 2001, www.scmdigest.com/SCMDigest/SCMDigest91.html (May 30, 2001).

Fingar, Peter, Harshna Kumar, and Tarun Shirma. 21st Century Markets: From Places to Spaces. *First Monday* v. 12 no. 4, www.firstmonday.org/issues/issue4_12/fingar/index.html (July 5, 2001).

Haughley, Wayne P. The Object Management Group Strategic Approach to Value Chain Integration. *Object Management Group,* October 18, 1999, www.omg.org/news/whitepapers/value_chain.htm (January 3, 2002).

Keen, Peter G. IT's Value in the Chain. *Computerworld,* February 2000, www.peterkeen.com/cworld40.htm (August 3, 2001).

———. Ready for the New B2B. *Computerworld,* September 11, 2000, www.computerworld.com/cwi/story/0,1199,NAV47_STO49842,00.html. (August 30, 2001).

Manufactuingnews.com. E-commerce combines with supply management to create a new industrial order. *Manufacturingnews.com,* October 13, 2000 v7.n18, www.manufactureringnewes. com/news/00/1013/art1.html (June 3, 2001).

O'Brien, Kevin P. Value-Chain Report—Evaluating the Functionality of B2B Marketplaces. *Industry Week's The Value Chain,* April 2, 2001, www.iwvaluechain.com/Columns/columns.asp?ColumnId=762> (September 31, 2001).

Say, Philip. The Buzz on C-commerce. *ClickZ.com,* April 30, 2001, www.clickz.com/article/cz.3827.html (May 30, 2001).

Stahl, Stephanie. Executive Reports: Cost Effective Customer Service. February 8, 1999, www.informationweek.com/720/costefct.htm (August 4, 2001).

Weston, Rusty. Executive Reports: Business Value in Communication. *Information week,* February 8, 1999, www.informationweek.com/720/value.htm (June 3, 2001).

## Chapter 12

Brown, Rick. Where Procurement Meets Accounting. *Line 56,* May 18, 2001, www.line56.com/articles/default.asp?NewsID=2517 (June 2, 2001).

Fingar, Peter, Harshna Kumar, and Tarun Shirma. 21st Century Markets: From Places to Spaces. *First Monday* v. 12 no. 4, www.firstmonday.org/issues/issue4_12/fingar/index.html (July 5, 2001).

Gellar, Dennis P. and Bradley L. Hecht. Electronic Procurement, the Extranet, and You. *Intranet Journal,* www.intranetjournal.com/articles/199912/ia_12_14_99a.html (August 4, 2001).

Gilbert, Alorie. Problems Behind the Promise. *Information Week,* November 20, 2000, www.informationweek.com/813/eprocure.htm (June 12, 2001).

Keen, Peter G. IT's Value in the Chain. *Computerworld,* February 2000, www.peterkeen.com/cworld40.htm (August 3, 2001).

Knowles, Anne. B2B : Bonanza or Bust? *Earthweb.com,* http://itmanagement.earthweb.com/ecom/ecomstrat/article/0,,12169_622471,00.html (June 9, 2001).

Meehan, Michael. Beyond Paperclips. *Computerworld* May 2001, www.computerworld.com/itresources/rcstory/0,4167,STO66623_KEY258,00.html (February 20, 2002).

Orlov, Laurie M. Wringing ROI Out of E-Procurement. *Forrester Research,* www.forrester.com/ER/Research/Brief/Excerpt/0,1317,12233,00.html (November 9, 2001).

SAP. SAP Solutions: E-Procurement. www.sap.com/solutions/e-procurement (July 31, 2001).

Seban, Larry. Does E-Procurement Deliver ROI? *CRM Daily.com®,* May 17, 2001 www.crmdaily.com/perl/printer/9821/ (June 19, 2001).

## Chapter 13

de Myer, Desiree. Speed up Financial Reporting., *SmartBusinessMag.com,* May 2001, pages 56–57.

Jacobs, Vernon K. E-commerce Accounting Systems. Offshore Press, 2000, www.rpifs.com/ecommerce/e-accounting.htm (August 15, 2001).

Keizer, Gregg. Account for Accounting. *ZDNet.com,* January 10, 2001, www.zdnet.com/smallbusiness/stories/general/0,5821,2673332-5,00.html (June 30, 2001).

Los Angeles Newsroom. Ariba Inks B2B Deals with Dell and Amex. *E-Commerce Times,* March 14, 2000, www.ecommercetimes.com/perl/story/2727.html (August 15, 2001).

Mangi, Naween A. Online Banking: The e-Perks Arrive But small companies still aren't tempted. *BusinessWeek Online,* October 8, 2001, www.businessweek.com/magazine/content/01_41/b3752618.htm (October 15, 2001).

Neuborne, Ellen. Happy Returns: How to deal with rejected Web purchases. *BusinessWeek Online,* October 8, 2001, www.businessweek.com/magazine/content/01_41/b3752625.htm (October 15, 2001).

Wendin, Christine Greech. Slash Purchasing Costs. *SmartBusinessMag.com,* May 2001, pages 66–67.


## Chapter 14

Duvall, Mel. Cultivating Profit: Business-to-Employee Apps Yield Savings, Greater Productivity. *Interactive Week,* July 2, 2001, page 25–26.

Extranet Strategist. If You Build it Will they Come?: Establishing Extranet ROI. *Extranet Strategist* Spring 2000, www.extranet-strategist.com/ (June 30, 2001).

Flash, Cynthia. Knowledge Management Meets e Portal. *Datamation,* November 28, 2000 http://itmanagement.earthweb.com/article/1,,622751,00.html (August 4, 2001).

Nelson, Emily. The Soft Sell: Kimberly-Clark decided that what works in other media may not work on the Web. So it came up with a different approach. *The Wall Street Journal*, April 23, 2000, page R24.

OpenConsult, Inc., Intranet Road Map, www.intranetroadmap.com/ (July 31, 2001).

Shein, Esther. The Knowledge Crunch. *CIO Magazine,* May 21, 2001, www.cio.com/archive/050101/crunch.html (August 1, 2001).

Telleen, Steven L. Intranets as Knowledge Management Systems Basic Concepts and Definitions. *iorg.com,* July 9, 1999, www.iorg.com/papers/knowledge.html (June 1, 2001).

White, Colin. Custom Fit: Personalization can greatly improve productivity and usability while providing key marketing advantages. *Intelligence Enterprise,* March 08, 2001, www.intelligententerprise.com/010308/feat1_1.shtml (August 14, 2001).


## Chapter 15

About.com. *E-commerce Tips.* http://ecommerce.about.com/gi/dynamic/offsite.htm?site=http%3A%2F%2Fwww.ibguide.com%2Fectips.htm (July 12, 2001).

CRMguru.com. The CRM Primer: What You Need to Know to Get Started with CRM. *CRMguru.com* May 2001, www.crmguru.com/members/primer/index.html (August 1, 2001).

Deise, Martin V., Conrad Nowikow, Patrick King, and Amy Wright. *Executive's Guide to E-Business: From Tactics to Strategy.* New York: John Wiley and Sons, 2000.

Elgin, Ben and Jim Kerstetter. Why They're Agog over Google. *BusinessWeek Online,* September 24, 2001, www.businessweek.com/magazine/content/01_39/b3750036.htm (March 3, 2002).

Fingar, Peter, Harshna Kumar, and Tarun Shirma. 21st Century Markets: From Places to Spaces. *First Monday* v. 12 no. 4, www.firstmonday.org/issues/issue4_12/fingar/index.html (July 5, 2001).

Gomes, Lee. Just Say No. *The Wall Street Journal*, April 23, 2001, page R33.

Graham, Jeffrey. E-CRM for Dummies. *ClickZ.com,* Wednesday, April 4, 2001, http://clickz.com/print.jsp?article=3698 (May 30, 2001).

Keen, Peter G. and Mark McDonald. *eProcess Edge: Creating Customer Value and Business Wealth in the Internet Era.* New York: McGraw Hill, 2000.

McTiernan, Chris. Putting the P Into e-CRM. *ClickZ,* February 12, 2001, www.clickz.com/article/cz.3364.html (May 30, 2001).

Neuborne, Ellen. Happy Returns: How to deal with rejected Web purchases. *BusinessWeek Online,* October 8, 2001, www.businessweek.com/magazine/content/01_41/ b3752625.htm (October 15, 2001).

OpenConsult, Inc. Intranet Road Map, www.intranetroadmap.com/ (July 31, 2001).

Phillips, Michael R. and Salli Rasberry. *Marketing Without Advertising: Inspire Customers to Rave About Your Business to Create Lasting Success.* Berkeley, CA: Nolo Press, 1996.

Say, Philip. Seven Great B2B Marketing Initiatives. *Clickz.com,* March 5, 2001, www.clickz.com/b2b_mkt/b2b_mkt/article.php/838111 (June 29, 2001).

Shashi Tripathi. Challenges and Main Components in CRMS. *CRM Forum,* www.crmforum.com/library/art/art-069/art-069.htm (July 31, 2001).

Siebel, Thomas M., Tom Siebel, Charles R. *Schwab Cyber Rules: Strategies for Excelling at E-Business.* New York: DoubleDay, Inc.,1999.

Stahl, Stephanie. Executive Reports: Cost Effective Customer Service. February 8, 1999, www.informationweek.com/720/costefct.htm (August 4, 2001).

Steingold, Fred S. Building Excellent Customer Service. *Quicken's Small Business* excerpted from the Fred S. Steingold's "Legal Guide for Starting and Running a Small Business." www.quicken.com/cms/viewers/article/small_business/40613 (August 4, 2001).

Szydlik, Sherry and Lamont Wood. *E-trepreneur: A Radically Simple and Inexpensive Plan for a Profitable Internet Store in Seven Days.* New York: John Wiley and Sons, 2000.

Vanscoy, Kayte. The Truth about Business Plans. *ZdNet.com Smart Business,* October 2000, www.zdnet.com/smartbusinessmag/stories/all/0,6605,2620618-3,00.html (August 5, 2001).

Whyte, Gordon. How to Monitor and Improve Your E-Business Processes. *About.com,* http://ecommerce.about.com/library/weekly/aa050901a.htm (June 3, 2001).

### Chapter 16

Arjona, Luis and Vikas Agrawal. Surviving in the Aftermath of the B-to-C Crash. *Business 2.0,* August 1, 2000, www.mckinsey.com/articles/surviving_aftermath.html (June 30, 2001).

Bakuli, D. L. B2C Internet Marketing Strategies. E-Commerce 620 Lecture 4, University of Maryland, http://polaris.umuc.edu/~dbakuli/ecom620/Lecture04.html (May 24, 2001).

Cox, Beth. Is Pure Play the Wrong Play? Yes, Says New E-tail Study. *Start-Up Internet Marketing: Tip of the Week,* www.startupinternetmarketing.com/ezines/pureplay.html (August 20, 2001).

Daniels, Jim. Opinion: Step-by-Step to Your Own Profitable Web Business. *BizWeb2000,* December 20, 2000, http://sellitontheweb.com/ezine/opinion072.shtml (April 24, 2001).

Deise, Martin V., Conrad Nowikow, Patrick King, and Amy Wright. *Executive's Guide to E-Business: From Tactics to Strategy.* New York: John Wiley and Sons, 2000.

Elgin, Ben and Jim Kerstetter. Why They're Agog over Google. *BusinessWeek Online,* September 24, 2001, www.businessweek.com/magazine/content/01_39/b3750036.htm (December 12, 2001).

E-marketer. B2C E-Commerce Revenues Continued to Grow Worldwide as Consumers spent nearly $60 Billion over the Net in 2000. *E-marketer.com,* March 20, 2001, www.emarketer.com/about_us/press_room/press_releases/20010320_b2c.html (August 5, 2001).

Ernst and Young. Global Online: Retailing: 2001. www.ey.com/global/vault.nsf/International/Globalization/$file/Globalization.pdf (January 12, 2002).

Fingar, Peter, Harshna Kumar, and Tarun Shirma. 21st Century Markets: From Places to Spaces. *First Monday* v. 12 no. 4, www.firstmonday.org/issues/issue4_12/fingar/index.html (July 5, 2001).

Gomes, Lee. Just Say No. *The Wall Street Journal*, April 23, 2001, page R33.

Graham, Jeffrey. E-CRM for Dummies. *ClickZ.com,* Wednesday, April 4, 2001, http://clickz.com/print.jsp?article=3698 (May 30, 2001).

Keen, Peter G. and Mark McDonald. *eProcess Edge: Creating Customer Value and Business Wealth in the Internet Era.* New York: McGrawHill, 2000.

Miles, Stephanie. People Like Us. *The Wall Street Journal*, April 23, 2001, page R30.

Neuborne, Ellen. Happy Returns: How to deal with rejected Web purchases. *Business Week Online*, October 8, 2001, www.businessweek.com/magazine/content/01_41/b3752625.htm (October 15, 2001).

Pastore, Michael. Increase in Ad Spending Predicted. *Internet.com,* March 15, 1999, http://cyberatlas.internet.com/markets/advertising/article/1,1323,5941_154521,00.html (July 15, 2001).

Say, Philip. Seven Great B2B Marketing Initiatives. *ClickZ.com,* March 5, 2001, www.clickz.com/b2b_mkt/b2b_mkt/article.php/838111 (June 29, 2001).

Purdie, Geo and Andy Rogers. Marketing Strategies Understand the A to Zs of B2B marketing. *Puget Sound Business Journal,* July 21, 2000, http://seattle.bcentral.com/seattle/stories/2000/07/24/focus8.html (July 30, 2001).

Ross, Fiona. Make the Most of Web Marketing. *SmartBusinessMag.com,* May 2001, pages 64–65.

Siebel, Thomas M., Tom Siebel, Charles R. Schwab. *Cyber Rules: Strategies for Excelling at E-Business.* New York: DoubleDay, Inc., 1999.

Steingold, Fred S. Building Excellent Customer Service. *Quicken's Small Business* excerpted from the Fred S. Steingold's "Legal Guide for Starting and Running a Small Business." www.quicken.com/cms/viewers/article/small_business/40613 (August 4, 2001).

Walker, David. Behind the Gloom: Continued Audience Growth. *Shorewalker.com,* April 10, 2001, www.shorewalker.com/pages/audience_growing-1.html (July 14, 2001).

Weisman, Jon. The E-Business and Technology Supersite Report: E-Commerce To Grow 57 Percent in 2001. *E-Commerce Times,* January 08, 2001, www.ecommerce times.com/perl/printer/6530/ (May 30, 2001).

Whyte, Gordon. How to Monitor and Improve Your E-Business Processes. *About.com,* http://ecommerce.about.com/library/weekly/aa050901a.htm (June 3, 2001).

### Chapter 17

B2BMarketingBiz.com. The Five Easy Steps to Running a Successful B2B Web Chat. *B2BMarketingBiz.com,* May 18, 2000, www.b2bmarketingbiz.com/sample.cfm? contentID=1654 (June 15, 2001).

B2BMarketingBiz.com. Special Report: Top 10 B2B Internet Marketing Tactics That Worked Best in 2000. *B2BMarketingBiz.com,* January 2, 2000, www.b2bmarketing biz.com/sample.cfm?contentID=1300 (March 2, 2001).

B2BMarketingBiz.com. 54% of Business Buyers Find New Suppliers Through Directories. *B2BMarketingBiz.com,* October 9, 2000, www.b2bmarketingbiz.com/ sam ple.cfm?contentID=944 (May 9, 2001).

Deise, Martin V., Conrad Nowikow, Patrick King, and Amy Wright. *Executive's Guide to E-Business: From Tactics to Strategy.* New York: John Wiley and Sons, 2000.

Katz, David M. Branding the B2B. *Brandera.com,* 2000, www.brandera.com/b/B/fea tures/00/05/02/business.html (July 24, 2001).

Ogden, Michael. B2B Largest Growth Area in Direct Marketing: Small Business Insights. *Smart Marketing,* May 1, 1998 print edition.

Palmer, Elaine Morris. B2B Advertising—The Fundamentals Apply. December 29, 2000, www.digitrends.net/marketing/13638_13097.html (May 25, 2001).

Purdie, Geo and Andy Rogers. Marketing Strategies Understand the A to Zs of B2B marketing. *Puget Sound Business Journal,* July 21, 2000, http://seattle.bcentral. com/seattle/stories/2000/07/24/focus8.html (July 30, 2001).

Ross, Fiona. Make the Most of Web Marketing. *SmartBusinessMag.com,* May 2001, pages 64–65.

Say, Philip. Seven Great B2B Marketing Initiatives. *Clickz.com,* March 5, 2001, www.clickz.com/b2b_mkt/b2b_mkt/article.php/838111 (June 29, 2001).

Walker, David. Behind the Gloom: Continued Audience Growth. *Shorewalker.com,* April 10, 2001, www.shorewalker.com/pages/audience_growing-1.html (July 14, 2001).

### Chapter 18

About.com. 75 Percent of Online Buyers Abandon Shopping Carts According to Bizrate.com Survey. *About.com,* October 23, 2000, http://retailindustry.about.com/ industry/retailindustry/library/bl/bl_bizrate1023.htm.

Atanasov, Maria. The Truth About Internet Fraud. *ZDNet: Smart Business,* April 2001, www.zdnet.com/smartbusinessmag/stories/all/0,6605,2688776,00.html (May 11, 2001).

Co-creative.net. Building an E-Commerce Trust Infrastructure. *SSL Server Certificates and Online Payment Services,* www.co-creative.net/ecommerce/BuildingAn E-CommerceTrustInfrastructure.htm (July 30, 2001).

Deise, Martin V., Conrad Nowikow, Patrick King, and Amy Wright. *Executive's Guide to E-Business: From Tactics to Strategy.* New York: John Wiley and Sons, 2000.

Jennings, Jennifer. CyberSource® Enhances Payment Solutions with New B2B Services. *Cybersource,* June 27, 2000, www.cybersource.com/press_room/2000/view.xml?page_id=202 (August 30, 2001).

McTiernan, Chris. Putting the P Into e-CRM. *ClickZ,* February 12, 2001, www.clickz.com/article/cz.3364.html (May 30, 2001).

Metz, Cade. Design Primer: It's Not Just the Visual. *PC Magazine,* February 20, 2001, www.ecommerce/filters/resources/0,10385,2181778,00.html (May 30, 2001).

Regan, Keith. Online Payment Firm Targets B2B Market. *EcommerceTimes.com,* December 5, 2000, www.crmdaily.com/perl/story/5705.html (June 30, 2001).

Saliba, Clare. Study: E-Gift Market Hinges on Reliability. *EcommerceTimes. com,* June 4, 2001, www.newsfactor.com/perl/story/10232.html (August 30, 2001).

TecBrand. E-Mail Marketing: TecBrand's 20 Principles of Email Best Practice. 2001, www.tecbrand.com/email-marketing.htm (June 30, 2001).

Tripathi, Shashi. Challenges and Main Components in CRMS. *CRM Forum,*www.crm forum.com/library/art/art-069/art-069.htm (July 31, 2001).

Warkentin, Merrill, Ravi Bapna and Vijayan Sugumaran. The Role of Mass Customization in Enhancing Supply Chain Relationships in B2C E-Commerce Markets. *Journal of Electronic Commerce Research,* vol.1 no.2 2000 ISSN 15266133, www.csulb.edu/web/journals/jecr/issues/20002/paper1.htm (June 15, 2001).

Whyte, Gordon. How to Monitor and Improve Your E-Business Processes. *About.com,* http://ecommerce.about.com/library/weekly/aa050901a.htm (June 3, 2001).

### Chapter 19

About.com. 75 Percent of Online Buyers Abandon Shopping Carts According to Bizrate.com Survey. *About.com,* October 23, 2000, http://retailindustry.about.com/industry/retailindustry/library/bl/bl_bizrate1023.htm (December 20, 2001).

Atanasov, Maria. The Truth About Internet Fraud. *ZDNet: Smart Business,* April 2001, www.zdnet.com/smartbusinessmag/stories/all/0,6605,2688776,00.html (May 11, 2001).

B2BMarketingBiz.com. Special Report: Top 10 B2B Internet Marketing Tactics that Worked. *Best in 2000 B2B Marketing Biz.com,* January 2, 2000, www.b2bmarketing biz.com/sample.cfm?contentID=1300 (December 23, 2001).

Co-creative.net. Building an E-Commerce Trust Infrastructure. *SSL Server Certificates and Online Payment Services,* www.co-creative.net/ecommerce/BuildingAnE-CommerceTrustInfrastructure.htm (July 30, 2001).

CRMguru.com. The CRM Primer: What You Need to Know to Get Started with CRM. *CRMguru.com* May 2001, www.crmguru.com/members/primer/index.html (August 1, 2001).

Deise, Martin V., Conrad Nowikow, Patrick King, and Amy Wright. *Executive's Guide to E-Business: From Tactics to Strategy.* New York: John Wiley and Sons, 2000.

Internet Labs. Getting Transparent. Using Your Security and Privacy Policies as a Marketing Vehicle. *Internet Labs Article Archives*, December 1, 2000, www.internet labs.com/transparent.htm (May 23, 2001).

Jennings, Jennifer. CyberSource® Enhances Payment Solutions with New B2B Services. *Cybersource*, June 27, 2000, www.cybersource.com/press_room/2000/view.xml?page_id=202 (August 30, 2001).

Katz, David M. Branding the B2B. *Brandera.com* 2001, www.brandera.com/b/B/fea tures/00/05/02/business.html (July 30, 2001).

Keen, Peter. Ensuring E-Trust. *Computerworld*, March 13, 2000, www.peterkeen.com/cworld41.htm (July 13, 2001).

Park, Andrew and Peter Burrows. Dell the Conqueror: Now the king of cutthroat pricing is looking beyond PCs. *Businessweek Online*, September 24, 2001, http://ads.businessweek.com/html.ng/Params.richmedia=yes&site=bw&chan=s pmz&spacedesc=special&var=715652325205583500? (February 24, 2002).

Saliba, Clare. Study: E-Gift Market Hinges on Reliability. *EcommerceTimes*, June 4, 2001, www.newsfactor.com/perl/story/10232.html (August 30, 2001).

Siebel, Thomas M., Tom Siebel, Charles R. Schwab. *Cyber Rules: Strategies for Excelling at E-Business.*New York: DoubleDay, Inc., 1999.

Stone, Deborah L. Companies Must Draft Privacy Plans for Websites. *The Business Post*, June 2001, p. 2.

TecBrand. E-Mail Marketing: TecBrand's 20 Principles of Email Best Practice. 2001, www.tecbrand.com/email-marketing.htm (June 30, 2001).

### Chapter 20

Berry, John. Eye on ROI: Acquiring Customers Is Costly but Critical. *About.com*, September 18, 2000, http://ai.about.com/compute/ai/msubmining.htm (May 23, 2001).

Berson, Alex, Stephen Smith, and Kurt Thearling. *Building Data Mining Applications for CRM.* New York: McGraw-Hill, 1999.

Co-creative.net. Building an E-Commerce Trust Infrastructure. *SSL Server Certificates and Online Payment Services*, www.co-creative.net/ecommerce/BuildingAnE-CommerceTrustInfrastructure.htm (July 30, 2001).

Compton, Jason. Know Your Customers. *Ziff Davis Smart Business*, April 12, 2000, www.zdnet.com/products/stories/reviews/0,4161,2453070,00.html (July 30, 2001).

Fingar, Peter. Transforming the Supply Chain. *Logistics Management and Distribution Report*, http://home1.gte.net/pfingar/logisticsmag04-00.htm (March 2, 2002).

Howard, Karen. Beyond Personalization 101. *Digitrends*, April 30, 2001, www.dig itrends.net/ebiz/13644_15550.html (July 30, 2001).

Internet Labs. Getting Transparent. Using Your Security and Privacy Policies as a Marketing Vehicle. *Internet Labs Article Archives*, December 1, 2000, www.internet labs.com/transparent.htm (May 23, 2001).

Katz, David M. Branding the B2B. www.brandera.com/b/B/features/00/05/02/business.html (June 15, 2001).

Keen, Peter. Ensuring E-Trust. *Computerworld,* March 13, 2000, www.peterkeen.com/cworld41.htm (July 13, 2001).

Lorek, Laura. Have-It-Your-Way Web Sites Start to Catch On. *Interactive Week,* July 25, 2001, www.zdnet.com/intweek/stories/news/0,4164,2779511,00.html (July 30, 2001).

Say, Philip. Seven Great B2B Marketing Initiatives. *Clickz.com,* March 5, 2001, www.clickz.com/b2b_mkt/b2b_mkt/article.php/838111 (June 29, 2001).

Siebel, Thomas M., Tom Siebel, Charles R. Schwab. *Cyber Rules: Strategies for Excelling at E-Business.* New York: DoubleDay, Inc., 1999.

Stackpole, Beth. Targeting One Buyer—or a Million. *Datamation,* March 2, 2000, http://itmanagement.earthweb.com/datbus/dtmine/article/0,,12239_621 301_3,00.html (July 23, 2001).

Stahl, Stephanie. Executive Reports: Cost Effective Customer Service. *Information Week,* February 18, 1999, www.informationweek.com/720/costefct.htm (August 4, 2001).

Stone, Deborah L. Companies Must Draft Privacy Plans for Websites. *The Business Post*, June 2001, p. 2.

Webtomorrow.com., Definitions. www.webtomorrow.com/definitions.htm (March 4, 2002).

### Chapter 21

Covey, Stephen. *The 7 Habits of Highly Effective People: Powerful Lessons in Personal Change.* New York: Simon & Schuster Trade, 1990.

Eriksson, Kristina. E-business and E-commerce by IBM. www.dbai.tuwien.ac.at/staff/dorn/Seminare/IM/EC/X2/ (March 2, 2002).

Ernst and Young. *Global Online: Retailing: 2001,* www.ey.com/global/vault.nsf/International/Globalization/$file/Globalization.pdf (January 12, 2002).

Fingar, Peter, Harshna Kumar, and Tarun Shirma. 21st Century Markets: From Places to Spaces. *First Monday* v. 12 no. 4, www.firstmonday.org/issues/issue4_12/fin gar/index.html (July 5, 2001).

Kamm, Steve.Turning Your Competitors' Strength to Your Advantage. *BusinessWeek Online,* September 17, 2001, www.businessweek.com/magazine/content/01_38/b3749026.htm (October 15, 2001).

Kautz, Judith. Strategic Alliances A Key Business Tool for Entrepreneurs. *About.com,* http://entrepreneurs.about.com/library/weekly/aa061500a.htm (January 2, 2002).

Knowles, Anne. B2B: Bonanza or Bust?. *Earthweb.com,* http://itmanagement.earth web.com/ecom/ecomstrat/article/0,,12169_622471,00.html (June 9, 2001).

Malone, T.W., J. Yates, and R.I. Benjamin. Electronic Markets and Electronic Hierarchies. *Communications of the ACM*, 30, 6 (1987), pp. 484–497.

McGarvey, Robert. Find Your Partner. When industry giants and dot.coms come together, it's profits that fly round and round. *Entrepreneur* magazine, February 2000, www.entrepreneur. com/article/0,4621,232631,00.html (January 17, 2002).

Rappa, Michael. Business Models on the Web. http://ecommerce.ncsu.edu/busi ness_mod els.html (June 8, 2001).

Canadian Business Network. *The CBNC how to Network Book: A Practical Guide for Successful Strategic Alliances*, December 6, 2001,http://strategis.ic.gc.ca/SSG/mi03 279e.html (March 2, 2001).

Webtomorrow.com. Definitions. www.webtomorrow.com/definitions.htm (March 4, 2002).

Weintraub, Arlene. The Mighty Mini-Dots: Small frugal and unflashy, they are making money where the big guys couldn't. *BusinessWeek e.biz*, March 19, 2001.

## Chapter 22

Advancing Women Network. Going Global...Study Your Markets, Develop a Strategic Plan or Take a Shortcut with Net B2B Marketplaces. *AdvancingWomen Network, 2000,* www.advancingwomen.com/web/going_global.html (October 20, 2001).

Betts, Mitch. Global E-commerce Still Faces Big Challenges. *Computerworld,* May 3, 2001, www.itworld.com/Tech/2418/CWD010503STO60164/ (May 10, 2001).

Boulton, Clint. What's in Store for Global IT in 2002? *Clickz Email Strategies,* January 3, 2002, www.internetnews.com/ent-news/article/0,,7_948091,00.html (March 2, 2002).

Drummond, Rik. Is Security Inhibiting Global E-Commerce? *E-Business Advisor,* www.advisor.com/Articles.nsf/aid/DRUMR11 (January 3, 2002).

Engler, Natalie. Global E-Commerce: How products and services help sites expand worldwide. *Information Week,* www.informationweek.com/755/global.htm (May 2, 2001).

Ernst and Young. Global Online: Retailing: 2001. www.ey.com/global/vault.nsf/ International/Globalization/$file/Globalization.pdf (January 12, 2002).

Fjetland, Michael J. If Not Everywhere You are Nowhere (Globally). http://cibs. tamu.edu/fdib/fjetland.htm (February 28, 2002).

Mahoney, Michael. *E-commerce Times,* March 21, 2001, www.ecommercetimes.com/ perl/story/8331.html (May 30, 2001).

Mosquera, Mary. Global E-Commerce to Hit $5 Trillion in 2005. *InternetWeek,* May 24, 2001, http://content.techweb.com/wire/story/TWB20010523S0011 (May 12, 2001).

Sawhney, Mohanbir. Go Global. *Business 2.0,* May 2000, www.business2.com/arti cles/mag/0,1640,13580,FF.html (July 30, 2001).

## Chapter 23

Compton, Jason. How to Build an Online Training Program. *ZDNet Techupdate*, May 8, 2001, www.zdnet.com/smartbusinessmag/stories/all/0,6605,2711906,00.html (January 4, 2002).

Distance-educator.com. *Knowledge Netbook: Distance Educator: Quickstats*. www.dis tance-educator.com/knb/de_quickstats.html (August 20, 2001).

Jeffries, Michael. The History of Distance Education. *IPSE—Research in Distance Education*, www.ihets.org/consortium/ipse/fdhandbook/resrch.html (October 20, 2001).

Kontzer, Tom. Video-to-Desktop Set to Emerge as Killer App. *InfoWeek*, October 12, 2001, www.informationweek.com/story/IWK20011012S0032 (October 20, 2001).

Latour, Almar and Kevin J. Delaney Paris. Reluctance to Fly May Boost Teleconferencing Cost. *The Wall Street Journal*, September 24, 2001, www.wsj.com (September 24, 2001).

Levine, Daniel. Seeing Eye to Eye. *PC Computing*, 1997, www.zdnet.com/pccomp/ features/fea0297/sub5.html (June 24, 2001).

McCartney, Laton. Fear of Flying. *Smart Partner*, October 8, 2001, www.zdnet.com/ sp/stories/issue/0,4537,2816702,00.html (October 21, 2001).

Moore, Cathleen. Videoconferencing takes control. *InfoWorld*, September 7, 2001, www.infoworld.com/articles/fe/xml/01/09/10/010910fevidconf.xml (October 21, 2001).

Reddy, Anitha. A Training Solution that Clicks. *Washingtonpost.com*, August 11, 2001, page E01, www.washingtonpost.com/ac2/wp-dyn?pagename=article&node= education/distancelearning&contentId=A64663- (October 20, 2001).

Smart Computing. Take the Travel out of Training. *Smart Computing*, November 1999, v.10 n.11, www.smartcomputing.com/editcat/SMART/INTERNET%2FWEB% 2FONLINE/69/11335/ (October 21, 2001).

Smetannikov, Max. Content Distribution Meets E-Learning. *Interactive Week*, May 28, 2001, page 24.

## *Chapter 24*

Compton, Jason. How to build an online training program. *ZDNet Techupdate*, May 8, 2001, www.zdnet.com/smartbusinessmag/stories/all/0,6605,2711906,00.html (January 4, 2002).

Ernst and Young. Global Online: Retailing: 2001, www.ey.com/global/vault.nsf/ International/Globalization/$file/Globalization.pdf (January 12, 2002).

Grossman, Wendy M. Wireless Wonder: A Dark-Horse Standard Could Win the Broadband Race. *Scientific American*, August 2001, www.sciam.com/2001/0801 issue/0801scicit4.html (February 23, 2002).

Harvey, Fiona. The Internet in Your Hands. *Scientific America* 2000, www.sciam.com/ 2000/1000issue/1000harvey.html#author (July 23, 2001).

Keen, Peter. Go Mobile Now. *Computerworld*, June 2001, www.peterkeen.com/ cworld54.htm (July 30, 2001).

———. Wireless Productivity. *Computerworld*, November 2000, www.peterkeen.com/ cworld49.htm (July 30, 2001).

Kontzer, Tom. Video-to-Desktop Set to Emerge as Killer App. *Information Week*, October 12, 2001, www.informationweek.com/story/IWK20011012S0032 (October 20, 2001).

Latour, Almar and Kevin J. Delaney Paris. Reluctance to Fly May Boost Teleconferencing Cost. *The Wall Street Journal*, September 24, 2001, www.wsj.com (September 24, 2001).

Levine, Daniel. Seeing Eye to Eye. *PC Computing*, 1997, ww.zdnet.com/pccomp/features/fea0297/sub5.html (June 24, 2001).

McCartney, Laton. Fear of Flying. *eWeek*, October 8, 2001, www.eweek.com/article/0,3658,s%253D723%2526a%253D16096,00.asp (January 2, 2002).

Moore, Cathleen. Videoconferencing Takes Control. *InfoWorld*, September 7, 2001, www.infoworld.com/articles/fe/xml/01/09/10/010910fevidconf.xml (October 21, 2001).

Reddy, Anitha. A Training Solution that Clicks. *Washingtonpost.com*, August 11, 2001, page E01, www.washtech.com/news/media/11822-1.html (October 20, 2001).

Smart Computing. Take the Travel out of Training. *Smart Computing*, November 1999, www.smartcomputing.com/editcat/SMART/INTERNET%2FWEB%2FONLINE/69/11335/ (July 3, 2001).

Smetannikov, Max. Content Distribution Meets E-Learning. *Interactive Week*, May 29, 2001, www.training.org/news/recent.html (January 2, 2001).

Wilson, David. The Future Is Here. Or Is It? *Scientific American*, October 2000, www.sciam.com/2000/1000issue/1000wilson. html (July 23, 2001).

### *Chapter 25*

About.com. How to monitor and improve your E-Business processes. *About.com*, http://ecommerce.about.com/library/weekly/aa050901a.htm (May 24, 2001).

Cyberatlas.com. http://cyberatlas.internet.com/ (July 26, 2001).

Ernst and Young. *Global Online: Retailing: 2001*, www.ey.com/global/vault.nsf/International/Globalization/$file/Globalization.pdf (January 12, 2002).

Fonstad, J. Start-Ups Going Global; Global Strategy for Start-Ups. *Red Herring*, June 2000, www.ilg.bigstep.com/generic.html?pid=16 (August 20, 2001).

Forsyth, John E., Alok Gupta, Sudeep Haldar, and Michael V. Harn. Shedding the Commodity Mindset. *The McKinsey Quarterly*, 2000, No. 4, http://mckinseyquarterly.com/article_page.asp?articlenum=950 (August 4, 2001).

Gates, Bill. *Business at the Speed of Thought: Using a Digital Nervous System*. New York: Warner Books, 2000.

Keen, Peter. Ready for the New B2B. *Computerworld*, September 11, 2000, www.computerworld.com/cwi/story/0,1199,NAV47_STO49842,00.html (August 4, 2001).

———. Wireless Productivity. *Computerworld*, November 2000, www.peterkeen.com/cworld49.htm (July 30, 2001).

Mitchell, Donald, Carol Coles and Robert Metz. *The 2000 Percent Solution: Free Your Organization from Stalled Thinking to Achieve Exponential Success*. New York: AMACOM, 1999.

Say, Philip. Seven Great B2B Marketing Initiatives. *ClickZ.com*, March 5, 2001, www.clickz.com/b2b_mkt/b2b_mkt/article.php/838111 (June 29, 2001).

Say, Philip. Five Important B2B Marketing Concepts for 2001. *ClickZ.com,* November 27, 2001, www.clickz.com/b2b_mkt/b2b_mkt/article.php/832991 (January 20, 2002).

Webopedia.com. Cookie. www.webopedia.com/TERM/c/cookie.html 7/27/01 (May 25, 2001).

Wurster, Thomas S. *Blown to Bits: How the New Economics of Information Transforms Strategy.* Cambridge, MA: Harvard Business School Publishing, October 1999

# *Index*